Colombian Women

Para Alsita
con un
abrazo afectuoso
de tu
prima

Elena

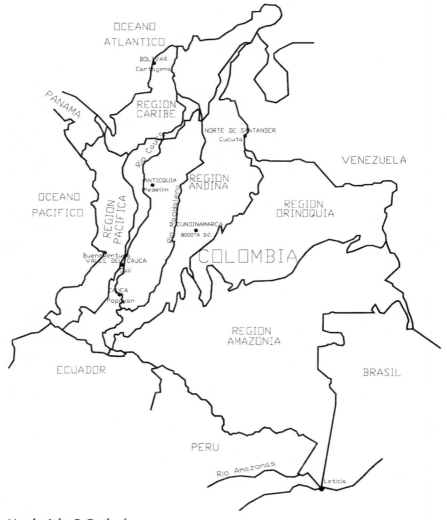

OCEANO
ATLANTICO

PANAMA

BOLIVAR
Cartagena

REGION
CARIBE

NORTE DE SANTANDER
Cucuta

Rio Cauca

VENEZUELA

OCEANO
PACIFICO

ANTIOQUIA
Medellin

REGION
ANDINA

REGION
PACIFICA

Rio Magdalena

REGION
ORINOQUIA

CUNDINAMARCA
BOGOTA D.C.

COLOMBIA

Buenaventura
VALLE DEL CAUCA
Cali

CAUCA
Popayan

REGION
AMAZONIA

ECUADOR

BRASIL

PERU

Rio Amazonas

Leticia

Map by John F. Cardenás

Colombian Women

The Struggle Out of Silence

Elena Garcés

LEXINGTON BOOKS

A DIVISION OF
ROWMAN & LITTLEFIELD PUBLISHERS, INC.
Lanham • Boulder • New York • Toronto • Plymouth, UK

LEXINGTON BOOKS

A division of Rowman & Littlefield Publishers, Inc.
A wholly owned subsidary of
The Rowman & Littlefield Publishing Group, Inc.
4501 Forbes Boulevard, Suite 200
Lanham, MD 20706

Estover Road
Plymouth PL6 7PY
United Kingdom

British Library Cataloguing in Publication Information Available

Library of Congress Cataloging-in-Publication Data

Garcés, Elena.
  Colombian women : the struggle out of silence / Elena Garcés.
     p. cm.
  Includes bibliographical references and index.
  ISBN-13: 978-0-7391-1626-5 (cloth : alk. paper)
  ISBN-10: 0-7391-1626-6 (cloth : alk. paper)
  ISBN-13: 978-0-7391-1627-2 (pbk. : alk. paper)
  ISBN-10: 0-7391-1627-4 (pbk. : alk. paper)
  eISBN-13: 978-0-7391-3011-7
  eISBN-10: 07391-3011-0
  1. Women—Colombia—Social conditions. 2. Women—Colombia—Interviews.
I. Title.
  HQ1552.G37 2008
  305.48'868861—dc22

                                                          2008010348

Printed in the United States of America

♾™ The paper used in this publication meets the minimum requirements of American
National Standard for Information Sciences—Permanence of Paper for Printed Library
Materials, ANSI/NISO Z39.48–1992.

To the women of Colombia

Contents

Acknowledgments

I would like to say thank you to all those who were supportive of my work, especially to my mother, and father, who declared near the end of his life that he was a feminist. To my two grandmothers and my innumerable aunts who were Colombian feminists in their own right *avant la lettre*, my appreciation is profound. Thanks to Henry J. Eder, the father of my sons, for sharing this project for so many years. To my sons Santiago, Harold, Enrique, and Alejandro who were always supervising if I was working and doing well. I would like to thank those who opened the doors of the Human Sciences for me at various stages of my life: Libardo Bravo, Estanislao Zuleta, Peter Caws, Ines Azar, Jean Menetrez, Alf Hiltebeitel, Gail Weiss, and John Kafka. I thank Diane Bell for her many inspirations; Isabel Vergara for her good advice and friendship. To Janet Mancini Billson, thanks for her generosity, advice, long-term support, and editorship for a chapter by me in her book, *Female Well-Being*. Thanks also to the other professors who have inspired me throughout the years: Roberta Rubinstein, Eli Hiller, Phyllis Palmer, Ruth Wallace, Janet Billson. I would like to thank my cousins Maria Antonia Garcés and Laura Garcés, and my friend Helga Kansy, whose examples I have followed. To my cousins, nephews and nieces, I always appreciated your encouragement and interests. To my friends, all of them, thank you. To Rosa Maria Martinez who helped me with my daily life and to find my books, notes, papers that kept disappearing, *gracias*. Thanks to Carmencita Mallarino who read my drafts over and over again, giving me good insights, and with whom I discussed so many times how we had been educated. To Oscar Marulanda, thanks for encouraging me to go on. To Jana Svehlova and her husband Tony Svehla, thank you for reading my drafts, and for your comments. Thank you to Juan Santiago Uribe, also for giving me comments after reading the book in a late stage of preparation. Thank you to Enrique Garcés, Emma Garcés, Maria Eugenia Garcés—my brother and sisters—and Maria del Socorro Perez, my sister-in-law, for their support, and to Emma for her insightful commentaries when we discussed issues about women's lives. Throughout every stage of this project I've been thankful to the women whose interviews have been so central to this book. I would like also to express my gratitude to Eli Hiller, whom I turned to in the last stages of this project, for editorial advice. More than just thanking her for her help in tightening nuts and bolts, I am gratified to have in Eli a Spanish-speaking editor who is well informed about Colombia from several years of living there. I feel the book has been much enriched by her contributions. I thank her for sharing so many pleasant hours in the company of our dogs, going back and forth and generating new ideas, and for the pleasure I have felt in working along with an enthusiastic reader.

Thanks to "Life" for having given me this opportunity. And to Placido Domingo for his version of the song *Gracias a la vida que me ha dado tanto* . . .

Diary

Following James Joyce's A Portrait of the Artist as a Young Man *I am inspired to recall what I wrote as a young girl of merely eleven years old, in the pages of a small diary written during a Spiritual Retreat in my convent school.*

Mater!

. . . Our sins incriminate us. Black pages are our personal sins. White pages what I did correctly. Hidden sins: those sins that were spoken in a misleading way to the confessor so that he would not understand the real meaning of what I was saying. Non-spoken sins: those that were not revealed because of shame or fear. *Other people's sins*: I enticed them to do so, to sin, thus I am responsible. Others might sin with their thoughts and desires because I am careless in the way I dress or because of behavior. In the morning I go to communion; in the evening I go practically naked to the party. *Scandal*. How many souls were eternally condemned because they showed their bodies in public pools. . . . Our bodies were redeemed by Jesus' blood and yet, we may be condemned. *The majority of the sins committed in the world is the fault of women*, said a Colombian bishop. We belong to a Christian family. We have the opportunity to do *spiritual retreats*. There is too much freedom in Cali. . . . I may be considered old fashioned if I don't go to parties or if I don't bathe in swimming pools. If only we could think about the list we have to present the last day of our lives, we would change those lives.

Spanish

Mater!

. . . Nuestros pecados nos incriminan. Paginas negras, pecados propios. Paginas blancas lo que puede hacer bien y lo hice. Pecados ocultos: decir las cosas maliciosamnete para que el confessor no entienda. Pecados callados por verguenza o miedo. *Pecados ajenos* son los que comete otra persona por mi culpa. Descuidada en trajes, modales, puede hacer que otra persona peque por pensamiento y deseo. Comulgo por la manana y por la tarde me presento al baile casi desnuda. *Escandalo.* Almas que se condenaron porque en las piscinas, en los banos mixtos mostraron sus cuerpos. Ustedes son almas rendimidas por la sangre de Jesus y pueden perdersen. La mayor parte de los pecados que se estan cometiendo en el mundo, son por culpa de las *mujeres*, dijo un Obispo colombiano. Tu vienes de un hogar cristiano. Recibes una formacion cristiana . . . aqui hay en Cali demasiada libertad . . . me pueden considerar pasada de moda sino voy a las fiestas o sino me bano en la piscinas. Si pensaramos en la cuenta que tenemos que presentar al final de nuestras vidas, cambiariamos de vida.

CHAPTER ONE

Myself: My Life

By writing herself, woman will return to the body which has been more than confiscated from her. . . . Censor the body and you censor breath and speech at the same time.

> Hélène Cixous, "The Laugh of the Medusa" (1976)

The main interest in life is to become someone else that you were not at the beginning. . . . The game is worthwhile insofar as we don't know what will be the end. . . . Each of my works is part of my own biography.

> Michel Foucault, "Truth, Power, Self: An Interview with Michel Foucault" (Martin et al. 1988: 9, 11)

This book grew out of my own experience as a Colombian woman. I was born in the city of Cali, in the southern portion of Colombia. The country is famous for great rivers, snowy mountain peaks, and majestic volcanoes. The Amazon rainforest and a magnificent river run through the lower part of the country. Vast prairie lands lie to the east, and the coasts slide into two great seas: the Pacific to the west and the Atlantic to the north. Cali is situated in the fertile Cauca Valley. The lowland is surrounded by Andean mountain ranges we call *Los Farallones*, one of which is known as the *Cordillera Occidental* (Western Range) and the other *Cordillera Central* (Middle Range). The Cauca Valley is crossed by rivers and streams that cool even the hottest months. The climate is tropical, but the air is dry and comfortable in the evening, because this area is situated a thousand meters above sea level. In the afternoon, light breezes blow between the mountains and the sea. Sweet sugarcane extract adds a lovely scent to the wind, which is perfumed by *camias* and other fragrant flowers. Orchids grow in great profusion, and wildflowers decorate the hillsides, valleys, and woods. As in all tropical climates, nature is lavish with its beauty. The people of the Cauca Valley love the outdoors, and their lives are intertwined with the seasons. In *el Valle*, the sun always shines. Skies are clear and bright, and the fertile land hosts enormous trees that are centuries old. When looking at this area from a plane, all one sees are shades of green, ranging from the color of unripe lemons to deep emerald. The people of Cali call our region a "paradise" where spring is eternal.

As the eldest child in a family of three daughters and one son, I was born to parents who were quite young. Although my mother and father were hoping for a boy and my paternal grandfather wanted as many grandsons as possible, my arrival was heralded with happiness. At least, so says my father. Actually, my mother—who was nineteen years of age and fresh out of the convent—could only cry when she realized a girl had been born. She was embarrassed at not having produced the much-desired son her father-in-law was expecting.

"Another 'house slipper' is born," said my arrogant, *machista*, and none-too- friendly grandfather, each time a little girl entered the family. This expression meant that another woman had arrived—someone warm and cozy to scuff around the house, good enough for cooking and cleaning but a person for whom a husband must be found, so she could have children to make four grandparents proud. With regard to the matter of gender, my adorable but misogynist father often repeated sweetly, "Dearest, how wonderful it is for me not to have been born female!"[1] My response never changed: "How wonderful, I assure you, it is to be a woman—and not a man!" I was named after my maternal grandmother, the daughter of a Basque immigrant who was much admired for her highbrow and *finesse d'esprit*. Because of this honored name, I was forgiven for being the wrong sex.

My childhood was very happy. Growing up among sisters and a brother, as well as many cousins and the children of my parents' few friends, I enjoyed a secluded but carefree existence. At nine years of age, I started school—prior to which a female tutor taught my brother, my sister, and me reading and writing. After first communion, we all went to school in Cali. My sister and I attended the Sacred Heart Convent; my brother enrolled in a Jesuit school. When I was twelve years old, I was sent to the United States to the same convent school in Albany, New York. My parents got along well, so we children were fortunate to be raised in a calm home and rather peaceful country. We spent summer holidays high in the Andes where my father and his eldest brother owned a home, two hours from the city. For three months we had a splendid time, without ever coming to town. At sixteen, I began traveling. I went to school in England for two years and Italy for one, but we never dreamed of spending vacations any place other than in "our" mountains.

My education was not interesting. In Colombia, classes were geared toward behaving properly and becoming a dutiful wife, someday. We prayed a great deal; religious instruction was thought to be important for our spiritual development. Rather than academic concerns, the point of my education was learning to keep my mind off topics that might distract attention away from God. Silence was the golden rule, obedience the highest value. Instead of speaking about desires and disappointments, we were taught to conduct an internal dialogue with the Lord. During this early cultural instruction, girls learned not to express their thoughts. Such training becomes deeply ingrained and, later, is difficult to erase. Instead of expressing my thoughts in writing, I lost myself in silence. Language became increasingly remote, as did the notion of identity.

Pupils were forbidden from associating in twos; we had to keep company with at least three classmates at all times. During religion seminars and daily mass, we wore gloves and veils. On weekdays, the veils were black; on holidays and Sundays, they were white. We sat with our legs tightly closed. We acquired "feminine manners." No "tomboy" conduct—like pushing, shouting, or kicking a ball—was tolerated. Such behavior was considered vulgar. Girls, we were told, must remain calm, controlled, and gracious at all times. Our speech had to be discreet and free of the words men used. We were constantly supervised by the nuns and advised that if we were obedient, we would have no problems with the teachers. My friends and I conformed perfectly to the rules. Consequently, the sisters were affectionate and considerate.

Nevertheless, I didn't like school. Independent thoughts were crushed by the teachers. I wasn't interested in studying and found school boring. I did enjoy recreation, visits with cousins or friends on weekends, and, of course, summer holidays. Reading was always fun and absorbing. Since early childhood, books helped me cope with a dull or hostile environment. Reading at age five, I subsequently submerged myself in books—which gave me pleasure, intellectual satisfaction, and comfort in times of illness or loss. My tutor, a woman I dearly loved, as well as my mother and maternal grandmother impressed upon me the importance of literature.

Virginity was another quality we were taught to value. The nuns considered us "temples of the Holy Ghost." Honored by this notion, we conducted ourselves accordingly. Having been chosen for such a privileged position in the Catholic Church, we were expected to maintain purity in words, thoughts, and deeds. Nothing was allowed to soil our minds and bodies. Furthermore, we were taught that freedom, impurity, and insubordination could lead to prostitution. As was said since the time of Cervantes, "*Mujer romera, mujer ramera*" (A roaming woman is a prostitute).

Nevertheless, girls in our family were thought to be special. We were carefully protected because anything could harm us. Delicate as porcelain, we were treated differently from my brother and male cousins. Boys could do all sorts of things girls were forbidden to try, like climbing trees, playing rough games, and going without chaperones to movies or parties. Girls had to be supervised. We were never left alone. Guarded from the misdeeds of boys and certain men—such as drivers or gardeners, and even male friends of the family—we had to observe curfews when we got older and attended gatherings. Girls were never allowed to go out with boys alone. We were watched day and night, practically until we were married.

By adolescence, we were told, by the nuns and priests, how girls could tempt boys. We learned that women caused men to commit sin. In fact, all iniquity started when Eve tempted Adam in the Garden of Eden. We were repeatedly reminded that because of Eve's misbehavior, humanity lost paradise, forever. God condemned such ungrateful human beings to roam the world, cultivate the earth by the sweat of their brows, and give birth to children in pain. Our guilt was great. Women were obligated to repair the harm done by Eve. Becoming good women was the best way to achieve this goal. In addition to being pure and virginal, we were expected to act submissively, to be silent, and resigned. The Virgin Mary was our guide. While I was growing up, my mother, two grandmothers, and eight aunts served as my models. These women, each in her way a rebel, were strong, courageous, and committed to life.

In the United States and later in Europe, the classes I took were more interesting than the courses in Colombia. Gradually, a desire for learning awoke within me. In England I studied British literature—particularly Shakespeare's plays—as well as history and art, all of which opened a new world for me. I also learned French, Italian, sewing, cooking, typing, and tennis.

When I returned to Colombia, I followed the path that all my peers had already taken: marriage.[2] First, however, I wanted to attend college. My parents replied that, as a girl, I had no need to study. "And if you read too much, your eyesight will suffer," added my maternal grandmother. Still a virgin, I married. I was a good girl who did what she was told. No one had ever taught me about menstruation or the "facts of life." The first day I menstruated, my mother said I shouldn't worry about what was happening; it was something normal for women. My friends in school told me what I needed to know about female bodies and where babies came from, but I received no formal sexual education. When I married, I obtained permission from a priest and a judge to have intimate relations.

My entire life was supervised.[3] I always had someone looking at what I was doing. If I was quiet and well behaved, people left me alone. Then, I could relax. I didn't feel resentment or lack of privacy because I could retreat into myself and read, sew, listen to music, or simply relax. Later in life, I had to administer a house full of children (four sons of my own and many nieces and nephews) plus care for a husband and extended family. My education prepared me to accomplish these obligations; I enjoyed being a mother and an aunt.

After marriage, when I and a few friends started psychoanalytic therapy, we decided to form a consciousness-raising group to discuss our lives, interests, and worries. We also took courses on philosophy, psychology, and literature. Our professor was a psychoanalyst and Marxist philosopher. Once a week, eight to ten women met to discuss texts we wished to understand and apply to daily existence. For example, we began to inquire about women's issues by reading Simone de Beauvoir's *The Second Sex* (1952). One of us usually wrote some thoughts about the book or chapter under consideration. This group lasted eight years.

As time passed, we decided to apply what we had learned by founding a magazine that dealt with existential questions, political topics, women's issues, literature, poetry, and art. The magazine came out for seven years and enjoyed an enthusiastic reception, especially among university circles. The publication was called *La Cábala*.

From an early age, I participated in women's groups in an effort to help improve our communities. Such collectives varied in size and changed over time, as did the purpose of our meetings. At ten years of age, I joined a few classmates to sew baby clothes for poor expectant mothers. Generally, we met for two to three hours at school, on Saturday afternoons. We also attended spiritual retreats organized once a year by our school. As time passed and we girls grew up, we helped institutions like the Red Cross, Children's Hospital, Psychiatric Hospital, or University Hospital. We took educational seminars, for example, at the Red Cross, which trained us to do our work better. The opportunity for female bonding and demonstrating love and care for other women was part of our motivation.[4]

My quest to understand female destiny in a man's world started when I was just a girl. Today, this passion extends to Colombian women and their political context. According to Barbara Du Bois, comprehension can lead to theoretical strategies, which could help us act in the future (1983: 108). My thinking about feminist issues has always been tied to action.[5] Scientists contend that knowledge and power are united insofar as "thought has to be comprehended in the concrete setting of an historical situation" (Mannheim in Reinharz 1983: 163). My research conforms to this notion because the insight I am seeking affects Colombian women's lives, as we profit from collective observation.

In light of my upbringing and curiosity about whether my experience is unique, I decided to interview other women and learn whether their experiences were similar to mine. I also hoped to discover why women in my country still face discrimination and oppression. Today, many people in Colombia believe that gender inequality has been redressed by consensus and law; I do not think the problem has been corrected.

Social scientists like Barbara Du Bois (1983), Shulamit Reinharz (1983, 1992), María Mies (1983), and Janet Mancini Billson (1995) emphatically agree that feminist theory must stand firmly on women's realities, insight, and language, if the *status quo* is to be changed.[6]

In other words, when doing such research, women should remain the focus of attention. Through our own words, we can build a body of information, answer questions, and develop methodology. This documentary method will reveal our social history, says María Mies (1983: 23) because "all knowledge is constructed through the interaction of self and world." Without intimacy, I could not have learned as much about the Colombian women as I did.

I was an insider among the subjects I interviewed. We shared a common culture and similar experience both as women and compatriots. Indirectly, I have conducted cultural analysis throughout my life. I studied our culture, its norms and rules, talked to people, asked questions, wrote and published articles, and inquired about values and cultural artifacts[7] in the creation of a dissident view of society (Reinharz 1992: 242). A "heretic" of sorts, I have listened to other women's voices and spoken out in our behalf. Although what I do is not ethnography in any strict sense, the research I produced from oral histories, in combination with what I call a "lifelong fieldwork,"[8] helps me write about cultural "processes through which gender is socially constructed" (Reinharz 1992: 162) amid multiple connotations. In the construction of this project, my understanding of Colombian women has improved; yet, there is much more research to be done.

Notes

1. Simone de Beauvoir writes how "[E]verywhere, at all times, the males have displayed their satisfaction in feeling that they are the lords of creation. 'Blessed be God . . . that He did not make me a woman,' say the Jews in their morning prayers, while their wives pray on a note of resignation: 'Blessed be the Lord, who created me according to His will." *New French Feminisms: Anthology*, ed. Elaine Marks and Isabelle de Courtivron (Boston: Massachusetts University Press, 1981), 49.

2. Virginia Woolf gives a short description about the education and lives of the "daughters of educated men." She writes, "It was with a view to marriage that her mind was taught. She tinkled on the piano, but was not allowed to join an orchestra; sketched innocent domestic scenes, but was not allowed to study from the nude . . . it was with a view to marriage that her body was educated; a maid was provided for her; that the streets were shut to her; that the fields were shut to her; that solitude was denied her— all this was enforced upon her in order that she might preserve her body intact for her husband. In short, the thought of marriage influenced what she said, what she thought, what she did." *Three Guineas* (New York: A Harvest Book, 1970), 38.

3. In the study of how an individual is "subjectified" into the person he should become, see Michel Foucault's *Discipline and Punishment* (New York: Vintage Books, 1975) and *History of Sexuality* Vol. I (New York: Pantheon, 1978), which should preferably be looked at together since they give a clear picture of what it means to become a docile body through "disciplinary technology."

4. For four years I wrote a column in our local newspaper answering letters from readers who asked for help. This activity taught me a great deal about the riddles human beings face in the course of life. Most of my readers were women.

5. Steiner Kvale explains in *InterViews: An Introduction to Qualitative Research Interviewing* (London: Sage, 1996), 46, that for Paul Ricoeur, the interpretation of meaning includes not only written texts but also the "objects of the social sciences— meaningful action," among which are discourse and action.

6. María Mies writes that "the change of the status quo becomes the starting point for a scientific quest." "Toward a Methodology for Feminist Research," in *Theories of Women's Studies*, ed. Gloria Bowles and Renate Duelli Klein (London and New York: Routledge and Kegan Paul, 1983), 125.

7. Of "cultural artifacts," Shulamit Reinharz says, "People who do content analysis study a set of objects (i.e., cultural artifacts) or events systematically by . . . interpreting the themes contained in them. These products stem from every aspect of human life, including relatively private worlds, "high" culture, popular culture, and organizational life." *Feminist Methods in Social Research* (New York: Oxford University Press, 1992), 146.

8. About ethnography, Reinharz writes, "Contemporary ethnography or fieldwork is multi-method research. It usually includes observation, participation, archival analysis, and interviewing—thus combining the assets and weaknesses of each method. Nonpositivist methods—particularly open-ended interviewing and ethnography—must have a prominent place in feminist science." Ibid., 46.

CHAPTER TWO

Feminist Research and Methods

I consider it presumption in anyone to pretend to decide what women are or are not, can or cannot be, by natural constitution. They have always hitherto been kept, as far as regards spontaneous development, in so unnatural a state, that their nature cannot but have been greatly distorted and disguised; and no one can safely pronounce that if women's nature were left to choose its direction as freely as men's . . . there would be any . . . difference at all, in the character and the capacities which would unfold themselves.

John Stuart Mill, *On the Subjection of Women* (1971: 41)

Aleja: "With the Same Leather Whip Used on the Cows"

Introduction

Ninety years old at the time of the interview, Aleja worked for my younger sister. She was my nanny. Although eldest of the respondents, in many respects her experiences foreshadow those of most of the others, to include underlying violence at home; a mother's deference to and admiration of an unfaithful father; a strong religious upbringing in the Roman Catholic tradition; education in the traditional Catholic system; a mother's reluctance to discuss a woman's sexuality or even basic biology with her daughter; constant supervision of girls; fundamental mistrust between men and women.

These revelations are the product of feminist research described in Chapter 2. It rejects the constraint, established by male social scientists, that only quantifiable evidence is admissible as truly scientific. The woman's approach employs intelligent personal contact and involvement between interlocutor and subject of research. The researcher listens and reports. She compares testimonies, perceives patterns (here initiated with Aleja) that, with mounting evidence, invites analysis of cause and effect. Eventually, this more involved, participative and creative approach evokes methods and theories to remedy social problems.

Interview

"Aleja, how you were raised? Tell me as much as you remember of your childhood, your parents' home, your school years, sisters and brothers, cousins and other relatives, and friends."

"I was raised in the country. My parents came from a small town in Cundinamarca, called La Mesa, but we lived further north—about half an hour by horse. It was a beautiful farm that belonged to a family from Bogotá. My parents were the *administradores* (administrators) of the farm. My mother was in charge of the workers' food, my father of weighing and collecting the various crops—corn, cotton, etc.—and of the *aguardiante* (distilled liquor fermented from the sugar cane). My mother directed the women in the kitchen and dining room. She was a very organized person who was admired and respected by all. My father spent much of his time away from the *hacienda*. He had to go to other villages to talk to the people, buy goods for the farm, and sell crops, honey, and *aguardiente*.

"My parents had six children. Two boys died when they were young. I was the eldest of the other four; we were two sisters and one brother. Rafael was eight years younger than I, and Etelvina was eighteen years younger. My mother started having children quite young, and finished her reproductive cycle at a late age. Because I was the eldest, my mother was extremely strict with me. Thrashing was the way I was raised. My mother had a quick temper and was always ready to beat us up, especially me since I was a rebel! I must admit that I was very disobedient. Nevertheless, all of my mother's beatings didn't make me more docile. Finally, she understood that she couldn't force me to do things I didn't want to do.

"I attended an all-girls school. Girls and boys didn't go to the same school in those days. Our teacher, Abigail, was very strict. When we misbehaved, she used to beat us with a ruler or make us stand with a brick on each hand in front of the door. When I was seven years old, my parents sent me to the larger town, La Mesa, to study with the nuns: the Sisters of Charity. There, too, I bothered the nuns all the time. My father used to take me to school every day, riding with him on his horse. My father was very tender and loving with us; by contrast my mother was stern. She beat us—especially me with the same leather whip used on the cows. Nonetheless, my mother was very religious. She taught me all my prayers and the right way to behave toward other people. She instructed us to be discreet, not to mind other people's business, not to get involved in arguments, feel respect for our elders, and never judge people. She told us girls not to let anyone touch us. It was the custom—I still don't know why—for young men to handle our breasts. Then my mother told us that, without being rude, we had to be firm and make ourselves be heard, saying that the boys had to respect us.

"My mother was extremely respectful of my father. She took care of his clothes and food. She loved to see him clean and always wearing white, immaculate shirts. My father was, as I just said, an affectionate man. All of his love was for us, and he was never abusive. My father used to play a small flute and sing a lot. He was also a big flirt! He had a girlfriend, in another town. She was young; and with her, he had three daughters. When I went with him to the market place, on Sundays, I met her. Rosario was her name. She was very nice and used to buy me combs for my hair and earrings. I did wonder why she was so nice to me, until, one day, I understood that she was my father's mistress. One day, a friend told my mother about my father's "adventures." But, my mother told this woman, 'listen, dear, my husband, while he is here in our home, he is my husband. When he goes out, whatever he does has nothing to do with me. So please, I ask of you, never again come here to tell me stories about him. He can do whatever he likes; it is none of my business. His life is a private matter.' I was the jealous one. It was I who did not approve when the three girls (his other daughters) came to visit us. I told my mother that I didn't like them to eat at our house, but my mother always answered, dear, it is not their fault! Generous and discreet, my mother was also sensible and did not have grudges or resentment."

"Tell me Aleja about what your mother or your teacher told you girls how to behave as girls. Did they tell you anything about women's virginity, purity, about menstruation?"

"No! Nothing. They never told us anything about those subjects, much less about anything that had to do with our bodies or their functioning! Because I was afraid of my mother, I never had intimate conversations with her. At fifteen, I almost married a young man from La Mesa. One day, an older friend of mine took me to a place where I saw him with another woman. Then I disappeared from his life and never told anyone about this relationship. After that incident, I never had anything to do with men. The day I had my first menstruation, I went to the river to clean myself. I was very frightened and thought I was bleeding to death. I was terrified! I thought my mother was going to beat me up. I was twelve years old. A friend told me all about menstruation, and later my mother did explain to me how I had to take care of myself. She also said I couldn't eat certain things while menstruating, like beaten egg whites. Those were the things my mother told me about my body. Nothing else. There was little time for conversations. We all had to work. Moreover, no one ever told me how babies were 'made.' I never saw animals mating. I never was left alone; my mother was always supervising us. The only man I ever saw was my father. The farm workers were very respectful, and we never had a close relationship with them. I had cousins and uncles, but they lived far away. They came sometimes to visit, but only for one or two days. My father, well my poor father, he never said anything to us. We left him alone and didn't bother him, he was always so busy."

"Aleja, now tell me about your First Communion. Who prepared you? Where did you do it? With whom?"

"We celebrated our First Communion in the big town, La Mesa. It was an important religious ceremony. The nuns prepared us girls, and we did it in the month of May. Boys had their First Communion on a different day. As I said before, we girls we did not mingle with the boys. I never really played with boys. I didn't even know the difference between girls and boys—I mean, the difference in behavior. I didn't even look at them. And play? We did not have much time to play. The free moments I had away from school, I worked in the garden. I watered the flowers, hoed the earth in preparation for new plants or seeds, and gave water to the chickens and other animals. I was always helping on the farm. It was a difficult job—more so for boys than girls. Also, I did not like to cook. Only afterwards, when I went to your grandmother's house, did I learn how to cook. My mother always said that people with nothing to do would develop bad ideas. Nothing good would come from spare time. We children had to work hard, whether we liked it or not. Those were the rules. I always liked working, and when I was a girl, I preferred to work rather than play!

"Later, when I grew up and went to work with your grandmother, I met a chauffeur who offered me a love relationship. One of the women who worked there with me said, 'You have to be very careful of men. They lie. They need single women and if they marry you, they change and suddenly act as if they own you.' Gabriela, my friend, said that men were simply bad, and I believed her. I feared men and didn't believe them.

"Thus, I didn't want to have anything to do with men. I might also have been influenced by seeing my father's unfaithfulness to my mother and how, at times, he was also rude to her and how she had to defend herself.

"To a young woman I would say, 'study, learn, work and if you are busy your thoughts will always land on useful things. Always make your boyfriends respect you, until the day you decide to get married."

❧

This study concentrates on women in Colombia, where I was born and raised, and on the plight of Colombian women, the result of a patriarchal ideology. Research focuses on issues surrounding the sources of this oppression. To understand the construction of radical feminist knowledge in Colombia, I explore eighteen interviews with Colombian women, around the themes of socialization, violence, desire, and empowerment. I set these interviews against the background of the history of women in Colombia and the political, religious, legal, and socioeconomic issues that bear on their lives. My inquiry advances the hypothesis that oppression of Colombian women, perpetuated by a patriarchal model, continues today. Sexual oppression, or sexism, begins with patriarchal ideology. With its religious and governmental laws and institutions, and, importantly, with the help of older women, Colombian women receive continuous discrimination that affects their well being and their right to "a satisfactory personal and social life" (Lavrin 1987: 113). The causes of this oppression are various, but among them, I emphasize two: the male fear of female sexuality, which men may experience as obstructing their maleness or manliness;[1] and the belief that men have been, and are, the creators of culture and society, thus the controllers of societal power (see De Beauvoir 1952; Peristiany 1966; Pescatello 1973; Schneider 1971; Lerner 1986). One purpose of this research is to unveil sexist attitudes within Colombian *machista* culture, to gather data, to show and describe how such prejudice affects women and to discuss some of the ways Colombian women speak of their lives under these circumstances. My research exposes the root causes of this *machista* behavior.

Specific themes discussed are (1) the institution of the family which structures gender and determines where the laws of State and Church are transmitted, under the supervision of parents, in conjunction with legal authority and religious teachings; (2) the socioeconomic status that permeates people's existence with either positive or negative effects on their human destiny, depending on their social class; (3) open and/or covert violence turned against Colombian women by social, cultural, and religious rules; and (4) intertwinement of issues of virginity, purity, desire, discourse, *machismo*, and *marianismo* into a solid net that obstructs women's lives and ways of being, by creating adverse social patterns of beliefs and behaviors. This study attempts to understand the deeply buried roots of the oppression of Colombian women. It seeks to modify, change, and/or eradicate them. Finally, it defines visions of a better world for women in Colombia.

Foundations to Study Women Under Repression

Because patriarchal systems commit violence against women in both public and private spheres, violating human rights and political freedom, they must be studied and modified. Patriarchy repeats specific domination patterns of men over women and men over men. For Mitchell (1973: 64–74), patriarchy is not only "the rule of the father" but the rule of men who are taught, by socialization and ideology, to be dominant and are allowed to use force when they consider it necessary. "Patriarchy is all-pervasive: it penetrates class divisions, different societies, historical epochs. Its chief institution, the family, relies on 'inherited' culture and the training of the young." Moreover, Engels observes that the organization of agrarian communities heralded the demise of female power (Engels 1985:120–21):

> The overthrow of mothers' right was the *world historical defeat of the female sex.* The man took command in the home also; the woman was degraded and reduced to servitude; she became the slave of his lust and a mere instrument for the production of children. (my emphasis)

This arrangement marked the beginning of a society where the surplus value of male work acquired importance, whereas the reproduction of human beings lost significance (Mitchell 1973; Mies 1983; Beneria 1985). The family was organized around a core of contradictions. A salient issue that arose within households was the asymmetrical relationship between the sexes that divided men and women in terms of productive versus unproductive work— wage labor versus use labor for the home. Gayle Rubin (1975: 168) describes this uneven relationship between male and female as the beginning of patriarchal power, which entails a

> specific form of male dominance, and the use of the term ought to be confined to the Old Testament-type pastoral nomads from whom the term comes. . . . Abraham was a Patriarch—an old man whose absolute power over wives, children, herds, and dependents was an aspect of the institution of fatherhood, as defined in the social group in which he lived.

Abraham's ascent in Western culture also marked the start of a descent for Sarah and the rest of Abraham's wives, as Engels was quick to point out, nearly a hundred years ago.[2]

Unfortunately, patriarchal society has established a hetero-reality in which being female automatically endangers a person's well-being. Gender-based roles permeate every level of activity within families and communities. The cornerstones of patriarchy include sexism, obstruction of female autonomy, restricted property rights for women in many cases (Mies 1986), educational discrimination against girls, and professional and medical maltreatment of women, among other forms of violence against half the earth's population (Cabal, Lemaitre, and Roa 2001; Daly 1990). Oppression on the basis of gender in some Western countries is less severe today than in the past, but significant subjugation of women remains a problem. Equal education is the first step in eradicating misogyny,[3] which is at the root of patriarchy.

In her book on feminist methods, Reinharz (1992) explains that theorists draw strength from different disciplines within the renaissance of women's studies in order to compile a more reliable understanding of female truths. The wisdom acquired in this fashion will, undoubtedly, empower women.

Robyn Rowland and Renate Klein (1997: 14) suggest that, considering their differences of class, age, race, and sexual preferences, women as a group share a gender that unites them "unto themselves." Thus, women collectively, and as a sexual class, are compelled to fight each day in a revolution against the other class—men—in order to achieve liberation from patriarchal oppression.

Drawing on Reinharz's *Feminist Methods in Social Research* (1992), I listened to the voices of women from different social classes, ethnic groups, and ages. This collection of interviews illustrates "women's ways of knowing" as affected by a combination of personal and historical experiences. In this way, women's lives, perspectives, and standpoints are revealed, as are insights about those of men (Belenky et al. 1986: 8–9.) Whatever affects women, in a positive or negative way, eventually influences the men and children with whom they share personal lives and cultural norms.

This work draws together two main bodies of theory: general theoretical and interdisciplinary concerns of the human sciences as they bear upon deconstruction and interpretation; and specific issues in feminist theory that ultimately concern the empowerment of women.

This study is interdisciplinary. Michel Foucault (1973: 351) says, "The science of woman and man considers people insofar as they live, speak, and produce." Such research examines women's and men's interests as these factors affect their lives. With the aid of culture, women and men represent to themselves the world in which they live (Foucault, 1973: 351–353) as they continuously accrue knowledge about their perceptions of reality (Kvale 1996: 239). Aleja (and the other interviewees) told me, in her interview, how she perceived her reality based on experiences she inherited through her family and other institutions, such as school and the Catholic Church. The way the individual reveals her life opens that life to knowledge and interpretation, as scientific social knowledge is being built (Obeysekere 1990: 112).

The objects of the human and social sciences are language, myth, religion, art, and any other system that lends intelligibility to human life and the social world.[4] These domains should be examined and interpreted within a cultural perspective (Caws 1988: 23–24). History tells individuals how to devise their expression of social truths, as they create meanings of symbols (Foucault 1973: 353, 371; Dilthey, 1988: 23–24). Daily reality is a combination of secular and sacred, sensual and mythical, cultural and natural. None of these realms is less valuable than the other. They all play a part in creating the human universe of symbol and discourse. Ordinary events construct reality and contribute to the thinking process. Dilthey (1988: 24) writes, "Even the psychophysical living unity [woman/man] is known to itself through the same double relationship between *Erlebens* [experience] and *Verstehen* [understanding]."[5] At the same time, each person's reality is "objectified" in thought (Dilthey 1988: 14, 23). Everyone sees the world in a unique way. Life consists of lived experience (subjective reality), which is why Dilthey termed the study of such experience the science of women and men. According to him, the human sciences are grounded in the connection between experience and understanding.

Foucault's idea of history is a way of analyzing and criticizing society and its institutions. Foucault's historical approach is more like a genealogy, through which he looks into the origins of anything: be it an institution, an idea, or human beings observed as the objects of society and its political power (Gutting 1990: 328–29). For Foucault, it is essential to "arrive at an analysis which can account for the constitution of the subject within a historical framework" (Foucault 1984: 117). Foucault sees history as a way of analyzing and criticizing society and its institutions. He deals with the history of ideas, their origin, and their power (see Obeysekere 1985). Briefly, one cannot understand human life without understanding history.

As a contribution to feminist research, this study seeks to unearth the roots of suppression of Colombian women. A vision for social change could provide new alternative perspectives to free them. The lives of men and women are so intricately intertwined that hurting half the population invariably injures everyone. Much of Latin America suffers from the same type of gender inequality (see Sen 1999; Lavrin 1978; Cabal, Lemaitre, and Roa 2001; Mancini Billson and Fluehr-Lobban 2005; Wills Obregón 2007). Although Colombia is not unique, one can see the kind of changes that could produce a more just society with greater opportunity for all.[6] Once Colombian women gain greater control over their bodies and voices, they will cease to be invisible and inaudible. Janet Mancini Billson (2005: 23) explains clearly: "Well-being extends to a state of social, economic, political and individual well-being that implies the opposite of isolation, poverty, disenfranchisement, poor health, alienation or powerlessness." Greater political, religious,[7] and legal rights can create some measure of security, so that the privileges of the few can become the rights of all.

Gender Theory and Practice

To comprehend the greater picture, one must understand the sexual construction on which society is built. This work explores how (1) female roles are shaped within the family, (2) the family structures gender roles and organizes power, (3) family patterns affect women's lives, (4) society supports patriarchal institutions, and (5) gender discrimination injures women, physically and psychologically. Sexual differences are based on biology. As the roles assigned each gender are constructed from these differences, they are socially exaggerated and manipulated. As Elizabeth Grosz (1994: ix) explains in her book *Volatile Bodies*,

> Our conceptions of reality, knowledge, truth, politics, ethics, and aesthetics are all effects of sexually specific—and, thus far in our history, usually male—bodies, and are all thus implicated in the power structures which feminists have described as patriarchal, the structures which govern relations between the sexes.

Freud asks, "What do women want?"[8] Freud's question may be answered in as many different ways as there are women who are wanting. The experience of Colombian women is only one case, not unique in a world of emerging female consciousness. Presumably Colombian women want autonomy, dignity, physical and sensual gratification, productivity, an end to violence and humiliation, and much-deserved respect, and well-being (Mancini Billson and Fluehr-Lobban, 2005; Wills Obregón 2007). The question about female desires, wishes, needs, and dreams is not as obscure as the problem it seeks to hide. For example, historian Asuncion Lavrin (1978: 121) answered Freud's question in the following way:

> To the classic question posed by Freud "What is it that women want?" we could answer without much hesitation that a very popular sentiment among women calls for *capacitación*, or improvement in their own education, to be able to help their families more effectively. We cannot forget that, in several countries, between one-quarter and one-third of low-income families in urban areas are headed by women.

Whether they are feminists or not, all researchers who deal in women's issues attempt to dissect women's experiences and rebuild a reliable, accurate theory. Women have been challenged to answer Freud's question; after all, the response is essential to female destiny. Gender identity is essential to understanding female existence. Public policy, cultural discourse, and social institutions currently subjugate women. A new vision of Colombian, and all, women needs to be supported by radical feminist theory that emanates from female experiences, realities, and desires.

> Thus, the narratives of oppressed groups are important insofar as they empower these groups by giving them a voice in the struggle over interpretations. . . . [T]hey are not denied the "authority" of experience if, by "authority," one means the power to introduce that experience as a basis for analysis, and thereby create self understandings. What is denied is the unquestioned authority of unanalyzed experience. (Sawicki 1989: 307, my emphasis)

When people are oppressed they have no voice. Aleja, when she speaks of being beaten with a whip, becomes empowered. As she speaks she releases resentful memories because she understands. A woman's voice is a weapon against a prevailing power. Feminist theory is a theoretical framework based intrinsically on women's interests, usually expressed in the voices of women. It does not accept anything less than changing the status quo. It is a politics that is "a means, not an end; a process, not a dogma" (Morgan 1997: 6).

I agree with Asuncion Lavrin and other feminists who write mainly on women's issues, that practice and theory must begin with a basic understanding of the family's manipulation of individuals through gender roles. "Theory does not only explain facts, it also describes reality" (Marks and de Courtivron 1981: 213). The analysis and criticism of reality are tools for a politics of change (see Gutting 1990).

The term "radical," as Robin Morgan (1997: 5) says, "implies going to the roots (as in radish) of an issue or subject." Important matters that concern women's lives are not to be kept unanswered, or superficially handled. Radical feminism delves into women's problems, questions, and doubts to find appropriate theoretical answers. For French feminists Elaine Marks and Isabelle de Courtivron (1981: xi), "a radical feminist . . . is any woman (whatever her relationship to whatever theory) who believes that women's liberation is inseparable from radical change."

This study, then, adopts a multidisciplinary human sciences orientation, including anthropology, sociology, religious studies, literature, psychoanalysis, history, and philosophy, and it takes a feminist standpoint. Female experiences are examined along with women's personal meanings and definitions. Subjective feelings and interpretations, long dismissed by male researchers because of their emotional character and alleged lack of objectivity, are discussed. Women interviewed in the course of this research are considered "knowers" who assisted in understanding the stories they conveyed. They helped discover what is unnamed, unknown, or repressed. "What we do shapes what we can know," says Sandra Harding (1987: 185). (You know how to climb a tree if you have already done it.) Therefore, "knowledge emerges for the oppressed . . . through the struggles they wage against the oppressors." The female knower, writes Dorothy Smith (1989: 37), has as context her everyday activities; therefore her narrative "is always embodied." One feels one's experiences through mind and body.

The main theory chosen to analyze the oral histories comes from French feminist thought, as presented by Julia Kristeva. Combined with other theories on development and well-being (Mancini Billson and Fluehr-Lobban 2005), it clarifies not only the situation of women, but also women's general position in society according to gender, by female work, or the "housewifization" of labor (see Mies 1986).

The Process

I interviewed women from different social classes, ethnic groups, and stages in the life cycle. Because Colombia is more than 90 percent Catholic, all subjects were rooted in the same religious tradition. All interviews were conducted in person and taped while I took notes. We ate lunch or dinner and drank juices or tea, depending on the time of day and the weather. Some interviews lasted two to three hours. In exchange for the working class women's time, including the eight who participated in a focus group, I paid each the equivalent of thirty dollars. Rosie, a sex worker, charged thirty dollars for half an hour, so I paid her ninety dollars.

At times, I provided my own personal experience. The interviews were transcribed verbatim by a secretary. I translated the interviews from Spanish into English, without cutting anything, and extracted raw data from each before analyzing interesting themes.

The experiences of the women interviewed represent some of the salient issues discussed in this study. Three of the most important are virginity, tied to the issue of purity of the female body and its possible contamination through sexuality and unconditional freedom; *marianismo*, which implies an obedient, silent woman who does as she is commanded by the "law of the patriarch," who spends her life satisfying the rules given to females; and the violence women receive from social institutions like the family, and the Catholic Church. Lastly, this discussion underlines the challenges facing Colombian women and the means and opportunities my interviewees have taken to face and surmount these obstacles, by using new discourses, break-ing traditions and opening new paths.

The Researcher Among Her Subjects

Among other feminists researchers and social scientists, sociologist Janet Mancini Billson, in the "Progressive Verification Method: Toward a Feminist Methodology for Studying Women Cross-Culturally," (1991: 15), proposes a research approach in which the researcher and interviewed subjects partici-pate actively and together in the construction of theory, methodology, and recollection of data for finding accurate solutions. Mancini Billson has named this method "the progressive verification method." The relationship developed between the researcher and the women studied, "subjects of knowledge," is one of equal partnership. Women as subjects rather than ob-jects of research engage in preliminary analyses of the emergent data. Shu-lamit Reinharz also recommends that the feminist researcher's experience should not be hidden, as if the social scientist were ignoring the importance of her own background. She stresses the importance of the researcher's mix-ing objective and subjective positions to enrich the study (*Feminist*, 263).

During the sessions, I spoke about myself, too.[9] I did not want to perpetu-ate the "historic silencing of women researchers' active and often passionate reactions to our own research" (Stephanie Riger and Margaret Gordon cited in Reinharz 1992: 263). My participation struck me as an obligation. During the interviews, I responded while listening to the women, offering pieces of my personal life or worldview. For these reasons, I have included, in Chapter 1, a short history of my own life, so that the interviewees would not be iso-lated by my absence from the study.

This approach is at odds with that of male, and often, female sociologists and anthropologists, who, following Auguste Comte and the Doctrine of Positivism assert that "the only true knowledge consist[s] of scientific description of ob-servable phenomena, both physical and social (Jary and Jary, 1991: 373). In other words, the researcher keeps her distance from her subjects. This study rejects this outdated and impersonal approach, insisting on the validity of the researcher's and the interviewee's participation in the study. Jana Sawicki's (1989: 3) advice also rings true, to free "ourselves from rigid adherence to the standards and practices of our disciplines that constrain . . . [our] personal re-flection." Feminist thought rejects conventional chains that impede fair dis-course. It asserts female strength of mind and spirit.

My interviews with the women suggest that I was not alone in starting early to think about Colombian women's histories and the discourses that shape them; each woman did so, in her particular way. The difference is that I have pursued the research.

When the time came to conduct the interviews, I asked some of my acquaintances if they would like to participate in my research and tell me about their upbringing and its consequences. Because the discussions could veer toward intimate topics, I preferred the research subjects to be women I knew and with whom I could speak more comfortably about their private lives than would be the case with strangers. This way, I felt less like an "inquisitor." Even though I met Rosie, the Colombian sex worker in Amsterdam's Red Light District, I was at ease with her, because we both came from the same hometown. Rosie may have felt comfortable with me because, while overseas, she hardly ever saw anyone from Cali. Most important, we empathized with one another.

Of the eighteen interviewees, I knew all but four, before the project. Rosalia and Gloria, working-class women, were contacted by Soledad. I met Rosie, by coincidence; and Graciela was introduced by sister María Luisa, a Franciscan nun. Among other responsibilities, she cares for young women who have been rejected by their companions and/or families because they are pregnant, as is the case with Graciela. The other women were acquaintances, people I had known earlier, but whose intimate stories and thoughts were unfamiliar. Some—like Clara, Susana, Soledad, Manuela, María del Socorro, and Juliana—I had met in different parts of Colombia, and in different stages of my life. Aleja, ninety-one years old at the time of the interview, had been a nanny. At sixteen she played with my mother in the days when Aleja served in my grandparents' home. Most of the other women—Esperanza, Juana, María Isabel, Flor, Dora, and Gloria—I knew for at least fifteen years. I met María del Carmen (who helped me with the transcripts) just a few years ago; she is my father's secretary. Nora was introduced by a cousin of mine.

The ages of the women ranged from Aleja's nine decades to Graciela's seventeen years. Racial backgrounds were also varied: white, white mixed with Indian, white mixed with black, African Colombian, and Indian. No black or Indian person was in the primary group of interviewees. Later, to widen my research, Sister María Luisa—who works in a poor section of Cali, selected eight women who would participate in a focus group. This nun had been educating women for the previous twenty years. Among them were two African Colombians, two Indians, and three others who belonged to the African Colombian and Indian ethnic groups; they had mixed with whites and with each other. Only one woman of these eight was white.[10] Although all of the women had a Cali connection, they came from several of the Colombian regions—Amazonas, Tolima, Nariño, Cauca, Valle del Cauca, Costa del

Pacifico, Antioquia, Cundinamarca, Santander, Bolivar y Costa del Atlántico—and they represented most of Colombian ethnicities—European, Mestizas, African, Afro-Indian, and Indians. Thus, these subjects presented an ethnic and geographic microcosm of the country. The traditional values and norms of women from one part of the country coincided with those of Colombian women everywhere, as confirmed in the responses to questions in this study. Where the women came from was less important than their common cultural experiences. Data is interpreted for the culture as a whole, not for any specific region.

Following feminist scholars who affirm that feminist research is creatively formed by the researcher as she develops the investigative process, I draw on history, socioeconomic perspectives and analysis of such issues as virginity, contamination of the female body, the eradication of women's eroticism through the education they receive, and women's silencing. I would say that I did a *sui generis* kind of fieldwork (which I could call "natural") with respect to the women I interviewed. I did not physically live among the subjects or participate actively in their daily comings and goings. Because I share with these women a host of factors that unite our lives and our symbolic universe, I firmly believe I conducted an insider's fieldwork. I was in the "field" (mentally) with the subjects of my research while I spoke with them, listened to them, and shared their sorrows and joys, because I too am a Colombian woman. As an insider, I participated actively in the narratives of these women's "realities." On the other hand, because I expatriated myself from Colombia and lived in the United States for twenty-five years, I have been able to acquire a clear outsider perspective of my culture and its *machista* society, and on the enormous sociocultural, political, legal and religious rules that differentiate Colombian men from women (see Sen 1999; Cabal, Lemaitre, and Roa 2001; Mancini Billson and Fluehr-Lobban 2005). In other words, I have been able to adopt a liminal or betwixt-and-between view, such as Victor Turner (1970: 94, 97) describes as a state of transition. Nothing is fixed. Everything is in constant flux, moving, developing, changing, and dying, to be reborn once more. Separated from my culture, I move from one dynamic realm to the other, and back, literally flying back and forth between the two cultures, several times a year.

This project originated with my desire to answer a simple question: "What does it mean to grow up female in a Colombian family, and what are the consequences for women of that country?"

Research can begin long before the actual study is written down. The actual investigation starts with one person's desire to know more about a subject, that is, with the person's thoughts, ideas, readings, writings, questions, and searches for answers in newspapers, magazines, and the media. Conversations with others may give a clue to whatever one is looking for. The interviews originated with the idea that one day I was going to do research on Colombian women's perceptions about being female in our *machista* society.

In this way I started my research on issues about Colombian women's lives and destinies. My mental fieldwork started, as I mention in Chapter 1, at an early age (see Reinharz 1992). Over four years, I completed all the interviews.

The women were unaccustomed to analyzing their lives and sharing thoughts with someone recording their words. Nevertheless, all contributions were proved valuable. They spoke forthrightly, and most respondents answered the questions without hesitation. If they camouflaged or reserved some information, I am sure the aim was to maintain privacy for themselves or their relatives. This limitation was not an important matter, nor in any way did it harm the research.

Biographical Notes

Six of the subjects came from the working classes. The five who were employed said they had good jobs as housekeepers or cleaning women, from which they earned good enough salaries to help their families' economic well-being, but they did comment that they were hoping to find better-paid jobs than the ones they had, or find a second job that would help supplement their salaries. These women and their families lived in decent surroundings. They had completed enough schooling to read, write, and do some arithmetic.

The eight women from the focus groups, although extremely poor, have received from the nun a good supervised education on subjects concerning human and sexual behavior and development, and social services. Today, human scientists in their own right, they help the nun in educating other women from *Aguablanca*. Sister María Luisa also had them finish secondary school, so they could enter the university to do a short-term project on social service. Each woman then instructed sixteen other women.

By contrast, Gloria, in her late twenties, was finishing a degree in computer science, and María del Carmen, thirty years old, studied accounting and English. These women, too, belonged to the working classes. Three have children, and their youngsters go to school—their older ones even attend college, making the offspring better educated than their mothers and fathers.

Only three—Juana in her late forties, Flor in her mid-thirties, and Rosalia in her mid-twenties—were involved in ongoing, stable relationships with men. Gloria never had a boyfriend. María del Carmen, who was not seeing a man at the time of the interview, had enjoyed just one meaningful relationship in the past (with a person she met while pursuing her studies). Graciela, who is African-Colombian, came to stay with Sister María Luisa, after her boyfriend left her pregnant with a child he claimed could not be his, and after she was also rejected by her mother, who admonished her to take care of herself if she was going to have sex with her boyfriend. Aleja had never known a man intimately. Esperanza, in her mid-fifties, had not been involved with a person of the opposite sex in sixteen years: "The 'love' compartment has been closed for me. I am much better off the way I am. This way, I don't have problems." Rosie, in her mid-forties, who comes from a low-income family, was having a relatively steady relationship with an East-Asian man. All of the women mentioned above came from low-income families.

Differences among women from the upper and middle classes seemed to correlate with age and upbringing, rather than with economic status. All these women received a solid education—some through obtaining university degrees or becoming exceptionally good readers (like Clara and Soledad), others by gaining exposure to foreign cultures that enriched their perspectives on the world. Juliana was finishing secondary school. Each one answered my questions carefully and promptly. Among this group, five women were married and had children. Manuela, Gloria, María del Carmen, and Juliana are single, while María del Socorro was not married at the time of the interview.

The Interviews

The women came to my house where we had enough privacy and were not bothered by interruptions. The questions I asked were the same for each respondent. Most of the women gave detailed, specific answers. Some concentrated on one subject more than others, for example, their parents' attitudes toward women, or male versus female virginity. By the end, all the subjects were interested in the entire questionnaire and answered as much as they could. At times, I had to explain a question repeatedly, but as soon as it was understood, the interviewees responded diligently.

At the beginning of our conversations I advised the women that they were free to leave the project, at any moment. I also told them to speak only about what they chose, as there was no obligation to discuss anything they wished to keep private. Therefore, they retained control over their stories and involvement. This sense of ownership and active participation produced a strong rapport between the respondents and me. The women knew I cared about them because, as we say in Colombia, we had been "crossing over the same bridge all our lives." I was careful to transmit this idea to them before I started the interviews.

> The requirement that the feminist establish rapport stems from the ideology that women experience relationships through an ethic of care. . . . Rapport . . . validates the scholar as a feminist, as a researcher, and as a human being. It symbolizes her sisterhood, her interviewing skill, and her ethical standing. (Reinharz 1999: 265)

Only through an ethic of care does the scholar accomplish feminism's first concern: helping to construct a more humane type of scholarship.

A Woman's Space

I also shared a common culture, religion, and language with the subjects interviewed, although variations existed between individuals, depending on socioeconomic background, ethnicity, age, and other particulars. In this respect I aspired to what Harding (1987: 9) describes as the "best feminist analysis,"

> [which] insists that the inquirer be placed in the same critical plane as the overt subject matter. . . . That is, the class, race, culture, and gender assumptions, beliefs, and behaviors of the researcher must be placed within the frame of the picture that she attempts to paint. . . . Thus, the researcher appears to us not as the invisible, anonymous voice of authority but as a real, historical individual with concrete, specific desires.

Because the interviewees and I shared symbolic cultural and linguistic meanings, we instinctively recognized the significance of narrative events—like the importance of arguments between daughters and fathers or between husbands and wives. I understood nuances and was able to grasp subliminal dimensions of intimate details the women related. For example, at times, men in our culture do not like women to know "too much about sex" for fear they will "get damaged or soiled." Similarly, men in Colombia tend to believe that money matters are "men's business" in which women are not supposed to intervene, unless the partners have an explicit agreement that contradicts the way money normally is managed. If women work and/or have their own income, they handle such funds separately from their husbands' or companions' money. Several of the interviewees, specifically those from the *Aguablanca* working classes, confirmed that they never spoke of money with their partners. Usually, there was a tacit arrangement between the couple that each was responsible for certain family bills. Thus, the interviewees and I were familiar with the same cultural codes and social rules. We shared a country—its geography, food, and customs. We grew up amid the same mountains, valleys, rivers, seas, and skies. We understood, profoundly, one another as females in a man-made world. Some people may have believed that women in Colombia were finally on a par with men. United by sexual class, we knew otherwise, that ours was the second class, the second sex (De Beauvoir 1952; Cabal, Lemaitre, and Roa 2001).

Gender was one of many threads—and a very strong one—that I used in knitting our women's understanding of our female place in Colombian culture. But the experiences we had were as different as the contexts in which they took place. Still, we observed a phenomenon described by Jana Sawicki (1989: 306–10) in which the telling of different narratives promotes "liberatory politics" that help open up a psychological space free of violence into which women can move unafraid. In other words, I opened "a space" for women to speak without fear, to uncover the mistreatment to which women are usually prone in family relations and society. For every one of the interviewees, being female presented obstacles. Prominently, having female bodies led to "special treatment" that handicapped the interviewees, one way or another, as children or adults in relationships with others, and with social groups and with politics.

The women's standpoint[11] and our respective explanations forged an understanding of what it means to be female in Colombia. My research has sought to contribute to a feminist epistemology (theory of knowledge) regarding the world that can be constructed within specific cultural contexts (Reinharz 1983: 170). It has been suggested that the way the individual interprets culture and the way knowledge changes inside that culture determines the narrative, "Knowledge of the world emerges through this process of interrelating projects and accounts. . . It's a mutual process of discovering" (Lengerman and Niebrugge-Brantley, 1990: 327). The methodology is "collaborative" (Reinharz 1983: 320–327), in that the researcher is a student "rather than an expert, and the woman being studied is also a student of the problem forming the basis of inquiry."[12]

Widening Dialogue

Both interviewer and subject weave a tapestry of ideas, uncovering hidden threads, as they develop. The women I examined *do not* constitute a representative sample; my aim was simply to illustrate the effects patriarchy has on the perception of self among specific respondents.

Auxiliary questions involve why men discriminate against women in Colombia. Do males expect to maintain sole control of society? Are they motivated by fear of women and their sexuality? Is discrimination rooted in childhood memories of the relationship with an overpowering mother? Does the castration complex play a part?

Julia Kristeva proposes another view on this subject matter: that the mother could be seen as the one who offers other possibilities for a more amiable and just society, one in which love and respect for others is the main characteristic and where a different discourse will provide other life and cultural perspectives.

Through "inter-viewing," I have learned about the women's experiences and ideas, while they themselves listened to their voices narrating their lives. The interviews were in-depth and open-ended, as is often the case with oral history. I asked myself what critical choices these women made that even allowed them to speak about their private lives. They were courageous to open their personal stories in a formal interview. I was deeply interested in the women's analyses of their own experiences, which informed my understanding. Each woman concentrated on her personal history and spoke as much as she liked—not only about her own life but about others' experiences, as well as the cultural or social meaning she attached to these accounts. Most have confirmed that the interviews were part of a process by which they were able to speak about their lives, thoughts, and ideas in a private way that was rewarding for them.[13] They were able to get a different perspective on their lives. Some said that what they thought was the way things were, according to custom, was not the way things should be. Also, many of the women, with whom I have kept contact, continue to tell me about their lives. Our first conversation did not end with one interview. On the contrary, it widened our communication and reaffirmed the value of these interviews. Those who saw the transcripts of their interviews, like Clara, Soledad, and Manuela, corrected what they thought had to be clarified. But the usual response to my question, "Do you wish to revise your interview?" was, "No, what I told you is correct. Everything I said is the way it was with me."

In my study of Colombian women, I have tried to analyze all data carefully. I hope that the results can be used to generate further knowledge about gender discrimination, and initiate dialogues to criticize and alter or eliminate harmful behavior, and challenge the status quo and/or social power relations (Gutting 1990: 330). In collecting oral histories, one of the many aims was to raise the consciousness of the respondents so that they could examine the historical realities that shaped their lives, while they created self-knowledge by understanding "their worth as persons and as social beings"

(Lavrin 1978: 120). As change must follow insight, rights and freedoms must follow exposure of oppression (see Foucault 1973: 378–380). Radical feminism drives both theory and action to construct a more just world, if possible.

Illustration of Feminist Research: Interviewing Aleja

I am a human scientist, a social historian. I deal with theories, data, and methodologies. Now, I sit across the table from Aleja, in my sister's breakfast room. Before us, we contemplate cups of warm Colombian coffee and delicious *arepas* (made of corn, like the Mexican *tortilla*, but different). At eighty-eight, Aleja's mind is crystal clear, her countenance calm and pleasant, as it always has been, from the moment I remember her, when I was barely two years old. She had played with my mother. Later she became my nanny, then the nanny to my brother, my sisters, and my younger sister's two daughters. I have called on this other grandmother to be a subject in my research. I said that I would ask her a few questions, to use the information to do some interesting work for my university degree. I know that she is pleased to help me.

Aleja first came to my family through her mother's friend, who recommended her to my maternal grandmother as an intelligent, discreet, and lovely sixteen-year-old girl. My grandmother, from Medellin, Antioquia, brought Aleja to that city, to train her as an inside maid and as a companion to my mother, who was six years old, at the time. When I was born, Aleja was sent to help my mother, not only as a nanny, but as a housekeeper. At twenty-nine, she had learned from my grandmother the skills a woman needs to run a household, including how to cook the best family recipes.

After all we children grew and had our own families, Aleja chose to stay with my younger sister, to take care of her two daughters and her household. So, Aleja never left us. (When she died in 2002, surrounded by my grandparent's descendants, she had been with our family a total of eighty years.)

As the interview unfolds and I collect her replies to questions I ask all the other women, I find myself thinking of the basic tenets: the importance of understanding human life as a feature of history, that culture and family are progenitors of female roles. What does theory have to do with the life of a woman like Aleja? How do I remain objective and at the same time involved in Aleja's story? My job is, somehow, to sort out the right information in relation to theory, to examine the life of this woman who was so important to my maternal family, and later, to my own family.

She comes to us as a country girl. That simple statement holds plenty of implication. It means, first of all, that her education was probably inadequate, if she were to advance beyond rural poverty. Anyway, such advancement would unlikely occur. Country girls of that time, and even today, do not advance unless, like Aleja, they are brought into well-to-do homes of the city as servants, or, by chance, get a good education, which is unusual. The hard, menial work endured as a child—she claims to have enjoyed it more than play—would be normal.

At school and at home, she is subject to violence. She attends a rural school where teachers beat disobedient children, like Aleja, with a ruler. Later, the girls school in the larger town is a convent where the nuns are strict but do not strike the students. However, when she goes home, her mother beats her with the cow whip. Her mother, "stern" and "very religious," takes charge of the workers' food. (We may assume that her responsibility is for a good number of workers.) Bearing six children, two of whom die early, she keeps on having children until "late age." "Extremely respectful" of a husband who is unfaithful, who maintains his other family in town, she does his laundry with love, ignores his infidelity, as she considers it none of her business, and invites his other children to eat in her house. No wonder this woman has a bad temper and is impatient with her children.

On the other hand, Aleja talks about her father with affection. As farm manager, he does important work, communicating with neighbors, buying resources and selling crops. Whereas mother is "stern," father is "affectionate," "tender," and "loving." He plays the flute and sings. "All his love was for us, and he was never abusive." At the time, he has another woman, on the side. Aleja complains that she never has an intimate conversation with her mother. As for her father, ". . . well, my poor father, he never said anything to us. We left him alone and didn't bother him; he was always so busy."

My inquiry goes smoothly, until I ask a question like, *How did you learn about menstruation and about how babies are made and born?* Her answers to anything to do with the body or sexuality, accompanied by a sweet smile, are always; "*I don't know, no one ever told me about those things. I learned by watching things happen.*" Several times, she does mention that girls had to be "discreet," make men "respect" us women, and always be careful of men's bad intentions.

Fear of men notwithstanding, love for her father is a constant in Aleja's life. Like almost all the interviewees, "I was never left alone; my mother was always supervising us." This is the *special treatment* to protect the virtue of women, to keep them chaste. "The only man I ever saw nearby was my father." As a child, she never has much to do with boys, not with the farm hands, not even with male relatives. At fifteen, she considers marriage (secretly, perhaps because she is afraid of her mother), but catches the man with another woman. Later, she is tempted by "a love relationship" when she works for my grandmother. But a friend warns her of the duplicity of men: "They lie. They need single women and if they marry you, they change and suddenly act as if they own you." Everything in Aleja's life bears out the truth of this warning: her two romantic experiences and what she witnessed at home. She acknowledges her father's infidelity as a reason for her not marrying and admits that he was also "rude" to her mother. (Is *rude* a way to say that her father was *abusive*?)

Unlike other girls of Aleja's socioeconomic class, she could afford not to marry, because she held a position with my family. As long as she worked hard and well, she would be supported. Without income, either she would have to rely on her family (who would likely regard her as a burden) or she would have to marry. Candidates for marriage or cohabitation would have been the farm hands. She might have preferred someone in the town of La Mesa, difficult, as she did not live in the town itself. Nor did she socialize with the people there.

If Aleja had married someone she met in Medellin, while working at my grandparents' house, her destiny would not have been much better than the one she would have at the farm. Likely, she would become companion to a man. She would have many pregnancies, because the Catholic Church would not allow artificial birth control. Today, the Colombian government does supply the pill to the women who live in or near large cities, but not too many women are covered. Even with two incomes, Aleja and her companion could not support a large family, decently. If she were lucky to meet a good man who cared for her and their children, one who earned a substantial salary, probably, her life would be pleasant, but not opulent, since she would likely bear many children. If the man she chose were abusive, one who drank and went to "the women" on the weekends, which is often the case, she might expect poverty, violence, and infidelity, along with a large family.

Instead of living with a man, Aleja stayed single, with our family. She did not have her own children, but we, my brother, sisters, and I were her children. Our children were her grandsons and granddaughters. She enjoyed life, expressing herself as nanny, nurse, cook, making herself loved and indispensable. She did not own a house but was able, with her salary, to give a house to her younger sister, help her nephews and nieces to attend good schools in Bogotá, and thereby change their lives. Indirectly, she helped free her family from poverty, through education and self-advancement.

I return as the social scientist, reflecting that Aleja might have wanted what all women want: "autonomy, dignity, physical and sensual gratification, productivity, and an end to violence and humiliation," (see Mancini Billson and Fluehr-Lobban, 2005) though she would not express it that way. Oddly, this uneducated country girl achieved a great deal, though not all of such wishes, but more than some of the other women I interview. She takes her place in my enterprise, adding her story, replete with family violence; poor education, including little sexual education; fear of men, their control, duplicity, and promiscuity; among a litany of complaints unspoken, or whispered, by women.

Notes

1. Julian Pitt-Rivers in "Honor and Social Status." *Honor and Shame: The Values of Mediterranean Society*, ed. J. G. Peristiany (Chicago: Chicago University Press, 1966), 45, writes that men's masculinity, "is the natural basis of authority and the defense of familial honor . . . [it] means courage whether it is employed for moral or immoral ends . . . and the concept is expressed as the physical sexual quintessence of the male (*cojones*—testicles). The contrary notion is conveyed by the adjective *manso* which means both tame and also castrated."

2. Anthropolgist Milagros Palma, *La Mujer Es Puro Cuento: Feminidad Aborigen y Mestiza* (To be a woman is simply a story: Aborigine and "mestiza" femininity) (Bogotá: Tercer Mundo Editores, 1992), analyzes Colombian aboriginal myths and crossbreed stories with a feminine viewpoint that uncovers the perpetual violence done to women through these genres.

3. Humm, ibid.,173, says about misogyny: "Psychoanalysts argue that misogyny, or hatred of women, is rooted in the infant's primitive rage toward the mother because society allocates childrearing to women. . . . Adrienne Rich has characterized misogyny as organized, institutionalized, normalized hostility and violence against women."

4. As Jary and Jary, ibid., 147, indicate, Foucault uses the word "episteme" to mean any "structure of knowledge that contributes to discourse formation, which determines the way the world is experienced. Foucault disregarded individual authors, subjects, and books; instead, he focused on anonymous discourse that informs particular writings."

5. *Verstehen*, the German word for "understanding," "usually refers in English to meaningful information within a sociological context. Sociologists use the word to indicate the procedure through which individuals gain access to other people's ideas." Ibid., 544.

6. As Nancy Hartsock explains, "Consciousness must become deed, but the act of becoming conscious is itself a kind of deed." "The Feminist Standpoint: Developing the Ground for a Specifying Feminist Historical Materialism" in Nancy Harstock *Discovering Reality* (London: D. Reidel Publishing Co., 1983), 66.

7. In Colombia, for example, women are confronting opposition on the part of the Catholic Church to the "day-after pill" as a mode of contraception. The Colombian

government remains silent on the subject. This position is yet another way in which men retain control over women's bodies.

8. To Freud's question, Hélène Cixous answers: "What do women want? . . . What does she want? . . . Nothing . . . because she is passive. The only thing man can do is offer the question 'What could she want, she who wants nothing?' Or in other words: 'Without me, what could she want?'" in "Castration and Decapitation," *Signs*, Vol. 7, no.11 (1981), 45.

9. Shulamit Reinharz, "Experiential Analysis," in Renate Duelli Klein and Gloria Bowles, eds. *Theories of Women's Studies* (New York: Routledge and Kegan Paul, 1983:175), thinks social scientists could profit from undergoing psychoanalytic therapy to prepare themselves for doing research. The researcher brings to the study, as a form of data, feelings, ideas, and historical perspective as well as ideology, cultural symbols, and a host of influences from the society where a study is being conducted. In other words, the scientist participates in the research as a human being, not as a "data collecting machine." Liz Stanley and Sue Wise's article "Back into the Personal," *Theories*, ibid., 195, 203, 206, also speaks of the importance of considering personal experiences on the part of the researcher as data. What we know about the social world and how we relate to it are critical aspects of what we do on a daily basis. Constructing daily life constitutes valuable data. Feminist research should "explore the basis of our everyday knowledge as women, as feminists and as social scientists."

10. Colombia, like most countries in Latin America, is populated today by a conglomerate of races from around the world: indigenous people locally called "Indians," whites, black descendants of African slaves, and Oriental races. In the United States, all Latin American people are generally grouped into a single category termed "Hispanic" or "Latino." Thinking of everyone from the entire continent as conforming to one racial criteria is alien to Latin Americans. A Latin language, Spanish (and Portuguese in Brazil), is spoken, and the Mediterranean culture is shared by all even though there are variations depending on the strength of an ethnic group (like isolated Indian tribes). The majority of the population belongs to the Catholic faith, although all major religions are represented in that part of the world.

11. The "knowing subject" of research, as Dorothy Smith explains, is centered in "her own life, in herself as a unitary being, as a body active, imagining, thinking, as a subject situated in her local and particular actualities." "Sociological Theory: Methods of Writing Patriarchy" in Ruth A. Wallace ed. *Feminism and Sociological Theory* (London: Sage, 1989), 346–66. Also see Sandra Harding's introduction to *Feminism and Methodology*, 1987: 1–10, for another feminist point of view about keeping the researcher visible (in terms of her own ideas, perspectives, and feelings) when reporting findings.

12. Sociologist and feminist Janet Mancini Billson in "The Progressive Verification Method. Toward a Feminist Methodology for Studying Women Cross Culturally," *Women's Studies* vol. 14, no. 3 (1991): 201–15, proposes a research approach in which the researcher and subjects spoken to or interviewed both participate actively

and together in the construction of theory, methodology, recollection of data for finding accurate solutions for the problems affecting women's lives. See her *Keepers of the Culture: The Power of Tradition in Women's Lives* (1995).

13. On the issue of empowerment, see Magdalena Leon, ed., *Empoderamiento de las Mujeres* (Women's ways of empowerment) (Bogotá: Editorial Nuevo Mundo, 1998). Maggie Humm defines empowerment as "a term used to describe facilitating oneself or others to work toward or attain personal aims. In a feminist sense, it is used to describe an enabling power to do something rather than a power over someone. For example, feminist anthropologists distinguish between 'empowerment' and 'authority,' arguing that empowerment involves strategies of persuasion and other forms of non-coercive influence." *The Dictionary of Feminist Theory* (Columbus, OH: Ohio State University, 1995), 78.

CHAPTER THREE

Empowerment Through Our Own Voices: Reflections on Woman-Centric Research

This creative crystallizing is a translation of feminist journeying, of our own encounters with the unknown, into a chrysalis. This writing/ metamorphosing/spinning is itself part of the journey, and the chrysalis —the *incarnation of experience into words*—is a living, changing reality. (my emphasis)

Mary Daly, Gyn-Ecology (1990: 23)

Woman's *jouissance* carries with it the notion of fluidity diffusion, duration . . . one easily sees how the same imagery could be used to describe woman's writing.

Elaine Marks and Isabelle de Courtivron (1991: 37).

Soledad: "Compared to a Chair"

Introduction
Intelligent, articulate, analytical, and ambitious, Soledad is thwarted in her development, because she is female. Her father chooses her as the son he would have liked to have had and did not have. He only had daughters. He offers her, then, trust and responsibility and to a point, unconditional love. But he denies Soledad her intellectual capacities.

Here again is a home with a womanizing father and a subservient mother. Although the family is well to do and "comfortable," the mother has neither money nor even her own thoughts. Beyond homemaking skills, no one sees a need to educate daughters, because the only career for a girl is marriage and raising children. A woman is understood as a man's acquisition, something he owns, to produce children and to dress up, a display of his success. These "pure" girls grow up without dreams or opinions, or the right to think and speak of their desires.

Soledad opens the theme of purity, (i.e., the protection of a girl's virginity), the irrational fear of prostitution—only a prostitute would study to be an actress or a musician. She also presents the first of several accounts of unequal and unfair treatment of women by the Roman Catholic Church.

In Chapter 2, classical and contemporary writers from many countries refer to many of the same dilemmas reported by Soledad in Colombia. Established patriarchal cultures, which organize societies, provide language, the most effective tool women have to empower themselves. But inside a skewed ideology, a woman has little chance to express her wishes. As Soledad and others testify, a woman in Colombia is denied the voice she needs to assert herself.

Interview

"Tell me, Soledad, how you were raised? What education did you receive about being a woman? Relate both good and bad memories from your days as a girl."

"I grew up in a very strict, conservative family. My father was extremely *machista*. At the same time, he was affectionate and had a lovely, seducing personality. He dominated us—that is, my mother, three sisters, and me—with his seductive ways. He was on top of everything that had to do with our lives. He was concerned with our needs and always tried to resolve them. A rich man, he took care of our material needs—no matter what they were. He was an excellent provider and a loving, caring husband and father. But he was domineering and quite arbitrary whenever he had a 'wish.' My father was a very good-looking man, and women were after him all the time. My father was a womanizer, a *Don Juan!*

"By contrast, my mother was a quiet woman, although strong in spirit, and she accepted everything that came from my father. She loved him very much, and, as a wife, she thought she had to please her husband, no matter what. My mother followed the role of the good, self-abnegating woman; she was a considerate wife and mother. I think this is the case with all wives and mothers, even today, no matter where they come from. By giving in to my father's whims, my mother was able to maintain her marriage. My father was extremely selfish with my mother. He was a like a king! If there was one avocado for dinner, it was sliced into six pieces; my father served himself with the largest slice. He was arbitrary, like a military man. His rules had to be obeyed. He didn't like to come home, for example, and not find my mother waiting for him. Thus, my mother had a "curfew." He had a very strong character.

"This was the atmosphere in which I grew up. When my father died, I thought, 'How sad that he's gone, but finally my mother will have a life of her own!' My mother didn't have control over anything: her life, her money, or her thoughts. A woman who has no material needs accepts manipulation by a man more easily. She is comfortable and, thus, forgets about her misery.

"My parents were totally uninterested in their daughters' education. They said that girls could go to school until tenth grade; afterwards, high school was considered unnecessary. Young women were told to take courses in cooking and variations of home economics, including embroidery and child care. Music, painting, and art were also considered fit subjects for a girl, who sooner or later had to find a husband. Neither my father nor my mother (who always agreed with my father) encouraged me to finish my studies. Nevertheless, when I was a little girl in grammar school, he wanted us four girls to get good grades. As I started growing up, his interest in my grades diminished. The same thing happened to my female cousins. We were like objects to be looked at. Our parents, families, and teachers had in their minds only one fixed future for young women: marriage. We weren't thought to have the capacity to decide or have opinions about our future. You see, first we lived with our parents, who provided for us; later the idea was that a husband was going to take care of us. Parents, generally speaking, respect and trust unconditionally the sons-in-law who become part of their families and who will protect their daughters. This is the main concern of a father regarding his daughter's new husband. This view was (and still is) not the same toward young brides. Often, she is not respected by her in-laws. The husband is regarded as the woman's savior, just like her father before him. The woman is seen as an acquisition—a good or bad one, depending on her physical and material attributes.

"I really think that young men marry to be able to own and dominate their young wives. After I dated Antonio for four years, our families started to worry because we didn't speak of marriage. My family thought he was making 'fun' of me. We did get married and went to live in the United States; he was going to finish his studies. Meanwhile, I worked so that he could finish his degree—something I considered normal. It never occurred to me that I had the same right to get a university degree! One marries and gets used to the idea that a husband has to be satisfied. Antonio was not *machista*, but he did have a strong and willful character. He never considered me his friend.

"Sexually, my ex-husband never understood my needs, which were completely different from his; our minds didn't meet in our lovemaking. He was not tender. All expression of affection had to end in sexual activity. It didn't matter if I was tired or ill. With my husband, I relived my life with my parents: I had to please others and forget about myself.

"One day, I finally asked myself why I had to be submissive and obedient when I never received anything in exchange. This happened eight years into our marriage. I started to lose my love for Antonio when he tried to beat me. Such violence occurred daily, and it was also directed against our daughter. My mother helped me leave that terrible situation. I always considered myself rebellious, but I really wasn't. I am strong verbally, but at the end I did what others told me to do—be it my father, husband, or society.

"As we girls were growing up, we didn't have special dreams. Our future was to marry a marvelous man, and we were going to be marvelous wives, and together we would give our parents beautiful grandchildren. Our lives were irremediably tied to marriage and the children we were going to have. We never dreamed that, one day, we could become important people, that we could make decisions about our destinies or have opinions. We were not allowed to speak up about what we thought or liked. If we did, they would say, 'Be quiet. You don't have the criteria to say anything about this matter!' Only men were thought to be able to give their opinions when there was any discussion, especially on important issues like politics. A young woman was, and still is, quite often compelled to remain quiet. As I see it, the idea of a woman being like a 'pure' object, which cannot be stained, gives her a bad future. In the end, the idea is that women are only good for procreation, keeping the house clean for husbands and children and serving them unconditionally. We could be compared to a chair! Yes, they give us everything that fulfills our material needs, like dresses, shoes, jewelry, and comfort. They keep telling us how beautiful we are, how well-dressed and elegant we look, but at the same time they take away what is substantial for our existence. They teach us to be superficial and make us believe, while we are growing up, that we are wonderful, that we own the world and that we can conquer that world. But when we try to do so, they stop us and say, 'Yes, you are beautiful, you may have all the dresses and shoes you want, you can have all the dolls you wish to have, but that's all. Don't get other ideas; that is all you may have.'

"We are told these things precisely because they don't consider that we own a 'thinking mind' to help us act on our own behalf or allow us to express our opinions. We don't even have the right to feel. Some women experience more limitations than others. Men, by contrast, have all the leeway they need to create their own lives. When women want to do something different, we are stopped. I had a friend who hoped to study music and become an actress. She was never able to do so because her parents thought that only prostitutes attended conservatories of music. If you had certain abilities, your family would stop you from developing them, if these talents would take you away from accepted roles. I loved to play guitar, for example, but my father was after me—supervising the songs I sang. Some he forbade me to sing because he said they were 'immoral.'

"My mother is a practicing Catholic. My father wasn't, but he expected his daughters to be religious. I never understood why we had to do things my father didn't do. Why do men have the right to do what they want, the right to force others to obey their wishes, while women cannot do as they please? As it happens, the rules of the Catholic religion are the same for all people, women as well as men. Finally, I stopped going to church because, after I had my first child, the priest didn't give me absolution, since I used contraceptives. Antonio always received absolution, no matter what he said to the priest.

"I was educated by nuns. The nuns used to look into my personal things— drawers, handbags, the pockets of my uniform—to see if I had letters from my boyfriends. For me, this was a terrible violation of my privacy. The nuns preached respect for others, but no one respected me. I felt persecuted by the nuns. Their conduct was an affront to my integrity. The nuns were guarding our virginity and family honor, which are tied to the purity of women's bodies. Neither our sexuality nor our minds belonged to us. If women act in an intelligent way, we are labeled aggressive. What is considered a positive quality in men is thought to be a drawback in women.

"I was the rebel in my family; my mother and sisters were passive. This rebellious attitude didn't benefit me, however. On the contrary, it brought confrontations with my father. My father treated me like the son he never had, precisely because of my confrontational nature. He oriented me in masculine ways he didn't convey to his other daughters, who were more feminine. My father trusted me completely; I was the chosen one. It was an ambiguous situation, because he gave me all his trust and lots of responsibility, but he didn't want me to use my intellect. I couldn't give my opinions. I didn't have the rights men have in society. I was not a boy and, thus, did not have the trust men receive from an early age from the adults around them. Fathers promote their sons' shameless behavior—like going to prostitutes. Men go out without being supervised. They go partying, they can drink, and they use sexuality as they wish. My father tortured me about what he thought were my 'love affairs.' I never did anything physical before marrying. My father also complained to my mother about my independence, which made him hostile and belligerent toward me. My mother, too, supervised me like the nuns; she looked into my things in the same way. She was equally terrible. I was tortured by everybody: by my parents, the nuns, the priests, and my husband. Thus, I created a thousand different ways or mechanisms to help myself survive and, at the same time, to 'please' them. I felt that I was being spiritually 'raped' by everybody around me.

"Women who are treated in this obnoxious way end up not having any self-esteem—like my mother, who never thought much of herself. My mother is very intelligent; it shows all over her face and eyes. But she always accepted everything that came from those she considered powerful, like her brother and husband. Many women look for other possibilities to get through, but women like my mother—who lack strong personalities—have their spirits broken. Furthermore, those of us who have gained consciousness have the responsibility to help other women. Lower class women have fewer opportunities because they receive less education and economic resources. Life is harder for them. Women who have men near them usually experience the men as obstacles to success, simply because a man makes you give yourself to him. If you speak to him about your own dreams or triumphs, he disregards them as trivial. The man usually wishes to speak about himself and his accomplishments.

"In contrast to what I have told you, I have a half-sister—my father's daughter by a schoolteacher. This girl was very well educated, unlike her four other sisters. She didn't have all the economic privileges we did, because she was born out of wedlock and her mother was very poor, but my father gave them the necessities to have a decent life. Finally, he paid for this girl's education, on her mother's insistence, because my father thought she was less fortunate than we four, and, thus, needed an education with which to confront life! How mistaken he was to think that his other daughters—who were economically better off—didn't need an education! My sister is thirty-three years old, much younger than my other sisters and me—and she faces a better future than we. Her life is different than ours because she received an education and is economically independent of her husband."

"What advice would you give a young woman today?"

"My only advice to women today is to try and get the best education possible and have their own money in order to become independent from the men with whom they live. I would tell young women to rely on themselves, rather than others, for success."

❦

In the nineteenth and twentieth centuries, a number of male writers, philosophers, and scientists examined the destiny of being born female in a world where women's lives were filled with injury and disadvantage. Analysts expounded on the deplorable situation of women in society, within their own families, hoping to improve their adverse position. Writers such as Karl Marx (1867) in the *German Ideology and Capital*, Frederick Engels (1884) in the *The Origins of the Family, Private Property and the State*, and John Stuart Mill (1869) in *The Subjection of Women* wrote in defense of women and their human rights. Sandra Harding (1991: 277–279) comments that many European-American feminists "underestimate men's ability to engage in feminist thought . . . they appear to believe that men cannot generate feminist analyses, as John Stuart Mill, Marx and Engels" did. Is it, she asks, that "*only the oppressed can generate knowledge?*" She argues that it cannot be forgotten that "feminists are made, not born."

For centuries, female authors, philosophers, and critics have advocated the recognition of women as intelligent, capable, whole human beings who—like men—have a right to education, social and legal opportunities, respect and admiration, and control over their bodies and minds. Such convictions are expressed in Christine de Pizan's *The City of Ladies* (1404), which defends women's intelligence; and by Mary Wollstonecraft's *The Vindication of the Rights of Woman* (1789), in which she argues that because of the way women are imprisoned in their homes, they cannot develop their intellects and are socialized to obey and serve men. Also in the eighteenth century, the Mexican nun Sor Juana Inés de la Crúz decides to reject marriage and motherhood and instead enter the religious life, which allows her to study, think, and write on women's issues. Harriet Taylor (1851), author of many essays on women's rights, argues that women, like men, can handle their own money, among many other particulars. At the beginning of the twentieth century, Virginia Woolf's *A Room of One's Own* (1929) and *Three Guineas* (1938) set out a schema that would instruct women on how to become independent of the chains that keep them in captivity. Toward the end of that century, Robin Morgan produced *Sisterhood is Global* (1984), which presents "radical feminist contributors—plus encyclopedic statistics, 'herstory,' analysis, and bibliography—from more than eighty countries" (Morgan 1997: 6). These writers, in one way or another, have ideas pertinent to the adverse destinies of Colombian women, among others.

Colombia is a patriarchy, which may be defined as a system of relations of material resources and cultural and social exchanges between the sexes, which subordinates women under a *gender regime*. It imprisons women through political, social, legal, religious, and economic institutions. Women come to know themselves beneath this masculine authority. Through patriarchy, females are robbed of the right to their own bodies and identities as autonomous, thinking human beings. Patriarchy constitutes the primary violence committed against women by the cultures in which they live. Women have been and are marginalized within society and constrained from becoming active participants in the world, alongside the other half of the human species. As anthropologist Gayle Rubin (1975: 173) writes in her article *The Traffic in Women*, "In the exchange of women as a fundamental principle in kinship, the subordination of women can be seen as a product of the relationships by which sex and gender are organized." The French anthropologist Claude Lévi-Strauss further elucidates, in *The Elementary Structures of Kinship* (1969: 480), how women are used as a symbolic measure of exchange within the social contract of many cultures. The incest taboo organizes culture, says Lévi-Strauss, while "the rule of exogamy has social value—[insofar as] it provides the means of binding men together." Such a kinship system delineates men's rights from women's rights in a social context. And Elizabeth Grosz (1995: xi) observes, "All knowledge and social practices have thus far represented the energies and interests of one sex alone."

Unfortunately, sexual differentiation, as Germaine Greer explains in *The Whole Woman* (1999), still relegates females to the "niche" into which they have been consigned since the beginning of recorded, masculine time. Woman is perceived as man's "*Other*,"[1] the space where he constitutes himself as a transcendental individual and thinking subject (Butler 1990). This purview, accorded to women in a world constructed by men confiscates many of women's social rights, and thus subjects them to discrimination that harms them physically and psychologically.

Patriarchal culture provides the symbolic (not just linguistic) language individuals use to communicate. It unites them through values, ideas, sentiments, and behavior patterns, all of which depend on language for transmission (Roheim 1950: 440, 441). It locates people in a moment of history, a given space within the world. Culture centers human beings in the universe.[2] Society, culture, and civilization can be "separable from the individual who composes" a given culture, but no person can develop his or her humanness without culture (Benedict, 1934: 253). People are organized within societies through culture and cognition, outside of which they cannot function normally (Cole and Scribner 1974: 7). "All forms of culture and thought serve the task of building a common world of thought and feeling," says Cassirer (1944: 72). Culture provides the rational framework for individual lifestyles, but people are still free to think for themselves. However, the way one grasps the world is influenced by different ideologies, perceptions, and interpretations transmitted through discourse. Unfortunately, sociological research far too often ignores human beings' individual behavior and relationships, while reaffirming cultural patterns or social institutions, as if they were persons. Culturology often operates as though people did not really exist. As Durkheim (1938: 239) affirms, "Psychology will always have the last word."

Participant Discourse and Language as a Tool for Empowerment

Language is the essential tool for communicating one's wishes. Discourse helps structure our realities. We live inside language, and language envelops our existence; we are what language makes of us as a result of having been born, symbolically speaking, into it (Caws 1991).[3] Discourse structures our identities and the world humans construct as our material reality. As Kristeva (1981: 272) puts it, "Through the discursive system, the subject makes and unmakes itself."[4]

Through thought and language, the tools employed in the social construction of reality, cultural change becomes possible; hence, the creation of a better world for women and others is feasible.[5] An inability to speak as assertive, independent, individuals leads to social invisibility. Without speech, we cannot express our wishes, feelings, and desires (Daly 1990; Weedon 1987; Kristeva 1981), so we cannot change the cultural rules. Discourse empowers the individual with the stamina to participate actively in her or his living process.

Speech performances, or ways of speaking, are idiosyncratic to the individual. According to George Steiner in *On Difficulty* (1978: 50), one speaks in tune with one's own social, ethnic, historical, and gender conditioning. Reading of a discourse, or text, is an interpretative endeavor; it is the introduction of meaning into a text that is to be understood. Meaning is not fixed but open to perpetual revision, depending on the influence from other discourses (Weedon 1987). For example, the word "woman" has various meanings, determined by the context in which it is used. The words "mother," "wife," "daughter," "sister," "servant," or "prostitute" can qualify "woman" in diverse, contrasting ways. The intended connotation depends on the context of the discourse and the particular female being described.

Ernst Cassirer emphasizes that all symbolic forms not only represent the world to humans but also the way "by which human thought expresses the world to itself." The real world is comprehended by women and men in keeping with how it is made visible to them, becomes intelligible, and "presents itself to the mind as a message" (Caws 1991: 16, 27). Mental activity and language (and, subsequently, culture) are intertwined in a close relationship where each influences other "cultural resources" and "tools." However, culture constructs the real as well as the symbolic aspects of the human world (Foucault 1973: 112). In the end, everything is tied to discourse.

Discourse and Desire

Language and power are intrinsically connected to the body and its drives and passions. It gives the individual vital energy to construct life and the world (Foucault 1973: 116). Because, under the Colombian patriarchy, woman's language is repressed, so, too, is the expression of women's desires, whether physical, emotional, or intellectual. Chapter 4 explains the theoretical underpinnings and the consequences of such repression. It exposes patriarchal culture for denying language, knowledge, and expression to women, on the presumption that women have a "lack," something inherently missing (like a penis) that justifies their subordination, keeping them ignored and unimportant. Without the notion of male superiority (organized by patriarchal thoughts and ideas) men would have to surrender exalted notions of themselves. A woman can and should speak with her own voice, with authority and force, to participate openly and fully in her life.

Voices Hidden, Voices Found

The aim of this book is to bring forth discussion on subjects expatiated in each chapter, to give a perspective on the social and historical place of Colombian women today, and contribute ideas to help bring change, to benefit their lives. Fundamental to that perspective is the reality that Colombian women in the twenty-first century are held subordinate to Colombian men because they have been silenced. The system is simply accepted, the subject seldom mentioned, because the passive obedience of women is ingrained in the culture. But, an inability to speak as assertive, independent, individuals leads to social invisibility. Without speech, we cannot express our wishes, feelings, and desires (Daly 1990; Kristeva 1981), so we cannot change the cultural rules. Discourse empowers the individual with the stamina to participate actively in her or his living process.

Likewise, examining the unconscious dimensions of a society's collective experience can facilitate group change. Nancy Harstock (1983: 60) describes the relationship between personal and communal life as follows:

> Feminist emphasis on everyday life leads to a second area of focus: the integration of personal and political change. Since we come to know the world (to change it and be changed by it) through our everyday activity, everyday life

must be the basis for our political work. Even the deepest philosophical questions grow out of our need to understand our own lives.

Thus, feminist criticism contributes knowledge that can modify and ultimately dismantle the institutions and gender behavior upon which patriarchal societies are built. In the words of Robin Rowland and Renate Klein (1997: 34),

> The fact that women belong to the social group which has the capacity for procreation and mothering, and the fact that men belong to the social group which has the capacity to [perform] acts of rape and violence against women, must intrude into the consciousness of being female and male. . . . This analysis allows for *change* (emphasis in the original), in the sense that men themselves could change that consciousness and their actions.

In the twenty-first century, women are continuously discriminated against and silenced in the political and/or public arenas and economic spheres (Cordoba 2004; Wills 2007). They face great obstacles in areas of economic and political advancement, personal freedom and well-being (see Appendix I for statistics). Yet, women in Colombia today are being educated (see chapter 6). Even in the lower economic classes, girls are going to school just as their brothers are, which was not the case less than fifty years ago. For the middle and upper classes, it is not unusual that women go to college; many pursue advanced degrees. Likewise, although their representation in the legislative bodies remains dismal, the majority of women do turn out to vote (see chapter 5). Nevertheless, in matters vital to their welfare—for example, birth control, abortion, wage disparities, political representation—they remain an underclass.

Where education and enfranchisement ought to ensure power, in Colombia there is a disconnection. Either educated, politically aware women are not speaking or they are not being heard, or both.

To have a speaking voice is to know oneself. It enables one to express desires and needs, to own a political and social identity. Those who have written or lectured on behalf of women, or those on the receiving end of discrimination, confirm the utmost importance for victims to speak about their lives. For a woman to capture her voice, to use language to open a space for herself in the world, ought to be a birthright.

Speech is the main tool for attaining well-being and agency, (i.e., the right to act). To speak up, to have a voice in matters concerning social life or cultural matters, is the road to freedom (Sen 1999; Mancini Billson and

Fluehr-Lobban, 2005; Kristeva, 1981). In a democracy, women need to establish themselves as actors, not as passive recipients of what others may say. To speak, they must use language, the tool *par excellence* that defines what it means to be human.

Language helps humans build lives, construct societies, regulate religious and cultural laws, put together institutions. Its words tied to and aided by grammatical rules produce meaning. Language is the hatchet that cuts through to reveal thoughts and ideas, to construct institutions, to enable women and men to live in communities. It creates regulations for a just society and encourages hope for an equitable world. Not speaking is equivalent to not thinking and not contributing. One who does not speak is a passive entity who only knows how to follow orders. In Colombia, women with language but no voice do not contribute, but stay passively silent and follow instructions.

Women Without Voice

As youngsters, women are taught not to speak. They are assigned a set of ideas about themselves that, without a voice, they cannot refute. Here is the testimony of the interviews:

Susana: "I married simply to stop hearing my father stamping his feet because he did not agree with me" and "I never had any interesting conversations or any kind of communication with my parents. I always felt ignored by them. I was very much afraid of my father, who completely ignored me. . .Whenever I asked my mother anything concerning sex or the functioning of our bodies, she answered that I was too young to know about 'those things.' My mother never answered any of the questions I asked her. Never."

Dora: "We had to be respectful of adults. To be loved by adults, we had to be obedient and quiet . . . My mother did hear our opinions, but at the end, we kept quiet and did what she told us to do . . . But they (teachers and parents) never went deep into the subject (of virginity); nothing was clear, everything was kind of shady, and we never asked. We listened and we kept silence." Then, as Dora grows and marries an abusive husband, "If I cried because he used gross language against me, he hit me all over my body and face. The bruises lasted up to a month. I was just eighteen years old . . . No one ever mistreated me. I grew up in a secluded and loving atmosphere . . . (Now) I had no friends; I didn't tell anyone about my suffering."

Esperanza: "At the age of five, my parents forced me to do housework . . . he (father) used to put two or three bricks in front of the stove, so I could reach pots and pans and cook the food . . . I also had to wash the clothes for my father and brothers. The dirty blue jeans were the worst. And my father never stopped screaming at me. He always found a reason to yell. Even today, I don't know why he shouted at me and was not able to address me in a nice way. . . . This is what I remember, my father always screamed at me."

Here are the techniques for imposing silence: (1) Ignore a young girl. Do not answer her questions. Make her feel that questions about her biology are sinful, that she has no right to question anything, at all. (2) Teach that to be a good girl, she has to sit silently before her elders, preparing her to stay silent, even in the face of harsh physical abuse. (3) Shout her down, before she is old enough to formulate her questions: *"How do I do this work? Why are you asking me to do a job I'm too small for? Why don't you ask my brothers to help?"*

Clara, presently eighty-seven years old, the second eldest of the interviewees, confronts the same overpowering, deaf forces. Yet, as a child, she has the perception and strength to resist. Her formal education starts under the rules of German nuns: "The discipline was violent in regards of silence, school games and recreations, permission to go or not go out after class, and the like." More significant is her interaction with her father and his "harsh rules": "Clara, you shall not go out today!" Her response is: "Why, papa?" Intolerable that she should question, he answers, "Don't ask me why! You will not go out today!" He is ineffectual against his rebellious daughter: "In the end, it wasn't important what he did or said. What really bothered me was to have limitations on my beliefs, wishes, and thoughts. Such restriction I could neither accept nor understand." Later, when her father sends three unscholarly sons to study in Europe, whereas his academically gifted daughter is kept home, she protests, "Why does this have to be so?" He does not answer. She observes, "Still I am waiting to have my *whys* answered by someone."

Eventually, rebellious Clara goes on to be Secretary of Education for her state and even member of the national Congress. However, she finds politics repugnant: "I observed that politicians were liars, that they misused the money given to them, and that they conducted terrible fights among themselves . . . I was rarely in agreement with them or with the political system and kept asking my eternal *why* that never received a satisfactory answer. Because of my personality and tendency to speak up, I have been labeled 'strange' and considered a hostile person . . . I never accepted constrictions that would keep me down and prevent me from acting, thinking, or being."

All the techniques for shutting her up are employed—ignoring her and her questions, requiring her silent compliance, disallowing her expression as an individual, and calling her names for her nonconformity. None of these strategies work. Married, mother of five children, Clara forges ahead, unfazed, a magnificent demonstration of what a determined woman can accomplish, while maintaining her dignity. In her generation, she is an outstanding exception from the Colombian norm.

Without voice, women are invisible. They must settle for the roles assigned. Without speech, they cannot express wishes, feelings or desires. They cannot break from a destiny assigned by others. Clara, Soledad, Esperanza, Susana, Nora, Flor, Maria Isabel, and Manuela are of different ages. They come from different social classes and are born in different parts of the country. They all speak of arbitrary fathers who try to dominate their lives, as mothers are unable, or do little, to help them. In plain words, these women express the same experience: they are raised with one role in mind, to get married and have children. Nothing else is important in their upbringing, least of all, their education.

Those women who come from well-to-do families live in comfort, but their ideas and desires are not taken into consideration. Women from the lower economic classes, like Esperanza, Aleja, or Graciela, endure the same suffocation of their views, without the comforts. All of them, from whatever the class, mention that, at times, in different ways, they did speak back to contest the rules imposed on them. In the end, they always give in and retreat to silence and obedience. Some escape their families, only to fall into a worse situation, if they do not have economic means, alone and abandoned by all. If, by chance, a woman has been allowed to assume a role not assigned to females, as happens to Soledad, she cannot advance beyond a point:

> My father treated me like the son he never had, precisely because of my confrontational nature. He oriented me in masculine ways he didn't convey to his other daughters, who were more feminine. My father trusted me completely; I was the chosen one. It was an ambiguous situation, because he gave me all his trust and lots of responsibility, but he didn't want me to use my intellect. I couldn't give my opinions. I didn't have the rights men have in society. I was not a boy and, thus, did not have the trust men receive, from an early age, from the adults around me.

If a woman is idiosyncratic, she is rejected. On her twelfth birthday, Maria Isabel determines that she is "able to reason and make decisions by myself." Her parents' response is to call her "bad and dirty . . . crazy, strange, unreasonable, and different. . . . My mother thought I had ruined myself with strange ideas." For her inability or unwillingness to conform, she is rejected.

> I was left alone by my parents and my brothers. It was as if I had been thrown out of the family because I was different. My only wish was to receive approval

and affection from my father and mother. I told my parents in many different ways: 'Please love me! Look at me! I am nice!'

An impossible member of her family, Maria Isabel and all of the interviewees agree, in one way or another, without exception, that to fight against being silenced is useless. They are afraid of retaliation and hurt. In the end, they take silence as the easiest and safest route, rather than speaking back and going against the rules of family, society, culture or religion.

Occasionally, either by the force of her character, as with Clara, and with the help of an exceptionally supportive husband, her "best friend," a woman can skirt the rules. In the case of Juana, her in-laws support her, encouraging a marriage in which she is equal with her husband, resulting in "a wonderful relationship." Maria del Carmen, studying as a means to earn her living, is supported by her parents. Juliana's mother, her daughter's best friend, listens to her with respect. These are exceptions, not the rule. Cultural and social laws are strict and to the point. Those who do not follow face swift and brutal retaliation. Therefore, women are careful, remaining silent on the margins, even if they are lucky to have sympathetic sponsors.

Accordingly, women endure discrimination in many fields, especially in politics. Piedad Cordoba, one of Colombia's twelve female senators, an ardent feminist, fighting openly for many years on behalf of women's rights, laments political discrimination in her article *Mujeres en el Congreso de Colombia* (Women in the Colombian Congress) (2004). Colombia did sign the United Nations agreement of the *Convention of All Forms of Discrimination Against Women* (1979) (CEDAW). The new constitution of 1991, article 13, confirms that men and women in Colombia have the same legal and social rights, freedoms, and opportunities. Congress passed Law No. 518, in 2000, recognizing and establishing the rule that 30 percent of all administrative political posts in the legislative, executive and judicial branches had to be filled by women. This law is not followed. Only 15 percent of the highest political posts in Colombia are occupied by women. Further, it has proved impossible, according to Senator Cordoba, for Congress to mandate a law for women to achieve the same rights as men to participate equally in political organizations and posts. Historically speaking, Colombian women have been, and still are, excluded from acting in the political arena, even if there "has been great social and cultural transformation. . .in favor of women's legal status and their right to education has improved" (Cordoba 2004: 242; see also Mancini Billson and Fluehr-Lobban 2005; Wills Obregón 2007).

Numerous feminist groups press for women's issues. But, only a few women in the Colombian Congress have tried to force a perspective of gender during deliberations in the creation of laws, because women can be leaders without carrying on a feminist discourse (Wills Obregón, 2007: 23). Unfortunately, reports Senator Cordoba, there is little solidarity among Congresswomen. The attitude of Congressmen is one of indifference, permeated by a strict *machista* ideology.

Women derive their identities from the discourses by which culture and its institutions ascribe to them roles and characteristics. In that way, women are assigned or denied power, according to the way they are culturally defined (De Beauvoir 1952; Butler 1990; Mancini Billson and Fluehr-Lobban 2005; Wills Obregón 2007). Although government is among the most influential of these defining, power-controlling institutions, women in politics, in general, have little contact with feminist groups. Their not speaking to one another accounts for why women's rights are not part of the political agenda (Wills Obregón, 2007: 25, 58), and, therefore, why women are relegated to an invisible and silenced minority, subjected to the customary discrimination.

Currently, Colombia has sufficient democratic laws governing social and political rights for women, to protect them. Women ought to join, to determine their objectives, to develop the strength to speak those objectives, to insist on enforcement of prevailing law, ignoring the irrational censure they may expect heaped upon them. Finding, owning, bringing together and putting to use women's voices is the way for them to take control, to succeed in their struggles. The following chapters show why such actions, urgently needed, are easier said than done.

Notes

1. Simone de Beauvoir, in her book *The Second Sex* (New York: Vintage Books, 1952), explains women's role as representing the "Other" for men. Josette Féral, in her essay "The Powers of Difference" in *The Future of Difference*, Hester Eisenstein and Alice Jardin, eds. (Piscataway, NJ: Rutgers University Press, 1980), 89, also writes about woman being the "Other": "Thus a woman does not become the Other but his Other, his Unconscious, his repressed. . . . Enmeshed in man's self-representation, woman exists only insofar as she endlessly reflects back to him the image of his manly reality."

2. Cassirer says the various symbolic grammars of culture—language, art, myth, religion, philosophy, and science—help humans in the endeavor for survival and the construction or reconstruction of an empirical world they do not want to lose; see his *An Essay on Man: An Introduction to a Philosophy of Human Culture* (New Haven, CT, and London: Yale University Press, 1944), 137.

3. Cixous says, "For as soon as we exist, we are born into language and language speaks (to) us, dictates its laws, a law of death: it lays down its familial model . . . [and] masculine desire." *Castration*, 45.

4. Kristeva says, "A major part of 'values' and 'rights' as well as thinking patterns and psychosexual behavior has to do with language. . . . The social contract and social restraint are inscribed in the *existence of language*" (emphasis in the original). Ross Mitchell Guberman, ed., *Julia Kristeva: Interviews* (New York: Columbia University Press, 1996), 16, 27.

5. Some signifying systems "are types of languages," explains Kristeva, who quotes Freud: "Symbolism is not peculiar to dreams but is characteristic of unconscious ideation, in particular among the people, and it is to be found in folklore, popular myths, legends, linguistic idioms, proverbial wisdom, and current jokes to a more complete extent than in dreams." *Tales of Love*, trans. Leon Roudiez (New York: Columbia University Press, 1983), 386.

CHAPTER FOUR

The Symbolic and Social Construction of Female Sexuality: Theoretical Background of Desire, Discourse, and the Body

This humanity of woman, carried in her womb through all her suffering and humiliation, will come to light, when she has stripped off the conventions of mere femaleness in the transformations of her outward status.

Rainer Maria Rilke (1986: 77)

Clara: "All my life I saw my mother crying"

Introduction

So far, this study has observed that Colombian women are denied voice, the fundamental right to speak, to assert and defend themselves, to stop being invisible. To discover why such denial is imbedded in culture, chapter 4 consults classical and contemporary social scientists and scholars. They examine clues to the formulation of repression and give them meaning. Theories are important because they show us where we have been; therefore, where and why we are as we are now; and finally, where we may go. The theorists' own attitudes are likewise instructive: in Sigmund Freud's impatient question, "What do women want?" he seems to be asking, "What in the world do these unreasoning women want, and how can we expect anything like a reasonable reply?" As the discipline of the human sciences advance, enter female observers and the perspective changes. They deconstruct and find ways to disrupt the symbolic language (i.e. that of patriarchal culture), turn it over, and replace it with a language Julia Kristeva refers to as "semiotic," (i.e., a maternal language linked to poetry, music, and eroticism). As the theorists are singular in disentangling the vines through patriarchal control, they are equally steadfast in blazing a trail forward to the daylight of Kristeva's jouissance, a woman's particular route to joy, fulfillment based in intellectual and artistic endeavour.

In her youth, Clara, whose interview opens chapter 4, doubtless was unfamiliar with arcane theories. Yet, something in her makeup drives her to cast aside culturally imposed limits. An exception to the rule of subservience, she strikes her own path, becomes a political leader and a founder of institutions, as well as a wife and mother. "Why?" she asks, as she forges ahead, past a father who will not recognize her capacities, through a glum world of shady politics—and succeeds. Clara's motivation, intellect, and refusal to accept what the Law ordains stands as the kind of model in which an ardent theorist might take pride.

Interview

"Clara, tell me about your experiences while you were growing up, the positive and the negative experiences. Tell me whatever you wish to comment on these issues."

"I come from a very large family. We were thirteen brothers and sisters. Ten girls and three boys. I was the second born, and my sister Laura, was the eldest. We grew up on a very large farm that my father owned. For us, the two oldest of the children, it was a delight to come back from school and be able to run free—like wind in the fields—was delightful. We would climb the fruit tress and bathe ourselves in small streams that crossed the farm. We were free; yes, indeed, we were. When I was about eight years old, our main entertainment was to go and see the train go by. Even today, whenever I hear a train, I remember our old farm house. That sound brings back my grandfather, my father, and mother, along with that train of my childhood, which I adored.

"My parents married when they were very young. My mother was extremely intelligent. A good reader, she was, and very humane and understanding. She was always available for her children—ready to give us advice, sternly when necessary, but as an affectionate counselor. My mother had been educated at the only private school of our hometown, and finished high school. My sister and I we went to another school—an all-girls institution directed by German nuns. The nuns were strict in terms of academic discipline, but never gave us any rules to guide our lives. The discipline was violent in regards of silence, school games and recreation, permission to go or not to go out after class, and the like. We were tightly constricted with the Germanic rules of the nuns, since we were all 'rebellious' country girls who were free as the wind.

"By sixteen, I finished high school. Within my family, freedom lasted only until the age of fifteen. At this time, school rules, and father's dog-like discipline, really were enforced. My father was a hard, strict person who didn't have a good way to impose his order upon us. Whenever one of us broke his terrible rules, my mother pretended she hadn't noticed our disobedience. It was very difficult to control or change girls who had been allowed to roam free around the farm, and then, suddenly, because of their age and their gender, were harnessed and curbed. By contrast, my brothers didn't have to follow such rules. I was a rebel all my life and, therefore, had terrible confrontations with my father. Laura, whom I adored and was like another mother for me, was submissive and obedient; she never fought with him.

"My mother didn't bother us with rules and let us be responsible for ourselves. She told my nine sisters and me about menstruation. With the help of a book, she explained menstruation and its importance. My mother knew a lot about medicine because she kept reading about the subject. Even though she was a modern woman, she didn't tell us about the sexual act or explain that men had erections. No one told us in a straightforward way that girls shouldn't permit men to touch them, but we understood what had to be: we needed to be virgins when we married. And the funny thing about this is that men expect women to be active in bed, like professionals, which is something they appreciate, and they do not think badly of us if we do it with them, but doing it with other men is forbidden. If we break this rule, our conduct is considered a crime and we are labeled prostitutes.

"Going back to my mother, I must say that she was an exceptional being—free in her way of thinking. She was very intelligent, courageous, and very well-read, full of desires and dreams she couldn't carry out. Even as a child, I felt her yearnings. She was obliged to have child after child, and all my life, I saw my mother crying. Every time she had a baby, she cried. Throughout my adolescence, she told me that marriage was a terrible bondage and I should never get married. My mother was an excellent mother and a very special woman. She was, I would say, 'advanced' for her times. She was a 'woman 2000.' Now that the years have passed, I understand how important she was for me. I married at nineteen, and my first child was born when I was twenty-years old."

"Clara, did your father give you an explanation for his harsh rules?"

"This was one of the great issues: they always were punishing me because I constantly asked 'why?' For example, my father used to say, 'Clara, you shall not go out today!' I responded, *'Porque papa?* ['Why father?']' He would answer, 'Don't ask me *why!* You will not go out today!' Usually, I would say that if he didn't explain to me why I was being punished, I would not obey him.

I stood my ground against him, which was part of my problem. I wasn't afraid of him and didn't care. At times, he took my books away from me and annoyed me with all of his ideas. In the end, it wasn't that important what he did or said. What really bothered me was to have limitations on my beliefs, wishes, and thoughts. Such restriction I could neither accept nor understand. I felt violated by my father in terms of my human integrity, and for this affront, I have deeply resented him.

"As I told you, I married very young. In part, I married my husband because he was a good-looking, attractive man, and I loved him very much. But also, I married him because I did not see any future in my hometown. We married and went to live abroad for a year. Our honeymoon lasted one year. It was a beautiful trip, and I was very happy. I was looking at the world I had read about in books. Luis, my husband, was familiar with the world I was discovering. He spoke English and French and also read quite a lot. My father was all for education. He wanted to send his older children to study in Belgium. Everything was ready for us to go, when we were hit by the economic crisis of the thirties; therefore, those plans couldn't be realized. But my father sent his three sons to study in Europe, even though, the only one who really cared about education was me. Laura didn't say anything, but I started questioning my father's decision. His answer was that only my brother was going to Europe, because he was a man. I was not going, because I was a woman and women didn't need to study. I protested: 'Why does this have to be so?' He never answered. Still I am waiting to have my 'whys' answered by someone.

"My father *did* want all of his children to study, to learn other languages, but the priority to go to Europe was reserved for boys—not girls. Here began the enormous difference between men and women in my family. Women were to get married while men accomplished great things! In truth, the eldest of my brothers wasn't a very brilliant man. He was a normal guy. My mother knew which of her children were prepared to go to study abroad, and it wasn't Rafael. As usual, she was not listened to and her opinions were disregarded by my father, who ruled the house. Thus, my three brothers ended up studying in Europe, while Laura and I stayed home.

"After I completed school, I looked for a job, so that I didn't have to stay home. I became the secretary of a doctor. After work, I used to go around the small villages on my bicycle. I was trying to recapture the freedom I lost at fifteen. Father didn't know about my afternoon rides, but my mother did. When I returned home, I always brought her flowers. Thus, my memories of adolescence are filled with frustration. I wanted to leave the prison in which I lived and go away to study. This same frustration pushed me into marriage.

"My mother did know about my feelings because she was my confidant. She understood me, agreed with me, and ceaselessly tried to help. In the end, my own mother—who kept telling me not to marry—realized that if I wished to find other horizons in my life, I had to get married. Like me, my mother was a rebel, but she had to accept the life given to her. In response, she focused all her attention and worries on me. Of all her children, I was the one she loved the most. I was the person she would have liked to be. I represented the *rebellion* she had to stifle within her heart. Mother projected herself on me. In her generation, women were punished more harshly by society than was the case in my time. Mother didn't want me to follow in her footsteps because, in her mind, I represented her. She permitted my rebellion to construct and guide my life. My mother died at eighty-four years of age. Until the end, she told me about the terrible life she was forced to lead. She thought of herself as superior, capable of accomplishing greater things than simply having so many children.

"My husband was my best friend. He understood me from the beginning of our marriage and never tried to tie me to rules. He allowed me to be free. I married an exceptional man and never regretted my choice. My husband approved of my desires and pushed me to look for work, so that I wouldn't get bored at home. He helped me economically, whenever I needed it for my work. I had five children, which was the main purpose of my marriage. One of my girls died; this tragedy changed my life, completely. I started teaching in a children's school, which helped me enormously, since I displaced my wretchedness under the children's joy. Some time later, I became the Secretary of Education for my state. Colombian people from the lower classes are very intelligent but have never had the opportunity to study. Thus, I fought to create better schools for the poor. I also founded a museum. I became a member of the City Council, and for two years I served in Congress. But I thought politics was horrible. I observed that politicians were liars, that they misused the money given to them, and that they conducted terrible fights among themselves. I resigned because I couldn't work in a competitive, dishonest atmosphere among colleagues. I was rarely in agreement with them or with the political system and kept asking my eternal '*why?*' that never received a satisfactory answer. Because of my personality and tendency to speak up, I have been labeled 'strange' and considered a hostile person. I have been a woman who tried to overcome her boundaries while trying to become a better human being. I never accepted constrictions that would keep me down and prevent me from acting, thinking, or being."

"Clara what would say to a younger woman for her to lead a happy life?"

"I have come to the conclusion that men are still big *machos*. I have spoken to many women, some much younger than I, who have been well educated and supposedly are independent, yet they live according to norms dictated by society and by men (husbands or companions). Men are in total control; they dominate here in Colombia and in the United States. It doesn't matter where, men are in control. Women have advanced very little. Men have been taught to give orders and think that they are the kings of creation, and they believe the story. Thus, I tell young women to have a dialogue with their husbands or companions. Women must listen—the same way they have a right to be heard. A good relationship depends on communication."

～

Feminist theorists explore—among other topics—how women's desires have been constructed by Western culture, and French feminists specifically consider that "[W]estern thought has been based on a systematic repression of women's experience" (Jones 1985: 361). This chapter follows Julia Kristeva's theory on the importance of discourse in the making of the thinking individual, and in the necessity to retrieve the maternal side of language, which she names the semiotic, in the reconstruction of society and in the modification of the Symbolic order, which is culture. We shall see how the strict Cartesian Symbolic structure of language is modified by the maternal side of language, which is filled with love, eroticism, and poetry.[1]

Because women are made to feel alienated from their bodies, they often lose all desire for gratification, which includes not only libidinal desire but all types of wishes and needs. Having their sexuality repressed, and in the absence of the satisfaction of inhibited desires, women may lack self-esteem and/or other forms of personal autonomy, such as power over action and thought, decisions regarding cultural creations, and influence over political institutions. Because women have been required to repress one of the most intimate parts of the self, they may experience inability to express their most favored visions of their lives and experiences.

How Julia Kristeva Sees the Individual and the Patriarchal System

Sigmund Freud, the "father" of psychoanalysis and the French psychoanalyst Jacques Lacan vary in their gender theories, but both contribute to a view of Western society that supports a patriarchal system, (Grosz 1990:148). One need not agree with the theories of these writers, but understanding them is a key to any analysis of Western culture. As Gayle Rubin (1975: 198) explains,

> Since psychoanalysis is a theory of gender, dismissing it would be suicidal for a political movement dedicated to eradicating gender hierarchy (or gender itself). We cannot dismantle something we underestimate or we don't understand. The oppression of women is deep . . . and all of the female politicians in the world will not extirpate the roots of sexism.

If sexism that oppresses women is to be eradicated, it is essential to uncover its origins in order to understand better the behavior of men towards women in Colombia, and grasp why and how this behavior is discriminatory to females and empowering to males in that country. How gender is organized into female and male roles must be analyzed.

On a symbolic level, man owns the phallus (represented by the penis) that signifies desire, subjective activity, and autonomy (Mitchell 2000). Lacking this object (the phallus/penis), woman who is considered castrated as "a punishment . . . for her inadmissible impulses" towards the father (Freud 1986: 144), remains in silent passivity and at man's mercy. Freud continuously writes about the girl's recognition of her lack of the penis and how this issue makes her undergo "permanent effects on the development of her character. . . . [W]omen," he says, "feel deeply their lack" of the valued sexual organ and, thus, "regard themselves on that account as inferior . . . [which is] the origin of a whole number of characteristic feminine reactions" that are adverse to the development of their sexuality and personality (1986: 116–128). At the same time, we cannot ignore, says Freud, social customs that impose passivity on women (Vol. 22, 1986: 116–128) which is, metaphorically speaking, because of her lack of the penis or phallus.

Woman is the "sex" for man, according to de Beauvoir, who claims, "Man thinks of himself without woman. She cannot think of herself without man" (1952: xxii). When assigning characteristics to gender identity, a culture takes into consideration biological differences between female and male bodies, which are "explained in terms of a binary structure of active and passive, presence and absence, that grants primacy to male sexuality" (Grosz 1995: 36). Through the resolution of the Oedipus[2] complex and because of the incest taboo and the castration complex, human beings in Western society are assigned sexual roles that are defined by a biological "mark" (Rubin 1975: 36; Freud, 1986: 36–9). Within the Western family, this theoretical position contends unconditional power is given to the male, whereas the female is put at a disadvantage because of her reproductive, life-giving role, and her responsibility in the socialization of children (see Dinnerstein 1975). At the same time, her difference versus the male has created an aura of mystery around her sexual being, the *terra incognita* that Freud (1986: 212) named a "dark continent" while he advises anyone who wishes to "inquire about femininity: to look into one's own experiences of life, or turn to the poets [Kristeva's semiotic and/or *poetic* language], or wait until science can give . . . deeper and more coherent information" (1986: 135).

According to both Freud and, later, Lacan, but especially in the latter's terms, gender roles assign a part to each individual allowing the person to enter a culture's Symbolic order, which in patriarchal society, is ruled by the Law of the Father. This law requires the child to be separated from the mother's body; later, as the child enters the community's language, she or he is able to name the lost mother and thereby retrieve her in the naming process. With the aid of language and culture, the child becomes a speaking subject, after losing the body of the beloved and desired mother (Oliver 1993: 30). In the case of the male, the mother can be recaptured later through a heterosexual relationship. The incest taboo is necessary for resolving the Oedipus crisis and for the individual to become gendered and enter the speaking social group.

In the case of the female, the situation is more complicated; she too must abandon an incestuous love for the mother, but, at the same time (according to this theory), she resents her mother for not having given her a penis. The girl then turns to the father, but the incest taboo prevents her from loving him. Finally, she identifies with the castrated, passive mother and hopes one day to have a child who will represent for her the penis she lacks (Mitchell 2000: 75–91).[3] Freud affirms that woman has a "lack" that only man can help her fill. Women enter the Symbolic order (culture) with the aid of man's phallus, which represents power and language (Grosz 1990: 67–81).[4]

This interpretation of how the female and the male genders are constructed reflects and adds power to the patriarchal system. The passive female is subordinated to male culture and excluded from the full power that language and self-expression provide, including autonomous desire, which entails eroticism, sexuality, and free exercise of the mind.

> The turning away from her mother is an extremely important step in the course of a little girl's development. It is more than a mere change of object. . . . Hand in hand with it there is to be observed a marked lowering of the active sexual impulses and a rise of the passive ones. . . . The transition to the

father object is accomplished with the help of passive trends . . . The path to the development of femininity now lies open to the girl. (Freud vol. 21 1985: 239)

Thus, the repression or manipulation of desire—for example, by ideologies and cultural rules—has dramatic influence and terrible results on women, who, more often than not, suffer from it (Mitchell 2000: 413). Western culture's foundation is "phallogocentric"; that is, its "[s]ymbolic discourse (language in various contexts) is another means through which man objectifies the world, reduces it to his terms, speaks in place of everything and everyone else—including women" (Jones 1985: 362). In Freud's patriarchal world, says Jessica Benjamin (1988: 88–90), men own the phallus/penis, which gives them power and independence through sexual subjectivity, desire, activity, and the right to discourse. While woman is the object of man's desire, she remains passive, since she is "not the subject of her own desire . . . often expressed by choosing subordination."

Femininity is generally disparaged and obliterated by the social order while masculinity is celebrated. Because woman is man's opposite, female qualities are deemed negative, instead of being viewed simply as different. She is excluded from man's circle of identity and is repressed inside the social order, while man's desire and language, represented by the phallus (see Mitchell 2000), is associated with agency or power.[5] As man sees himself reflected in woman, the female offers him the role of speaking subject.

Woman is sexually different from man in that she lacks a penis. This absence threatens man's image of himself. If the law of the Father is not followed, the male fears castration, since in infantile thinking or imagination, the boy believes that the girl has been castrated.[6] The Oedipus complex, which solidifies relationships in the family, is based on this primeval fear of loss. Freud's theory of the Oedipus complex maintains that the male child needs to "exit from the imaginary orbit of maternal desire and return to the father;" it is the only way the infant may enter "the exigencies of the symbolization of desire through language" (Irigaray 1985: 61) and become a member of a social group that establishes gender differences. According to Freud's theories of gender and sexuality (Mitchell 2000: 95–104), the female child, considered castrated, longs to have an infant from the father as a symbolic replacement for the penis she lacks. For Freud and for Lacan, the Father's Law introduces the child into language and into the social realm while it ignores any influence coming from the mother (Oliver, 1993: 56).

To wrap up, it is important to have in mind that language and power are intrinsically tied to the body and its drives, feelings, and passions. Speech, as Michel Foucault (1973: 116) claims, is linked to "desire and power," giving the individual vital energy to construct life and the world. Language is the essential tool for communicating one's wishes. According to Rowland and Klein (1997: 16), "The patriarchal system is located within a language and knowledge system which constructs masculinity and femininity in support of the power balance." The power and symbolic meaning of patriarchal language keep women at the margins of culture.[7] Males tend to consider the female gender in terms of what women lack relative to men. Women are represented as the absence of desirable qualities, and as existing solely to fulfill the desires of men. Woman, the archetypal "Other," reflects back the masculine image where the male can see his narcissistic self. Woman represents man's power, says Judith Butler (1990: 45) in summarizing Lacan's theories of sexuality; woman "reflects the self-grounding postures of the masculine subject." This power, "if withdrawn, would break up the foundational illusions of [the] masculine subject position."

How Meaning is Constructed, According to Julia Kristeva

Julia Kristeva's theory of the semiotic and the symbolic elements in the making of meaning/language, leads to a better understanding of the situation of Colombian women in a culture that has been organized and handled by patriarchy. Her theory of the construction of signification recognizes the importance of female elements in the structuring of the human being in becoming a thinking, speaking subject.

Kristeva (Guberman 1996: 21) carefully explains how language is constructed, through the union of the symbolic rules given by culture, with the semiotic drives received from the mother's self and/or body.

> By the symbolic, I mean the tributary signification of language, all the effects of meaning that appear from the moment linguistic signs are articulated into grammar, not only chronologically but logically as well. . . . It concerns both the acquisition of language and the present syntactic structure. . . . By the semiotic I mean the effects of meaning that are not reducible to language or that can operate outside language . . . [and] the child's echolalia before the appearance of language, but also the play of colors in an abstract painting or a piece of music that lacks signification but has meaning.

Thus, the semiotic—which represents the maternal metaphor—is the hidden part of the symbolic. Like the symbolic, the semiotic conveys meaning. It is a language that erupts into the "closed socio-Symbolic order" of culture to create different meanings (Kristeva 1984: 81). For example, new meaning is created when female language invades society's patriarchal language. Occasionally, the semiotic disturbs the "authoritative language of *Logos* (the Word of the Father or Culture) [because the semiotic entails] the return of instinctual drives to pleasure" (Gallop and Burke 1980: 111). This eruption can accompany rhythmic intonations, music, play, laughter, and sounds; it may be observed in poetic language (see Lorde 1985). Because the semiotic has subversive characteristics, it is frequently repressed and, hence, stays in close alliance with the unconscious, where it "expresses itself as the organization of instinctual drives . . . [in the] psychic development of the subject . . . [and] precedes knowledge of self as distinct from other" (Gallop and Burke 1980: 111). In this way, the symbolic and the semiotic participate dialectically in the construction of syntax, language, and meaning (Oliver 1993: 8–10; Gallop and Burke 1980: 111) as well as in the psychological formation of the subject.

Just as the semiotic represents the body of the mother and instinctual psychic drives, the symbolic (with lower case) represents *Logos*, reason, and language, which belong to the Father's code. The Father's Law and his Name establish the rules to be followed by the Cartesian ego, which says, "*Cogito ergo sum*" ("I think; therefore I am").[8] This rationality, together with the creation of syntax and meaning, demands the mother's absence and silence, because she—as a metaphor for nature and instinctual drives of pleasure—could destroy the order of culture and meaning that the Word of the Father upholds. The semiotic is also considered violent (by the Law of the Father) since it has drives that can disrupt the cultural order, and, as such, it needs to be harnessed.

Kristeva (1981: 23) stresses the link between the Symbolic order and the Oedipal phase, which introduces both the "castration operation" and the incest taboo[9] that contribute to human subjectivity and the "Symbolic field" (culture). As the child separates from the mother, she or he enters culture and language, while the penis becomes the "referent" of the "lack" (woman) or the "desire" (man). Women, who are kept "on the borderline" (Moi 1985: 167) of the symbolic because of their "lack," may start from this premise to analyze their sexual difference and its consequences. Woman is not recognized as being "the subject of her own desire" but is turned into the "desexualized mother" who lacks subjectivity (Benjamin 1988: 88). She is at the disposition of patriarchal culture with its social rules and institutions (see Oliver 1993).[10]

With the resolution of the Oedipus complex, the individual becomes a structured, gendered subjectivity—male or female—and is socialized accordingly.

Kristeva (Guberman 1996: 110) further explains the separation of the infant from the mother as an experience that must be repressed or sublimated for the child to become a speaking, social individual: "[T]he incest taboo, which is constitutive of the social order as well as the order of language, is in the end a mother taboo for the boy and for the girl." As mentioned above, man finds a "maternal substitute" in a female sexual partner. Woman, by contrast, will be forever separated (if her sexual partner is a man) from the mother and the "archaic territory" the girl child once enjoyed.

Desire and the Body

One cannot speak of the human body without considering eroticism, sexual desire, discourse, and autonomy. They are all parts of the same whole. "Desire goes beyond rationality, and to a large extent, is part of the mysterious, the poetic, the ineffable—in a realm not readily pinned down with words, nor readily amenable to logic, to rationality" (Davies 1990: 501). The body, says Elizabeth Grosz (1995: 32), is culture's most important object. Culture writes its symbolic meanings on the human body, which, in turn, serves as society's manuscript. As Grosz (1995: 32) affirms, "As pliable flesh, the body is the unspecified raw material of social inscription that produces subjects as *subjects of a particular kind*" (emphasis in the original). Each culture writes its own codes as it imposes, according to the individual's gender, its requirements for human behavior.

Sexuality is an intrinsic part of being human. "Sexuality and desire . . . are energies, excitations, impulses, actions, movements, practices, moments, pulses of feelings" (Grosz 1995: 182). Sexual desire does not necessarily lead to sexual intercourse, nor is its end purpose the production of a relationship— or a child. Through sublimation of the libido and/or erotic drives, people create the world around them. We become artists, writers, and poets who amass the energy to fight for our goals, beliefs, or life itself. Just as we become subjects through the use of language, through our sexuality and erotic desires we become human. Kristeva (Guberman 1996: 212) puts special emphasis on the importance of the aesthetic process because she considers it to be the creative, life-giving energy of the individual. She describes it carefully:

> I think that the aesthetic process, which for psychoanalysis is a process of sublimation, consists in finding a certain harmony of the most violent drives, the life drive and the death drive. This harmony is obtained through the powers of language and, in the case of literature and poetry, is modified through music, through rhythms and rhetorical figures, and through pleasure.

These are the energies of the body and mind that help us relate to other people and the world around us. One's relationship with the environment can be filled with *erotic* urges or violent *death* drives. The choice depends upon how culture handles these drives and instructs the individual to use them, but also on how the individual decides to use them.[11]

Eroticism humanizes sexuality. Erotic desire allows people to relate to the world in positive ways and express creativity. Erotic energy lends stamina to the individual. Eroticism is quite different from genital arousal, reproduction, or even pornography. Eroticism gives women power, affirms Audre Lorde (1984: 55), "[since it is] an assertion of the life force of woman; of that creative energy empowered, the knowledge of which we are now reclaiming in our language, our history, our dancing, our loving, our work, our lives." Sandra Harding (1991: 260) complements Lorde's words:

> Women's erotic energy would infuse their work, their public lives, their community relationships. Men's involvement with their own "nonsexual" activity is often perceived as erotic . . . [but] heterosexual women are not permitted this infusion of their sexuality throughout their whole lives.

Regrettably, women have been deprived by different patriarchal institutions—legal and religious systems, for example—of their sexuality and eroticism (see Ranke-Heinemann 1990). Florence Thomas (1986: 200) in her studies on femininity and the mass media found, as approved feminine models, disembodied women who are made of "pure spirit castrated of their desires, and their sexualities." Because erotic feelings are an intrinsic part of being human, they influence our ability to use language and express ourselves. "Desire produces sensations never felt, alignments never thought, energies never tapped, regions never known" (Grosz 1995: 204). Lacan posited that when we are forcefully separated from our mother's body—within which the child found all pleasure—we face, for the first time, the issue of desire in the distance between need and fulfillment. Only then do we begin to feel emotion. As Bronwyn Davies (1990: 501) affirms,

> [D]esire is spoken into existence, it is shaped through discursive and interactive practices, through the symbolic and the semiotic. . . . Desires are constituted through the narratives and storylines, the metaphors, the very language and patterns of existence through which we are "interpolated" into the social world.

Nevertheless, the child must give up these erotic stirrings for the mother [that she or he will find again later in symbolic meanings] in order to enter culture and belong—supposedly as free agent—to a language community. Later she will find again these stirrings and express them as art, for example, or anyway she chooses.

Woman as Dissident—Feminist Analysis of Meaning Systems

Monique Wittig (1986: 66), among other feminists, believes that gender has deprived women of the "authority of speech" and of the possibility to use it on behalf of a world they, too, inhabit. Metaphorically speaking, females have been forbidden to use language as a tool for thinking and expression. In his epistle to Timothy, Saint Paul (1 Tim. 2: 11–14) recommends,

> Let woman learn in silence with all subjection. But I suffer not a woman to teach, nor to usurp authority over the man, but to be silent. For Adam was first formed, then Eve. And Adam was not deceived, but the woman being deceived was in transgression.

Because of their sexual difference, women have been excluded from making "any claim to the abstract, philosophical, political discourse that gives shape to the social body" (Wittig 1986: 67). Elaine Marks, in her essay "Women and Literature in France" (1978: 836), says it "is not the old meaning of difference as natural opposition but, rather, difference as what has been repressed in the signifying practices of our Western culture." Women have been repressed and thrown into a silence that has kept them unseen until recently.[12]

As an illustration, several of the interviewees speak specifically about feeling repressed, their not being considered by their families and/or the social group as thinking individuals with ideas, wishes, and desires in their own right. Clara speaks throughout the interview of having to follow the rules given to her, but never receiving answers to her "whys?":

> This was one of the great issues: they always were punishing me because I constantly asked "why". For example, my father used to say, "Clara you shall not go out today!" I responded "Why father?" He would answer: "Don't ask me *why*? You will not go out today!" . . . [and] when I participated in politics I kept asking my eternal "*why*" that never received a satisfactory answer. . . . I am still wondering about all those "whys" that never were answered for me.

In contrast, in Susana's case, it was her mother who never answered her questions. But worse, she says, "My word was not valued. At school we had to be silent. Thus, I had to be unseen and silent in my home and at school." Esperanza, too, speaks about her not being able to think when she was a child, only wanting to grow up rapidly in order to escape from her mental enclosure and sufferings. "I started to think for myself at twelve years of age," she says. It was then that she began to have her own ideas; she was able to rebel against all the injustices she suffered from her father and mother and begin to analyze her situation, have wishes and desires, plan for her future life, and know what she liked or disliked. Esperanza always rebelled against her given destiny.

María Isabel, too, remembers how as a child she had no ideas of her own, and how, when she entered adolescence, she understood that it was time for her to start developing her own ideas, judgments, and thoughts. She, too, dates this realization to her twelfth birthday:

> [that was] the day on which I told myself that I now was able to reason and make decisions by myself . . . To declare that I had the capacity to think meant, for my mother and my father that I was crazy, strange, unreasonable, and different. . . . I had ruined myself with strange ideas. Certainly, I agree, there is nothing more difficult than being responsible for one's actions. In other words, consciousness has its consequences. There is nothing crazier than this idea because responsibility entails loneliness. The result of self-awareness and liking to think meant that I didn't belong in the context of my family. . . . I was like a thorn in their side, an obstacle in their lives.

Soledad, also, tells how when she was young, adults around her thought that women had no good criteria from which to speak up or to consider that women, too, could think, make decisions, and become important people, and not only housewives and/or mothers.

> We [young women] weren't thought to have the capacity to decide or have opinions about our future. . . . We were not allowed to speak up about what we thought or liked. . . . Only men were thought to be able to give their opinions when there was any discussion. . . . A young woman was, and still is, quite often compelled to remain quiet. . . . They don't consider that we own a "thinking mind" to help us act on our behalf. . . . We don't even have the right to feel. . . . Neither our sexuality nor our minds belong to us.

For Clara, at eighty-seven much older than María Isabel and Soledad, things were quite similar. She says,

> Because of my personality and my tendency to speak up, I have been labeled "strange" and considered a hostile person. I have been a woman who has tried to overcome boundaries while striving to become a better human being. I have

never accepted constrictions that would keep me down and prevent me from acting, thinking, or being my own self.

And Dora describes what happened to her: "My mother listened to our opinions, but in the end we kept quiet and did what we were told. To be loved by adults we needed to be obedient and 'quiet.'" These women speak of their having been silenced, rejected, ostracized, or punished, whenever they spoke, trying to make their thoughts, wishes, and desires known.[13]

Culture and the Lives of Human Beings

Culture instructs people with rules and mores to direct approved behavior. Culture derives from the symbolic organization of signs and meanings attached to objects that surround us (Kristeva 1982: 134). The individual becomes human by relating to these meanings, through language. People create culture continuously, with the help of language and symbolic meanings. It is the process that socializes the individual. But it is also the process by which the status quo is challenged, and by which cultural beliefs can be altered.

Kristeva (Guberman 1996: 269) considers the symbolic to be the national language of society, which unites all members. However, the other side of language that Kristeva calls "the semiotic" is "transverbal." Human beings combine these two components of language in different ways, depending on personal history and psychology. Thus, they become both singular and universal individuals (see Oliver 1993).

Women have remained marginal to society's order because of gender differences, but with the aid of the semiotic elements, the symbolic unity of culture (its unity of meaning and signification) can be disrupted. The semiotic, which is located beyond language and is subjugated by the symbolic and/or culture, entails feelings, color, music, poetry, art, and laughter. Among the narrations I gathered, two of the interviewees possessed beautiful voices but their fathers forbade them to sing. Nora, whose family was not religious, says,

> I used to listen to *boleros* [romantic music] as well as opera. If my father heard me listening to suggestive songs, he turned off the radio immediately—saying the songs were immoral. When I was twelve years old, I asked my parents to let me study singing, since I had a nice soprano voice, but my father said that such profession was for streetwalkers!

And Soledad mentions what happens to a woman who likes music:

> I had a friend who hoped to study music and become a musician. She was never able to do so because her parents thought that only prostitutes go to conservatories of music. If you had certain abilities, your family would stop you from developing them, if these talents would take you away from accepted roles. I loved to play the guitar, for example, but my father was after me—supervising the songs I sang. Some he forbade me to sing because he said they were "immoral."

According to Kristeva, the semiotic drives have the power to disrupt the established order. In reading the words of these two women, one could say that their fathers feared the spiritual upheaval that music or art can bring to the individual. These men feared the disruption of the everyday, where there is only space for rules and obligations. Perhaps, they also feared the eruption of the erotic into the lives of their daughters, that it would derail their female responsibilities and lead them to other horizons that differed from those given by culture and society. (According to the interviews, the consistent parental fear is that of prostitution.)

Julia Kristeva in her essay "Women's Time" (1981: 204) says, "Woman's desire [is] to lift the weight of what is sacrificial in the social contract . . . to nourish our societies with a more flexible and free discourse, one able to name what has thus far never been an object of circulation in the community: the enigmas of the body, the dreams, secret joys, shames, hatreds of the second sex." Therefore, "[t]he dialectic oscillation between the symbolic and the semiotic opens up the possibility of new types of discourse that can alter the social" (Oliver 1993: 8).

For Kristeva, a feminine perspective is an intrinsic part of being female, and it springs from close contact with the semiotic. Through the aid of the unconscious, from which many of the arts come forth, women may begin questioning a social contract that they do not understand or accept, and that they may wish to condemn, because it is adverse to their welfare. Tapping the semiotic is a way to open up repression and look at it, deconstruct it, and consciously discard it. Woman, thus, can interrupt the discourse in progress and establish new ideas.

The unconscious, structured like a language, erupts into the symbolic order or culture with the aid of the semiotic elements, which are like a chain of meanings that carry what Kristeva calls "maternal music" (Oliver 1993: 95).[14] This different language calls into question what is central to social representation. Thus, a new Symbolic order (culture) is recreated. This new reality is the reality created by a heterogeneous subject, male or female, who does not believe in a fixed identity. It is "[t]he subject-in-process [who] is always in a state of contesting the law . . . [and] gives us a vision of the human venture as a venture of innovation, of creation, of opening, of renewal . . . [of] 'open systems'" (Kristeva in Guberman 1996: 26). While continually renewing the social code, such a subject is always in process and a revolutionary in her or his own right (Oliver 1993: 100). In other words, from the unconscious, women may create a new cultural language to confront the existing one, transforming society in a continuing process.

Kristeva (1981: 299) claims that only through dissidence will new thoughts emerge. Her views open the possibilities that patriarchal social codes will eventually be deconstructed by feminine dissidence. She (1981: 296, 298) affirms that the semiotic not only disrupts the symbolic and cultural rules and codes but helps restructure the socio-symbolic order of the master discourse. Eroding culture or the Symbolic level of reality is the work of the dissident—the subject of poetic language, who knows the unconscious. Since this being is in exile from a society to which she does not fully belong, she differs from the univocal ego who follows the conscious order of law and duty of the Symbolic order. Kristeva (1981: 299) explains:

> We must, therefore, attack the very premises of this rationality and this society, as well as the notion of a complete historical cycle, and dismantle them patiently and meticulously, starting with language and working right up to culture and institutions. This ruthless and irreverent dismantling of the workings of discourse, thought and existence is therefore the work of a dissident.

Dissidents differentiate themselves from the group and attack radically what they find unacceptable, specifically if the objectionable material represents the Law of the Father.

Kristeva's (1981: 200) political program entails the deconstruction of society by a new generation of women who bring "cultural innovation" to society. Kristeva favors the welfare of women at all times, and her work is best viewed as a political manifesto. Her detailed analyses are comprehensive, exact, and well structured. Her thought is radical when addressing the reorganization of the social milieu, and when speaking of the subject-in-process, who is never finished and always "becoming" (Daly 1990: 1), always autonomous, remaking the world (see Oliver 1993; Rowland and Klein 1997). As Catharine MacKinnon (1997: 46) asserts, "[T]heory becomes a way of moving against and through the world."

It is also part of such a program to envision a process that can help to liberate the oppressed. One can work toward a new discourse that will render obsolete both feminine silence and the phallic word of the Father, and offer the beginning of a new era that will see women utilizing their different language, their ideas, and their thoughts to speak about their experiences, their needs, and their lives.

The inscription of the feminine upon the volume of culture must leave its mark on language if a true revolution is to occur (Stanton 1986: 75–76). "For radical feminist poets and novelists, language becomes an essential code in redefining and restructuring the world with women at its center. . . . [Because] language is action" (Rowland and Klein 1997: 32). Language and praxis have to be intertwined in the "demolition of the old and the building of a new thought and being" as well as in the reconstruction of culture and its institutions (Stanton 1981: 80). Language is never separate from the social construct because Symbolic meanings structure society and the individual.[15] The subject constantly interacts with language and the social order.

The semiotic can contribute to a reorganization of reality; one that recognizes men and women who do not have a fixed identity. It will be women's word, thought, and consciousness that will illuminate and transform the rigidity and cruelty of a culture and of the social space that encloses people in a prosaic and mechanical life devoid of affect, color, music, and poetry.

Women's Time—Kristeva's Historical Analysis of Female Experience

Kristeva has been looking for ways to change the situation of women in a world still adverse to their deepest needs. Certainly, women's needs differ, depending on the culture they come from. Nevertheless, quite universally, the law of the Father underestimates and ignores women's interests. To help women in a man's world, Kristeva's "Women's Time" (1981) reviews the destiny of women in Western Judeo-Christian society. It is a feminist ontology that details what female existence has been like under these conditions, in order to propose a feminist epistemology (Humm 1989: 193).

Kristeva (Guberman 1996: 101) claims that any change would also be "a transformation of subjects because it alters subjects' social constraints, experience of pleasure, and, more fundamentally, language." In other words, social change produces personal change, and vice versa. Kristeva works toward deconstructing sexual differences that constrain personal freedom and force individuals into rigid molds. This deconstruction corresponds to a specific restructuring of the speaking subject within culture and its symbolic order (Kristeva summarized by Jardin 1981: 11). In the case of Western culture and its monotheism, women have been silenced and placed together at the margin of society away from men, who, actively, have been constructing Judeo-Christian law and history. Further, Kristeva considers most important "not the notion of gender but . . . [the notion of] singularity." The irreducibility of individuals—whether women or men—entails "a democracy of the multiple. It is seeing individual differences and singularities." With respect to women's "time," one can think in terms of history or projects, of "departure, progression and arrival" (Kristeva 1981: 190–192).

In Kristeva's scheme, the law of the Father and its *Logos* (Word) ruled the people, and only patriarchs whose essence resembled God's were thought to converse with Him. Woman was considered different. Lacking the sacred character and/or nature of man, she was set aside and given no right to relate directly with *Jahweh Elohim*. Man told woman about the law; he spoke, and she listened. Because of what woman lacked, making her different,[16] her conduct was deemed disorderly, her nature understood only in terms of pleasure and laughter, song and desire.

> [A] sexual difference . . . relative to reproduction—is at once translated and translates a difference in the relationship of subjects to the [S]ymbolic contract which is the social contract: a difference in the relationship to power, language, and meaning. (Kristeva 1981: 21)

Woman broke the order of culture. Since those times, wise elders affirmed that only *jouissance*[17] mattered to the female mind. Men believed that women lacked seriousness and earnestness about life, and that nothing of importance, apart from happenings related to nature and the instinctual drives of their female bodies, mattered to them. Thus, continues Kristeva (1981: 140), knowledgeable patriarchs gave women rules and roles: mother, wife, sister, daughter. But the female did not acquire a proper name; she was only a body.

Because woman is not identified as having personhood, explains Kristeva (1981: 144), she is obliged to stay out of the Symbolic order and remain on culture's borderline (see Ortner 1974; Moi 1985) where she maintains a difficult balance between thought and psychosis. She cannot use the Word of the Symbolic order (culture) and hence is forced to remain silent, absent, and ignored. Simultaneously, woman appears to represent "pure desire . . . which ensures the permanence of the divine paternal function . . . [in order] to continue the species" (Kristeva 1981: 142). Her female "specificity" is denied and reconstructed only as an equal for man: his mimesis with an invisible penis. This myth provides an easier "truth" for man to handle than woman's threatening difference provides (Kristeva 1981: 155). As Josette Féral (1985: 89) reflects, "Society itself is mad, possibly . . . [because of the] repression of women; it is founded upon the negation of her difference, upon her exclusion from knowledge and herself."

Motherhood, as seen by man, allows woman to participate in the symbolic order (to use the language of culture) on the condition that her difference is overlooked. In this way, "woman submits herself to a sexually undifferentiated androgynous being" (Kristeva 1981: 147), yielding to Him her right to use the Word. Banished from the reality of the Patriarchal culture or Symbolic order, women are placed in a vacuum. Motherhood is the way in. In *quid pro quo* she exchanges the child for an entry into that culture, giving up her right to sexual assertiveness, to her voice.

Silencing women is detrimental, since speech, as Michel Foucault (1973: 116) argues, is tied to both "desire and power" and is the tool for structuring reality and communicating desires, feelings, passions, and needs. Cultural values and individual rights, ideas, sexuality, and affects all depend on the medium of language. Likewise, the "social contract and social restraint are inscribed in the *existence of language*" (original emphasis) (Kristeva 1981: 268). Bereft of language with which to construct subjectivities, women are disadvantaged, relative to men, from the beginning of history.

When egalitarian doctrines speak of the relationship between production and reproduction and extend "the zone of egalitarianism to include the distribution of goods as well as access to culture," they ignore—says Kristeva (1981: 21; 1981: 142)—the fact that women are indispensable for reproduction and, thus, for culture. The Name of the Father and his "master discourse," which "centralizes eroticism," controls every area of the socio-symbolic contract—be it politics, legislation, religion, production, reproduction, or meaning. Woman is, therefore, considered nonessential, which makes her invisible (Kristeva 1981: 142). Her discourse has been marginalized with regard to politics, history, work, and science. Excluded from linear, or historical, time and language, females inhabit a space devoid of cultural meaning within the wilderness of nature, marked by repetitive reproduction. Hence women's time, says Kristeva (1981: 15–18), is "cyclical" since it shares the reproductive rhythms of nature. On the other hand, women's space is also mythical and monumental. It is filled with the powerful mythical mother who can only be feared (Dinnerstein 1975: 95–97; Freud 1986: 273). Because of her singularity and her difference, woman is feared as a "Daemon—or witch" (Kristeva 1981: 296).

Consequently, women have been robbed of female specificity and feminine subjectivity by the Law of the Father. The Name of the Father and his Word organize the symbolic order by repressing all that is different and cannot be explained. His Name survives alone, while the other, the unexplained sex, the female, is unnamable.[18] Confusion and disorder prevail, for women, and for men, too.

As an example of how religious men have ignored women, Uta Ranke-Heinemann in her book *Eunuchs for the Kingdom of Heaven* (1990: 323) offers an exhaustive research on the relation church men from the Catholic Church have had with women. Ranke-Heinemann mentions and cites the spiritual diary of John XXIII, in which he wrote, in 1948,

> After more than forty years I still warmly recall the edifying conversations that I had in the Episcopal palace in Bergamo with my revered bishop Monsignor Radini Tedeschi. About persons in the Vatican, from the Holy Father downwards, there was never an expression that was not respectful, no never. But as for women or their shape or what concerned them, no word was ever spoken. It was as if there were *no women in the world*. This absolute silence, this lack of any familiarity with regard to the other sex, was one of the most powerful and profound lessons of my young life as a priest, and even today, I thankfully keep the excellent and beneficial memory of that man who raised me in this discipline. (my emphasis)

Women's Position in the Symbolic or Cultural Order

Kristeva's essay "Women's Time" (1981: 13–35) reflects on women's position within the Symbolic order at a time when goddesses were still worshipped and nature was respected, rather than feared. She argues that civilization turned against women's subjectivity and thinking capacity at its own expense. Attempting to locate this change further, Sally Slocum (1975: 44–73) in her article "Woman the Gatherer" illustrates how, before patriarchy was organized through agriculture, women gatherers were important in their societies, because they were the main feeders of the community. Grain provided the essential part of the diet, rather than hunting—as is usually believed.

Kristeva (1981: 23) asks a question whose answer forms the backbone of her "Women's Time": *"What can be our place in the symbolic contract?"*[19]

(original emphasis). This query, which is actually a riddle, must be deciphered by women in the course of finding their place within the hierarchies of the Western world. According to Kristeva (1984: 75), the socio-symbolic contract, which is the law upon which Western civilization rests, is sacrificial and repressive for both men and women. This form of repression lends structure to society and is supposed to free human beings from unleashing violence (see Freud 1981 Vol. 21: 64–145). Once admitted into the Symbolic order, men participate in it actively and enjoy "its fundamental social bonding" (Kristeva 1981: 23–5).[20] But women were—and still are—marginalized from the Symbolic (culture), and are thus victimized (Moi 1985: 167).

Colombian Women and the Law of the Father

Quite a few of my interviewees spoke straightforwardly and with no hesitation about women being marginalized by the Law of the Father—their fathers' law. Clara specifies that her mother's word was never listened to by her father, no matter the issue at hand. "As usual, no one listened to her opinions, which were disregarded by my father who *ruled* our house and family." Nora says, "My mother was very unassuming and submissive. She never answered back to my father [who was ten years older than she]." Soledad spoke extensively about her father's domineering and arbitrary personality:

> My father was extremely selfish with my mother. He was like a king! He was arbitrary like a military man with his wife and us his four daughters. His rules had to be obeyed . . . he had a very strong character. . . . My mother always accepted everything that came from those she considered powerful, like her brother and her husband.

And Susana says,

> My father—who apparently was unconcerned about his children's intimate life—indirectly supervised us. He sent his *orders* through my mother. My father never said anything personally; she spoke for him. . . . He had an iron will over our obedience to his law.

Susana's mother never questioned her husband's orders, as they were the law in that household. María Isabel, whose family, like Susana's, represents the typical Antioqueña model (see chapter 5) where the mother is the father's spokesperson, experienced the same regulations as Susana. Everything was carried out in the family according to the father's will, whose established rules had to be followed:

> My mother was the gatekeeper of my father's sacred chamber, of his word and law. The rules were his. She spoke for him; he was silent. She was in charge of having things done the way he wanted them. Our home was an altar, a holy place where I didn't have a place. Because my mother belonged to "god" (my father), she had access to the heaven from which he ruled. Later, Fernando—my husband who was also like a god in that he was much older, more powerful, and presumably much wiser than I—became the divine authority figure in my life. I had to call him *señor* [master]. He had the power to dominate my life the way my father did, but my father exercised his will through my mother as an intermediary. My mother protected my father's Word.

As María del Socorro put it, "A woman's word is not respected."

Half the population of the earth experiences a socio-symbolic contract imposed "against their will." The repercussions of this imposition remain the most pressing problem that modern women are anxious to resolve (Kristeva 1981: 25).

Kristeva (1981: 26–30) analyzes how women are harmed by the social order that alienates them. She suggests that females ought to call "into question the very [social] apparatus itself," although without rejecting the Symbolic law. Women should question the existing social order, raising consciousness, but without rejecting culture's necessary and unavoidable rules. Otherwise, society would fall into chaos. Nevertheless, in assuming a dynamic and forceful role, women must be careful not to adopt the ways of the oppressor, lest they themselves become oppressors. By raising the consciousness of society, they can bring forth change.

Afterthoughts

Kristeva's thought is universal. She thinks about women's issues globally—although principally about women in the Western world—and her perspectives should be helpful to those interested in safeguarding women's well-being anywhere. Kristeva has been criticized for not accepting the principles of feminism and failing to declare herself a feminist. Yet, her article "Women's Time" (1981) reminds readers that, above all, this author is concerned about women who have been alienated by patriarchal ideology, with no specific country in mind. Kristeva carefully traces in "linear time" women's struggle for liberation against the law of a Father who does not recognize female differences, *jouissance*, or experience within families, where the Oedipus complex works against women. Kristeva's woman is never finished, is always a self-in-process, a dissident from culture and society, whose language makes her powerful, because it interrupts and modifies patriarchal culture and/or society.

Kristeva discusses the achievements and failures of different generations of women. She reviews the pain women have felt in being rejected from the socio-symbolic structure and in struggling for acceptance as subjects with rights over the use of language.[21] Kristeva "advocates for the organization of a feminist generation" that can raise consciousness and question the position of women within a Symbolic order that does not recognize the significance and value of women's biological and psychological experiences. And,

> [i]f we remember that what women really share is an oppression at all levels, although it affects us each in a different way—if we can translate *fémininité* into a concerted attack not only on language, but also directly upon the sociosexual arrangements that keep us from our own potentials and from each other— then we are on our way to becoming "*les jeunes nées*" (the newly born) envisioned by French feminisms at their best. (Jones 1985: 375)

Such a generation can help with "the demassification of the problematic of *différence*" (original emphasis) in order to destroy the "very nucleus of personal and sexual identity" (Kristeva 1981: 209), that is, the dismantling of the rigid boundaries of the ego who is fixed and does not accept the possibility of change or being always in process. Women are accepted and can remain within the social order, so long as they ignore their biological differences and see themselves as men's mimesis, that is, mimic them. "According to Jerome," writes David Kinsley in his book *The Goddesses' Mirror* (1989: 225), "the female virgin transcends her sex to such an extent that she comes to approximate the male!" To remain outside the social order because of their female specificity, or to participate in it with men's characteristics, implies that women are deprived of their female subjectivity, alterity, difference, and power. Kristeva proposes that women accept their own singularity and continue fighting for their own liberation as well as the redemption of a world that forgets about the human "subject of poetic language"[22] in favor of a rigid, Cartesian, rationalistic ego.[23] "Women's Time" locates the roots of female oppression and chronicles progress toward a more just world. The female discourse will be an alternative and liberatory discourse that will, at all costs, says Jones (1985: 366), re-create the world.

Notes

1. Kelly Oliver, *Reading Kristeva* (Bloomington, IN: Indiana University Press, 1993), 23, differentiates the Symbolic with capital S from the symbolic with small s. The former stands for culture; the latter represents the making of meaning, language. I shall follow her.

2. For the consequences of this arrangement see Nancy Chodorow, *Reproduction of Mothering*; Adrienne Rich, *Of Woman Born: Motherhood as Experience and Institution* (New York: Norton, 1976–86); Dorothy Dinnerstein, *The Mermaid and the Minotaur: Sexual Arrangements and Human Malaise* (New York: Harper and Row, 1977). Motherhood in patriarchal society has been strictly a woman's occupation.

3. For more explanations of the Oedipus complex and its resolution in the organization of human life, see the feminist psychoanalysts and theorists Benjamin, *The Bonds*, and Chodorow, *The Reproduction*.

4. Cixous tells how "Old Lacan takes up the slogan 'What does she want?' when he says 'A woman cannot speak of her pleasure . . . It's all there, a woman *cannot*, is unable, hasn't the power . . . Unable to speak of pleasure = no pleasure, no desire: power, desire, speaking, pleasure, none of these is for woman.'" *Castration*, 47.

5. Women's desire, as explained by many feminists—like Julia Kristeva (1983), Hélène Cixous (1981), Luce Irigaray (1985), Juliet Mitchell (1973; 2000), Nancy Chodorow (1978), Jessica Benjamin (1988), and Dorothy Dinnerstein (1975)—has been geared toward the family and cultural structures that maintain close ties with institutions that oppress women. Because we are human, our desires are attached to cultural objects that make up our social universe. See Mitchell, *Psychoanalysis*, 396, on Lacan for whom "Desire is desire of the other."

6. Freud, in "Feminine Sexuality," *The Standard Edition of the Complete Psychological Works of Sigmund Freud*. James Stratchey trans., (New York: W. W. Norton and Company, 1985), Vol. XXI, 223–243, says, "Quite different are the effects of the castration complex in the female. She acknowledges the fact of her castration, and with it, too, the superiority of the male and her own inferiority; but she rebels against this unwelcome state of affairs." Freud claims that the female child experiences her "lack" as a "misfortune" that she and all women suffer, including her mother, as a consequence of femaleness. This perception leads to the girl's contempt for the female sex. To understand how female sexuality has been reinterpreted by Jacques Lacan, see *Feminine Sexuality and the Ecole Freudienne*, eds. Juliet Mitchell and Jacqueline Rose, trans. Jacqueline Rose, (New York: Norton, 1982).

7. For a careful and detailed explanation of how women have been kept at the margin of society, see Sherry Ortner "Is Female to Male as Nature Is to Culture?" In Michelle Zimbalist Rosaldo and Louise Lampher, eds., *Women, Culture and Society* (Palo Alto, CA: Stanford University Press, 1974), 67; Gayle Rubin "The Traffic in Women," in Rayna R. Reiter, ed., *Toward an Anthropology of Women*. (New York: Monthly Review Press, 1976), 157; Toril Moi *Sexual-Textual-Politics* (London: Methuen, 1985), 78.

8. In the article "The Powers of Difference," *The Future*, 28, 29, Féral notes that "the self, which is constituted by thought and created by an act of thought, by the separation of the mind and body, is driven to master nature. . . . The 'state of nature' seems to be primarily populated by adult, single males whose behavior is taken as constitutive of human nature and experiences as a whole."

9. In "Women's Time," *Signs*, 7, no.1, Autumn, (1981): 22, Kristeva explains that "the reality of castration is no more real than the hypothesis of an explosion which, according to modern astrophysics, is at the origin of the universe: nothing proves it . . . it is an article of faith. . . . Numerous phenomena of life in this 'big-bang' universe are explicable only through this initial hypothesis."

10. Cixous writes, "[F]or Freud/Lacan woman is said to be 'outside the Symbolic' . . . that is outside language, the place of the Law, excluded from any possible relationship with culture and the cultural order. And she is outside the Symbolic because she lacks any relation to the phallus, because she does not enjoy what orders masculinity—the castration complex." *Castration*, 46.

11. For explanations of the death (Thanatos) and love (Eros) drives, see Herbert Marcuse, *Eros and Civilization* (Boston: Beacon Press, 1955); Sigmund Freud, *Civilization and Its Discontents*, ed. James Stratchey, 64–145, Vol. XXI (London: Hogart Press, 1961).

12. For an overview of what has been women's history, see Rosalind Miles, *The Women's History of the World* (London: Michael Joseph, 1988); Gerda Lerner, *The Creation of Patriarchy* (New York: Oxford University Press, 1986).

13. Chantal Chawaf says about words, "[they] have a sensorial quality. Their role is to develop consciousness and knowledge by liberating our unconscious as well as to bring back hope," 117, in Marks and de Courtivron eds., *New French Feminisms*.

14. On the unconscious being structured like "the maternal music in language" Oliver says that Kristeva comments that her unconscious is "beyond both Freud and Lacan because . . . neither of them liked music? Or because of repression of the primary identification with their mothers? Or, ultimately, because they weren't mothers?" In *Reading Kristeva* (Bloomington, IN: Indiana University Press, 1993), 95–6.

15. Jane Gallop and Carolyn Burke, in their article "Psychoanalysis and Feminism in France" in *Future*, 106–114, write, "We learn who we are through the acquisition of language. . . . Using language, we internalize the laws of the world, especially those that reflect patriarchal powers."

16. Kristeva in "Women's Time," 27, writes, "the real fundamental difference between the two sexes: a difference that feminism has had the enormous merit of rendering painful, that is reproductive of surprises and of symbolic life in a civilization which, outside the stock exchange and wars, is bored to death."

17. *Jouissance* means "pleasure," the maximum of human happiness; it is also the name given to orgasm in French. On this subject, consult *New French Feminisms: Anthology*, eds. Elaine Marks and Isabelle de Courtivron (Amherst, MA: University of Massachusetts Press, 1981), 37, note 8: The verb *jouir* (to enjoy, to experience sexual pleasure): "This pleasure, when attributed to woman is considered to

be of a different order from the pleasure that is represented within the male libidinal, economy is often described in terms of the capitalist gain and profit motive.
Women's *jouissance* carries with it the notion of fluidity diffusion, duration. It is a
kind of potlatch in the world of orgasms; a giving, expending, dispensing of pleasure without concern about ends or closures." Further, for a vivid example of
women's lecherous, deceitful, and mean nature as thought of by the "wise" Judeo-
Christian patriarchs of antiquity the opera *Salome* by Richard Strauss pictures well
this male-imagined female.

18. Elaine Marks writes in "Women and Literature in France," in (*Signs* 4, 1978:
841), "Women are the absent, the unacknowledged different, and the dead (the
buried, the decapitated, the alienated)."

19. Kristeva in "Women's Time," 20, notes: "No matter if this context is humanist, socialist or capitalist, and of a Catholic, Protestant or Jewish creed," because
Western civilization is ruled by patriarchal ideology.

20. See Freud's "Civilization and Its Discontents" in *Standard*, 64–145.

21. Kristeva says in an interview by Eliane Boucquey, "*Unes Femmes:* The Woman
Effect," in Guberman, ed., *Julia*, 112: "I believe the problem lies elsewhere: how can
we offer the economic and libidinal conditions they need to analyze social oppression
and sexual repression so that each woman might realize her specificity and difference
in the context of what is unique about the way she has been produced by the vagaries
and necessities of nature, families, and societies?" In other words, how can we make
women understand and articulate their personal situation as individuals belonging to
a social group?

22. The way women use language and express themselves is in itself a "poetic"
form because it is unconsciously tied to their feelings. (Of course, not all women are
able to do so, and some men are more in contact with their "feminine" side, thus enabling them to be in touch with their feelings.) Kristeva spoke about language and
expressing oneself to Boucquey, ibid., 112, "[T]he feminine condition should merely
be a way of enabling each woman to speak about her own uniqueness. This act of
speaking is no more 'male' than 'female'; it cannot be generalized, for it is specific and
incomparable. Only then can it be an innovation or a potential contribution to a civilization that is lucid and aware of the constraints it imposes without creating new
forms of totalitarianism."

23. Kristeva recalls Hegel's idea of "the eternal irony of the community," meaning
"a sort of vigilance that keeps groups from closing up, from becoming homogeneous
and so oppressive." Kristeva considers women's role a matter of fact and duty: "a sort
of vigilance, a strangeness, as always to be on guard and contestatory." In Suzanne
Clark and Kathleen Hulley's interview of Kristeva, "Cultural Strangeness and the
Subject in Crisis," in Guberman, ed., *Kristeva*, 45.

CHAPTER FIVE

Family Models and Colombian Women's Participation in History and Politics

Manuela and Juliana: "Two Women Twenty Years Apart with a Similar Life Experience."

Introduction

Manuela and Juliana, from well-to-do families, learn early that as females their au-
tonomy was limited. Manuela, twenty years senior, argues for expansion of any
kind of experience. Juliana, the younger, speaks for the traditional female behavior.
Both recognize the double standard: that for men, independence is total and any-
thing they decide to do is not regarded as bad behavior. They also advise on the im-
portance of a woman's economic independence through education. They have
learned not to depend on men.

The lessons drawn by such Colombian women are not unique. They are born
into a history of male dominance. It is a history that weighs on women's talents
and rights. In chapter 5, that history is traced from the country's inception to the
present.

Manuela, age 37, and Juliana, age 17, attended the same school twenty years
apart. What has changed? What has remained the same?

Interview

On Childhood:
Manuela—"Well, I had a nice, happy childhood. I grew up in the countryside and was practically an only child. . . . I had a close relationship with my
father. I received lots of attention from both my parents. During my first few

years, I played a lot with my brothers and cousins; they were all boys. We lived in the countryside and had great liberty . . . a very healthy childhood. We played lots of sports and different kinds of games. We went horseback riding with my father and used to swim a lot because we had a swimming pool. We climbed trees, played hide-and-seek, and ran all day long in the fields. We also had several dogs that were our playmates."

Juliana—"I entered nursery school when I was three years old. It was the American school in my hometown . . . a school for boys and girls. I felt perfectly well in a classroom with boys. I was a tomboy! . . . I wanted to be a boy. I wanted to be like my father and do everything he did. I played soccer and all the games boys played among themselves, like running around the fields. I always tried to be the best. I wanted to have the power and authority girls do not have by playing with dolls."

On Gender Differences for Boys and Girls:
Manuela—"My brothers and cousins liked to play soccer, but they discriminated against me in this area. They wouldn't accept me as a participant . . . 'You are a girl, and you cannot play soccer,' they reminded me. I felt excluded, not rejected. I remember my brothers and cousins playing soccer, while my mother said to me: 'Manuela, come and help me set the table; today, we don't have a maid.' I used to get furious at my mother, because, first, I wondered why the boys couldn't help with lunch; and second, because my mother was supposed to be a feminist and here I was doing housework. My mother used to write about women's issues, but she was telling me to help her, while the boys went about their business. This situation infuriated me. . . . I used to play with dolls and girls' games, like pretending to run a school. . . . As we started growing up, we began differentiating ourselves: boys on one side, girls on the other, and our games were not so democratic. The real difference between the boys and me started when I reached puberty and they began calling me '*la nina*' ('the girl') and kept reminding me that I was a girl, that I was different, and that I could not do certain things men did. I felt enormous rage when they treated me this way."

Juliana—"In school, we had gym classes with boys, but we were separated during sports; boys are stronger, faster, and rougher. Girls playing games like . . . 'housewife' forced them to stay closed up in their homes, and this I didn't like. As I grew up, things started to change very slowly. It all happened as my body started to change and . . . develop. Really, it all started in the classroom. My behavior changed; I stopped being outspoken and interrupting class. I stopped trying to be competitive in math or any other subject or sports. I stopped fighting to be best in everything, to have authority and . . . control, outside and inside the classroom, as boys do."

On Father-Daughter Relationships:

Manuela—"My father used to tell my sister and me how he wanted our bodies to look. He kept saying that we were too fat. He also wanted us to have breast implants. We had them, to please him. Personally, I think a father should look at his daughters with a father's eyes—not as women who have to satisfy his ideal of feminine beauty. Our mother, by contrast, promoted our interests, like ballet dancing.

"My mother was very intelligent and she wanted to explore other possibilities beyond being a wife and mother. Since my father didn't like the example she was setting for me, he decided to do something about it. Once, a young maid was breast-feeding her child, and my father told me to identify with her, because, one day, I, too, was going to feed my baby the same way. I was only fifteen, and, frankly, quite immature. . . . At the time, I liked animals and running through the countryside; I was very emotional. An argument broke out. . . . My father was a womanizer, and, in the middle of my terrible rage, I told him what I thought of him: that he liked prostitutes and, therefore, (he) fell off the pedestal where I had placed him, all my life. I went to my room, to pack my suitcase, because I decided to leave home. When my father saw what I was doing, he took a broomstick and started running after me. . . . He hit me very hard with the broom. This violent episode marked . . . my relationship with my father for the worse. I realized my father could be very violent, and I felt rejected by him. At the same time, part of my rage sprang from the fact that I couldn't understand my mother's attitude. She wanted the best for her children, but how could she accept my father's unfaithfulness? . . . I also heard that my grandfather was a womanizer. Thus, I concluded that all men were allowed to be womanizers, no matter what! Within the family, you learn what men can do and women cannot do!"

Juliana—"My father . . . he didn't worry about the way I dressed and what I did. My father was happy the way I was. I was completely free to do as I wished. I have never felt that my privacy has been invaded by either my mom or my dad. About manners, well, yes, they always teach you about good manners, for the sake of tradition, and because you have to know how to behave properly. My parents always spoke about their having the same level of authority in our household. . . . This does not happen too often in other families. My mother is not Colombian and this, I think, can make a difference."

On Sexual Education and Sex:

Manuela—"When I went to high school, some girls my age had sex, but it was understood that 'good girls' didn't do it.

"In school, they didn't give us any sexual instruction. My mother told me about menstruation and a bit about sex. My parents never spoke with me about virginity or purity. I heard my friends dividing girls into 'virgins' and 'non-virgins,' putting the women into two groups. My father went around with bad women but my mother was a good woman. The intrinsic message was that I had to be careful or else I could become a prostitute.

"If a woman takes risks, she is considered a prostitute. A 'good woman' likes to dress well and cares about her physical appearance. . . . But men can do whatever they wish, especially with respect to their sexuality. My brothers acted like 'real men,' by taking the car in the evening, going partying, visiting prostitutes, and watching whatever movies they wanted to see. If I had been an adventurous person, I could have done quite a lot, but I wasn't. I think parents usually push male children to be more adventurous than female children. Yes, being a man is quite different from being a woman. To be a man, at the time, meant to me that they could go to bed with as many girls as they wished. It meant being able to 'have a girl' for sexual purposes. To be a man meant being able to exercise sexual freedom, just like my father did. I think girls should also be able to explore freely, just like boys do, with regard to everything: sex, the world, likes, and dislikes."

Juliana—"In fifth grade, they taught us anatomy. Then, in seventh grade, they told us about venereal diseases and all the problems they cause. Once, a teacher even showed us a film about intercourse. I don't think it was a wise idea to have shown that film; you provoke the students with those explicit sex scenes. In this class, they also told us about menstruation, in front of the boys, which was rather annoying, because they (the boys) made a fuss about it and made us girls feel uncomfortable. In my case, it was my mom who told me all about menstruation. So, it was not new when it happened to me or when they told us about it at school. I think those classes should be more about sexual ethics than anything else. We were too young to understand what they were showing us. Also, some of the boys I know go to the prostitutes, which I think is awful. If the boys don't have 'willing girlfriends,' then they go to prostitutes. This very well could have been the result of those classes and the films they showed us.

"If a girl from the 'good' girls starts having sex with her boyfriend, it is because they've had a very long relationship. Usually, these girls believe that they will marry their boyfriend, after a year or so, which usually does not happen. For us Catholic girls, it is a sin to have sex; but if we marry the boy, nothing happens; it's okay. Nevertheless, you don't do it, not because it is a sin, but because it is something learned in your family and this is the way you want it to be. You have to weigh the consequences. For boys, things are different; they don't worry about sin. For men, everything is a seduction and a conquest. Nevertheless, I think us women, we should keep our virginity till the day we marry. This is one of the traditional rules I think we should follow: to keep our virginity for our husbands. They started telling us about this, since our first Communion. Only girls are told to do so; boys are never told anything like this."

Advice to Young Women:

Manuela—"I would say that the most important thing is to trust her [a young woman's] desires and wishes. I would tell her not to be afraid to explore, to take risks, to experiment with life. Doing so is part of living. It is important for her to follow her heart and live consciously. By experimenting, she will learn what she likes and dislikes. To be autonomous will help her not to be influenced by the wishes of her parents. She should also strive for as much education as possible. Education will give her freedom, especially economic freedom, and she won't have to marry a rich man in order to survive. A woman who depends economically on a man will be under his grip. I would tell my daughter or another young woman that having a man at her side isn't very important, compared to having valuable experiences to enrich her life. If she lives with someone, she shouldn't let that person mistreat her. Instead, that person should understand her and be a companion and friend."

Juliana—(with regard to a young girl's having sex at an early age) "I would tell her to wait, because the way men deal with women is not worth it. . . . With time, men get bored with the same girl and they want a different one. I would tell her to be very careful. . . . Men feel that they are more of a man when they have sex with many women and they talk about it between them. They like to boast about it. The best way . . . not to have such an experience, of being dropped by a boy and talked about by him and his friends, is by not doing it. Moreover, girls who have experience on these matters say that what is normal is for the man to be on top and the woman at the bottom. . . . If you know too much about sex, you are dirtier . . . like a prostitute.

"To a young woman, I would also tell her that what is essential in her life is to study, so that she can be economically independent. And to think well before having an intimate relationship with a young man, as I just told you."

❧

The Cuban-American historian Asuncion Lavrin[1] affirms that history must be the solid basis for research on the construction of gender—and on "woman as a discrete category" (Hoff 1996–1997: 398). At the same time, Diane Bell and Renate Klein (1996–1997: xxiii) emphasize that "[W]omen's history . . . is a critical component of developing a consciousness about the ways in which knowledge has been politicized and women written out of historical scripts."

This chapter examines the types of family structures that developed in the kingdom of New Granada, as the colonizers named the upper region of South America that became Colombia, after the wars of independence. It will explore cultural and social relations that resulted from the encounter between Spaniards and Indians, initially, and later, with black slaves. Particular conditions developed for women and men, because of the cultural upheaval brought about by the colonizers, that set the stage for later participation by women in Colombian history.[2] It is important to look back to the sixteenth century

[a]nd see a pre capitalist new world in which the encounter of several cultures produced important cleavages in culture concepts of family and social order. New forms of familial and personal relationships developed in the fissures created by the confrontation and eventual adaptation of conquered and conqueror to each other. (Lavrin 1987: 110)

Colombian anthropologist and scholar Virginia Gutiérrez de Pineda has written the classic history of the different variations of Colombian families,[3] four different family models, which still form the basis for social life in Colombia today (1975). From the fifteenth century to the twentieth century, these family structures solidified, as did their idiosyncratic cultures and historical contexts. Gutiérrez de Pineda's study of the Colombian family shows that Indian, black, neo-Hispanic, and Antioqueña[4] families evolved from the three races that populated the country, since the arrival of the Spaniards in the sixteenth century.

The whites, who came from Spain, brought with them their own customs, civil laws, and religious laws. The Spaniards encountered the indigenous people in the New Kingdom of Spain and/or of New Granada and tried to influence them from the beginning with their European customs, especially with Christian Catholic ways of looking at the world and at women and men. Later, with the arrival of black slaves from Africa, other intra-family relations were created.

Family Structure, Religion, and Sexuality

The Catholic religion helped model the Spanish worldview with its monotheistic philosophy, mythology, and Christian beliefs.[5] Moreover, the civil laws of Spain were, and are, solidly based on Christian doctrine. Thus, for example, marriage, considered to be a sacrament, cannot be dissolved by human law.

The nuclear family was ruled by laws that, intrinsically, were dictated by Catholicism and approved and supported by the judiciary. The wife was to obey the husband; the husband could rule his household at his wish, as ordained by St. Paul to the Corinthians. Also, Catholic marriage had strict rules such as monogamy, no possibility of divorce, and bride dowry, which were unknown to the aborigines. While "sin" had no place in the worldview of the Amerindians, the Europeans' lives gravitated around the notion of "sin" (Restrepo 1995; Rodriguez 1995; Gutiérrez de Pineda 1975).

When the Spaniards arrived, with all the arrogance of the colonizer, they believed that the Other, the different stranger, could have no say over the settlers' power, ideas, and wishes. In addition, observes Roberto Restrepo (1995: 28), the Spanish society of the sixteenth century was xenophobic.[6] The *conquistadores*[7] were convinced they were to conquer the world so that they could Christianize the heathen; theirs was a mission in the name of God, a holy war they came to fight and win in the New World.[8] The Catholic Church needed more souls to be converted for the kingdom of Heaven. The Spanish kingdom was going to help Rome to accomplish its main purpose: the conversion of the world to Christianity. Latin America was a good target for the Spanish empire and its Catholic monarchs (Restrepo 1995: 5–6).[9]

For the indigenous peoples of North, Central, and South America, the arrival of the white Spaniards was filled with human calamities and spiritual distresses. These men brought with them illness, death, and the destruction of the Indian cultures. The Spanish worldview was difficult for the Indians to understand. They did not comprehend what the foreigners meant with their laws and mythologies. Terror and despair filled the Indians' lives, including their social lives. Many of their cultures and languages were eradicated, as they were killed in great numbers.

Meanwhile, Spanish women in the sixteenth century were subjected to a double and hypocritical sexual morality. "A lady adhered strictly to the model of the virginal, chaste woman, submissive to the male, dedicated to perform domestic work, as the only status given to her was that of spouse" (Restrepo 1995: 29). While, says Roberto Restrepo, husbands had innumerable lovers from all social classes, women encountered jealousy and confrontations between themselves. Later, as Pablo Rodriguez (1995: 73–75) demonstrates, in the times of the *colonia* or colony, the ideal woman was constructed by masculine fantasy. The feminine virtues were chastity, modesty, piety, discretion, obedience, prudence, and an affable nature. The ideal woman was expected to be a good administrator of her home. According to Jaime Humberto Borja (1995: 49), "[W]omen's virginity and purity was a proof of their having vanquished their intemperate nature. . . . Virginity became the Christian ideal, and marriage the only space where sexuality was practiced, while benefiting procreation. Beyond physicality, virginity was an obsession created by and for the use of men" (Sanchez and Martinez Cruz 1978). Simultaneously, sexual pleasure, even in marriage, was to be discounted.[10] Mary became the symbol of the ideal woman[11] while Eve portrayed evil (Ranke-Heinemann 1990). The white woman was represented as the good woman, Mary. Eve was pictured as the Indian, the black, and the female of mixed races (Borja 1995: 51). For the "honest woman," her only and best destiny was considered enclosure in her home or in a convent.[12]

Five hundred years later in Colombia, the idea that women are responsible for the "fall" of the human race is still firmly believed. Some of the women interviewed spoke about this issue. Flor and Rosalia were taught, in preparation for their first Communion, that Eve was bad (Ranke-Heinemann 1990). Eve "made Adam sin and go against God by making him eat the apple. This is why they sinned and how evil in the world began. And that small lump men have in the middle of their neck is the symbol of the apple Eve[13] forced Adam to swallow," said Flor. Rosalia affirmed, "Eve and Adam sinned when Eve gave Adam an apple and made him eat it." According to the women who spoke about the myth of Adam and Eve, religious teachers did not make clear what sin was committed at the time. Susana, from the upper class and in her early fifties, emphasized how the nuns taught her that Eve gave the apple to Adam, thus making it invariably clear that women, even today, are responsible if men sin. "We (women) had to be aware of our bodies, for they could be a cause of trouble to others," Susana continues. Christian interpretations of the Bible connect sex with disobedience and sin, since Adam blamed Eve who, in turn, blamed the serpent.[14] Catholics tend to believe that eating the apple represents sexual activity, even though no such connection exists in the Old Testament where the word "sin" is also absent.[15] (Only Rosalia mentions that she never believed that "we women were bad because Eve offered and made Adam eat the apple.")

These ideas were brought to New Granada by the Spaniards. The bourgeois world and the patriarchal ideology were starting to be part of the world of the Spanish universe, influencing the New World and the life of its peoples (Restrepo 1995: 5; Segura Graiño 1995: 48). Castilian law was different for men, to whom it gave privileges, and for women, who were disadvantaged by its codes (Segura Graiño 1995:44, 48). Women were considered to be feeble, unable to defend themselves, the inheritors of Eve's impure and sinful nature; they had mean personality traits and an inclination towards sin.[16] Restrepo (1995: 5) writes that the Catholic Church has instructed its priests since the twelfth century that "woman is temptation made feminine flesh, while the only way for the pure male is to sublimate his carnal desire."[17] The belief arose that after human beings were thrown out of Paradise, men were to care for and protect women, who were not to be left alone without a father, brother, or husband (Segura Graiño 1995: 57). The Bible specifies that woman's self and her place in the creation of the world was to be acknowledged only if she was to be recognized as a gift from one patriarch to another, God to Adam, to remedy the latter's aloneness: "a help meet. . . [a] Heaven's last best gift"(Nyquist 1987: 173).

And this practice remains: "We girls were not allowed to go out. We had to be near our parents or grandparents. . . . Adults didn't worry about the comings and goings of young boys, but they did take care about girls because of the issue of *virginity*," says Flor. Susana recalls, "I was treated like a female; I was considered fragile. Thus, I had to be taken care of very carefully. My brothers were allowed to do as they pleased. They went out alone while I was chaperoned, up until I was eighteen years old." Rosie also confirms this norm; she says, "My parents took great care of my sisters and me because they said girls have to be supervised more than boys. My sisters and I were not allowed to enter nightclubs or *cafés* nor participate in parties or dances." And Dora, forty-five years old and from the flourishing middle class, who was supposed to draw inspiration from its model of femininity and purity, says, "Our parents took care of my sister and me in an exaggerated way. We never were allowed to go out of our homes alone. My mother thought that girls were always in great danger of being harmed by bad men. . . . Usually our mother accompanied us everywhere." Dora was sent to a convent boarding school, until she finished secondary school. Her parents considered that the ideal place where girls could be "protected against all dangers" of daily life and the world and molded into the "ideal woman."

Yet, although men's adultery is a sin according to the Catholic Church, Virginia Gutiérrez de Pineda (1997: 148) points out that it has always been socially accepted, because of the acceptance of the male's "libidinous" nature. Among the interviewees, Soledad's father was openly a "womanizer" who had a daughter by another union. And so did Aleja's father, who had three other daughters and "many women." Aleja's mother accepted her husband's extra-marital relationship to the point that she often had his children over to eat at her house because, she said, "they are not responsible for what has happened." Esperanza's and Flor's fathers openly went to visit "the women" on weekends, and their mothers accepted this arrangement as custom. Indeed, in June 2001, the Colombian government gave bigamy a legal status, simply because it was impossible to punish the bigamous man; he is protected not only by society, but also by the women who share him. Colombia's main newspaper, *El Tiempo* (Bogotá, June 24, 2001: 1–5) writes that bigamy is a practice accepted by Colombian culture. Men have been allowed to experience their sexuality freely, a practice condemned for "honorable" women.[18] The lawful acceptance of bigamy, undoubtedly, promotes further infidelity among spouses.

The interviewees were clear about this issue. Soledad says, "Fathers promote their sons' shameless behavior—like going to prostitutes. Men can go out without being supervised. They go partying, they can drink, and they *use* their sexuality as they wish." Juana gives further details:

> Men usually go to prostitutes. Even if they are married, they visit whores, since doing so is a tradition in this part of the world. Such conduct is part of *machismo*. Men belong to the streets and women to the home! A man who lives only with one woman isn't a real man, according to this philosophy. Drinking is also part of their lives.

Dora, on the other hand, tells how she and her sister were ignorant about sexual matters. Her sister, she says,

> Came back from her honeymoon with her virginity intact (she was sixteen). She came back worried, speaking "about all the things" she had to do with her husband, and she didn't understand why . . . that topic was the last thing we would think to discuss.

On the same topic, Clara says that "husbands" expect their wives to act as "prostitutes" in bed, but if they did it with other men, then they would be labeled "prostitutes" and their conduct would be considered a "crime." Indeed, Manuela shows that prostitutes define what it is, in her opinion, to "behave like a man," which was the way her brothers behaved:

> To act like a real man is to take the car in the evening and go partying, visiting prostitutes, and watching [certain] movies. . . . They go to bed with as many girls as they wish. It means being able to "have a girl" for sexual purposes. To be a man means being able to exercise sexual freedom, just like my father did. Yes, being a man is *quite different* from being a woman.

Meanwhile, the adulteress, until not long ago, could have been punished by her husband with death while he was absolved by law, as his crime was considered the outcome of great rage and enormous sorrow. The unwed mother, even today, can be thrown out of her home;[19] and the prostitute is considered to be the scourge of society. Nevertheless, the prostitute has been accepted by the Catholic Church as a necessary evil (Simone de Beauvoir 1952) needed to defend the honor and the purity of maidens and protect the cohesion of the family, by being responsible for the biological needs of men and, more particularly, husbands (Gutiérrez de Pineda 1975).

These continuing main strains of *machista* culture need, however, to be seen against the background of a more complete social fabric.

The Family Structure and Culture of the Indigenous People

The Indian family was a utilitarian unit. Its sole purpose was to benefit the community and its members. "Matrimony was an obligation for the maintenance of the family, which was the social and economic nucleus of the State" (Restrepo 1995: 15). There were innumerable indigenous groups all over the Latin American continents. These people moved around the land quite easily, had wars, and had a well-structured commerce among their societies. The Aztecs of Mexico and the Incas of Peru were not the only developed indigenous groups. In Colombia, for example, the Muiscas, the Tayronas, and the Chibchas reached a high culture between the fourth century BC and the sixteenth century. When the Spanish troops of Gonzalo Jimenez de Quesada arrived, they completely destroyed these three millenarian civilizations and cultures (Restrepo 1995: 38).[20]

The Spaniards found that within the Indian family nucleus, the man was responsible for the woman and the children. These cultures' matrimonial laws were based on exogamy with a maternal filiation, and they forbade incest. Everywhere, the Indian laws protected women against the physical or sexual violence of men. Women were respected and much appreciated. The leaders of the societies paid women benefits during pregnancy, widowhood, and old age (see Gutiérrez de Pineda 1975; Restrepo 1995).

Marriage, although extremely important, could be dissolved if it did not work out by the wife and/or the husband. Either could ask for a divorce and could remarry someone else, without fear of stigmatization. Children usually stayed with the mother, but it was preferred that the couples who had children did not separate. Sexual life, started practically at puberty, was "practiced with no restriction" (Restrepo 1995: 34). For the woman, the beginning of adulthood was the first menstruation, which was considered an important rite of passage. To be a virgin did not bring respect for the woman. On the contrary, virginity was deemed a "shortcoming," meaning that the woman was not desired or good enough for a man to want to be with her. It was a cause of shame instead of pride. Purity and virginity were not concepts belonging to the Indian worldview. Young women and young men could choose each other as love partners. If the relationship worked, and the woman became pregnant, then the marriage was celebrated, and the man symbolically owned the woman and the child. He was made responsible for his family (Gutiérrez de Pineda 1997: 127). Faithfulness for women or men was not an obligation, nor was infidelity considered a crime. However, a woman could be sanctioned by her husband and sent back to her family. On the other hand, men also practiced polygamy (Restrepo 1995: 30). The chiefs had many wives, six or seven.

Usually, the first chosen was the head of the co-wives or concubines. Polygamy was a discriminatory practice where women were always at a disadvantage, and by which they suffered terrible discriminations and extreme and vicious mistreatment, according to Virginia Gutiérrez de Pineda (1997: 111–14). Simultaneously, lovemaking was considered an art that provided the partners immense pleasure. A sign of friendship to a friend or foreigner who visited a household was to offer him a daughter, a sister, or a niece for him to sleep with, if the woman accepted. Not to offer the woman to the visitor was to reject him and devalue him as a friend (Gutiérrez de Pineda 1997: 121; see also, Restrepo 1995). The Spaniards were astonished by this practice, which they also profited from, but considered "savage" and immoral. Furthermore, women were given to the enemies as a prize, when wars were lost. Women were also exchanged or bartered for other material goods and/or favors.

Married women had to take care of household chores, cooking, raising children, crops, and animals. They made the family's clothes and looked after the husband's happiness (Gutiérrez de Pineda 1997). Sewing, pottery, and bodily designs of the members of the family were women's business.[21] Giving birth for the Indian women did not seem to be an ordeal or something to fear. Strong and practical, they gave birth near a river, alone or with a friend, while the husband prayed to the deities for a good delivery. Usually, after the birth, the women bathed in a river and cleaned the baby, before showing it to the father and other members of the group. Children were breast-fed up to three years, no matter the social class in which they were born. Indian women practiced natural birth control and abortion when the pregnancy was not desired (Restrepo 1995: 25–34). As shown, the Amerindian cultures in Colombia were patriarchal. With the aid of certain cultural practices, like adaptive sexual and marriage rules that allowed women the same freedom of choice that men had over their personal lives, patriarchy was sometimes not evident. But between the social regulations, men ruled over cultural and social codes. The Indian women often had to exist within the patriarchal system with humility and resignation. It is recorded that, in many groups, women killed their female children after birth, to spare them the hard destiny women had in a world where men enjoyed unrestricted leisure and wellbeing, with the aid not only of cultural beliefs but also of their women (Gutiérrez de Pineda 1997: 115–21).

The personality of the Amerindians, as described by the *conquistadores* (Restrepo 1995: 25), including Columbus himself, was a sweet and gentle nature. They smiled a lot and had happy countenances. These people, Columbus wrote, did not seem to have material cravings. Their languages were filled with soft sounds.[22] The women were beautiful, discreet in their demeanor, and their nakedness did not shock the eye. The Spanish chronicles described the generosity and the loving attitude of these people towards others; they also describe the beauty of their naked bodies and the elegance of their movements. Some of the Indians covered themselves with blankets that the women wove. The colonizers were surprised to see the freedom men and women had over their sexualities, and how they enjoyed sexual practices as a means for their personal delight. Marriage was desired and much respected, but men and women had total sexual freedom and could change partners at will, with no grave repercussions (Restrepo 1995: 34; Gutiérrez de Pineda 1997: 102). Indians knew about love. Their love was discreet and silent, their lovemaking unhurried and engaging, writes Roberto Restrepo (1995: 16, 27–28), all of which differed from the love practices of Europeans.

The Spaniards, as soon as they got used to the challenges in the New World, started fighting and killing the Indians. They took the men as slaves and the women as concubines, after having violated their carnal intimacy. They destroyed the world life of the Indians and left them impotent against a world impossible to decipher. The colonizers not only physically killed the inhabitants of this land, but worse, they annihilated them spiritually. Those who did not perish were absorbed by the Catholic Church, where they found some solace and peace for their misery and traumas. The survivors of the Spanish massacres started to adopt the culture of their enemies, and, in their religion, they found a new belief system that could support and protect them from total despair and nihilism. Today, Colombia has more or less eighty indigenous groups. Unfortunately, society in general has forgotten them. Their survival and their cultures are at stake.

The African-Colombian Family

On the other hand, Africans came to Latin America as slaves to help the Span-ish conquerors work the gold mines, serve them as soldiers to fight the wars against the insurgents, and do work the white people would not perform because of their higher status. Like the Indians, blacks were placed in a disadvantaged position beneath the masters. The Africans were in a worse position than the Indians, however, since they came from a far away world, without speaking any of the languages encountered in the new lands, not knowing the people's cul-tures, and being poor and miserable after having been dispossessed and sepa-rated from their families, their loved ones, and their countries. The social val-ues and cultural structures transmitted to the Africans were a mix of the social values the Spaniards brought with them and the cultures of the different Indian groups that existed in Colombia at the time of the Spanish conquest. The blacks, writes Gutiérrez de Pineda (1997: 239), were culturally influenced by the Indians, and, specifically, by their myths, beliefs, and values. Thus, whites, In-dians, and blacks created their own cultural milieu with different cultural influ-ences and constituted the social structures that now are found in Colombia. Un-til their liberation in May of 1810, the status of the Africans was one of enslavement. But, as Virginia Gutiérrez de Pineda (1975; 1997) indicates, it is problematic to speak about their culture and their social lives, because no good bibliography about them exists. Nor are there historical documents explaining how these people were culturally assimilated by the cultures of the New World. Little is known about the black slaves, apart that they did not have freedom, and that they did all the menial and hard work, to help serve the men and women from the upper classes. Instead, the Spanish chronicles went deeply into the Spanish, Indian, or mixed ethnic family structures, explaining how the so-cial lives and roles of women and men were organized in their newly developed social institutions.

The slave or black African was always an extra in the Amerindian and/or Spanish cultures (Virginia Gutiérrez de Pineda 1997: 156–59). The country was strange to them, and so were the values, rules, and codes. Blacks were un-able to reproduce their own cultures in the New World. This loss was their greatest tragedy. Africa was lost for them, and so were their languages. "It was a radical transplant" that did not give these people the possibility to repro-duce in this new land what they knew and had lost (Gutiérrez de Pineda 1997: 158).

Furthermore, in Colombia, black immigration was not as massive as it was in the Caribbean or Brazil. Thus, the black population's only alternative was to mix with the other people they met in their new destiny, organize themselves as best they could, and live wherever they were allowed to live. The black slaves had to be reborn by creating another culture, as they acquired new cultural and social values. And so they did, especially when they started to establish themselves in certain parts of the country near the Pacific or Atlantic coasts.

Today's Colombian black populations are the most underdeveloped in the country: they are the least educated, the poorest, the most disadvantaged, and those who have the least cohesive social and cultural structures (Gutiérrez de Pineda 1975: 235). The male's only way out from misery, and to forget the enslaved past, usually has been to use his sexuality in an erratic, "explosive way" (Gutiérrez de Pineda 1975: 404). This tendency leads to abandonment of women and children at a higher rate than in other family groups, relatively more female-headed households (which in any group tend to be the lowest income households), and less societal respect for the group.

Mixtures and New Formations

Thus, two groups organized the new country's cultural and social tapestries, the white Europeans and the Indians or indigenous groups. It needs to be remembered that the Spaniards developed laws to protect themselves from losing their culture. The Spanish language was maintained with no great effort. From the time of the conquest to the present, this maintenance of culture has had great influence in the organization of the Colombian world. The Catholic Church and its doctrines have had great importance, too (Gutiérrez de Pineda 1975). Catholicism was easily assimilated by everyone, after the Indians were forced to scatter away from their villages. The Spaniards have always used strict laws, to protect themselves from outside influence. Whites were forbidden to marry Indians and blacks. They brought from Spain white women with whom to marry and have children. Sometimes this ethnic separation was successfully kept, but innumerable times it weakened as different types of relations between women and men developed. Apart from the religious marriage practiced by the upper classes, there were *de facto* unions, concubinage, and prostitution. From such unions, children were born, races were mixed, and classes failed to maintain desired "blood purity." As the ethnic groups climbed the economic ladder, they, too, started to practice the rules of the upper white classes, such as getting married in the Catholic Church. Ethnicity stopped being the measure of high status in the country. But whites tried to maintain their race "clean"; and they still do, even if they are unable to keep their higher economic status.

From this mix of Spanish and Indian values, the neo-Hispanic family and the Antioqueña family resulted. The former developed in the northern part of Colombia, and the latter at the country's center and southwest. There are exceptions—for example, black and very poor communities usually do not marry in the Catholic Church; they have multiple, sporadic relationships (Gutiérrez de Pineda 1975; Bermudez 1992, 1993). These family structures represent, to a large extent, today's Colombian culture, with variations depending on geographical zone and the specific group of people.

The Neo-Hispanic Family

The neo-Hispanic culture structured itself strictly around patriarchal ideology, which, in this type family, organizes the relationships between men and women quite rigidly. At the same time, it drastically influences and infiltrates all social institutions, making social relations inflexible (Gutiérrez de Pineda 1997:160–219). The father and/or the male is the main cultural figure; his word is what counts. He has all the power needed to handle whatever relationship he has with women, children, and other men. The male character is aggressive, stern, violent, and willful. To contradict a man, one runs the risk of receiving his rebuttal, mistreatment, or contempt. Male children are socialized very young to develop a strong, stubborn personality; they are taught to do as they wish, from an early age. Women and children are under the control of the masculine head of household, be it father, brother, or uncle. The masculine will rules every family. In the working or poor classes, male domination over the family is more obvious and more aggressively carried out than in the middle and upper social classes. Men who are absent for long periods of time, because of their businesses or farms, usually have relationships with women other than their wives. They, typically, establish unions outside the law, with women from the working or poor classes, or they have sporadic mistresses who usually become poor unwed mothers. In this way, women from the poorer classes help protect the reputation, the virginity, and the purity of women from the middle and upper classes. Rich businessmen or farmers have their extra-marital affairs and relationships customarily with women who are grateful to these men for having looked at them while not heeding their social class. Also, to have children fathered by men of the upper classes is an honor for poor women. It is a way to climb the social ladder or to fight poverty, as, usually, the men will see to the woman's and the child's economic well-being. Wives try not to acknowledge what is going on between their husbands and other women; what is important is to maintain the family cohesion and honor.

Men fight and protect to death their women's honor and purity. A woman who dishonors her name dishonors the family name too. But a man from the neo-Hispanic culture shows his virility and *machismo* through the women he possesses. He soils both his wife and his mistress in order to make sure that his values are kept (Gutiérrez de Pineda 1975: 404). Men's honor and worth are exemplified by their amorous adventures and by their economic success. The demonstration of manhood starts at puberty, when the young man is taken to the prostitutes by one of the adult males of his family.

Female Crimes and Punishment

One of the features of *machismo* in early Colombian families had to do with the strength by which men exerted power over their women, actually a duty. Women, by their nature, deemed "treacherous, ignorant, unconquerable, indomitable, arrogant, disobedient, scandalous, loud, uppity, dependent and vengeful," required control by forceful men. The law accorded husbands the right to punish their wives, "for excesses," without reference to truth or the gravity of a man's complaint. Adultery, real or imagined, could be punished by death. Most punishment had to do with sexual conduct, inadequate housekeeping, or inadequate attention to the husband. But if a wife cut her hair, or visited her family, without permission from her spouse, he had a reason to punish her. The "uncontrollable wrath of husbands was abetted by their being 'pickled with alcohol.'" And the forms of punishment could be extremely crude: for example: "a husband who sleeps with a knife under his pillow; one who burns his nude wife with a bunch of burning straw, another who ties her to the beam, whips her and forces her to spend the night outside in inclement weather. . . . Imprisonment for days, with or without food, spikes, daggers, mule bridles and hot water" were weapons against wives perceived as disobedient, in some way. Other forms of punishment included verbal abuse, abandonment, bringing a prostitute to live in the house, and buffeting with fists. Because women were physically weaker than men and, as a rule, they had few economic resources, they endured violence and humiliation (review by Maria Teresa Mojica and Rene Salinas on Juana Salamanca's book "Mujeres Castigadas") (*History of Punishing Women El Tiempo* 2006: 5), as many do, today.

The Antioqueña Family

Virginia Gutiérrez de Pineda (1975: 373–493) pictures the Antioqueña culture as being totally opposed to the neo-Hispanic culture that gives all power to the patriarch or the male figure. The Antioqueña family, on the contrary, acknowledges the mother or the female figure as very important for the functioning of the family. The mother participates actively in the family's economic happenings and decisions of the household, even if she does not contribute monetarily. The Antioqueños are hardworking, religious people. From their state in north-central Colombia, they have moved around the country whenever they have been in need of work, populating all the regions of Colombia. In this way, they have spread the seeds of their culture, which is based on courage, hard labor, desire for success, and generosity. Antioqueños help others who are in need—family members, friends, or poor people who have fewer opportunities because of lack of resources or education.

What gives status to Antioqueños is money, and not purity of race, as it used to be (Gutiérrez de Pineda 1975: 410–12). He who has money goes automatically up the social ladder. The ethic of the Antioqueño male is work and economic success. Morality is based on progress. He is prone to take risks and to fight his way through, no matter if he has failed once or twice. He cannot be overwhelmed by hardships; his strength of character helps him to conquer unfriendly situations. From this idea springs his tenacity, creativity, and versatility; his being able to adapt to anything from geographical niches to whatever he encounters that is new and different (Gutiérrez de Pineda 1975: 413). A zest for life, his love for work, his desire for success impels him wherever destiny and luck carry him. And behind this desire for accomplishing a fruitful and leisurely life, there is God, to whom the family prays, so that it will reach its goals and dreams.

The Antioqueño male needs a woman to help him out in his endeavors. He needs someone he can trust with his family, who means so much to him, and his culture. He, thus, finds a woman who is strong in character, responsible, cunning, and good at handling the family finances—a woman who, like her man, is not afraid of hardships, work, or different worldviews. This woman, above anything else, is loyal to her husband or companion and to her family. Her honor is based not only on the family's accomplishments, but also on her purity and her virginity. Once again, we encounter a culture that is respected through women's chastity, but essentially and foremost on the economic successes of men.

Families survive men's "biological needs," carnal desires for other women who are not their wives, through prostitutes (Gutiérrez de Pineda 1975). Prostitutes, in a different way from wives and/or companions, help sustain the pillars of these men's households. Wherever the men go, the prostitutes go with them. Instead of having other unions like the neo-Hispanic family man does, the Antioqueño uses the services of sex workers to help liberate him from unrestrained, carnal desires that in the male are considered normal by culture, society, and religious philosophical concepts and teachings.

Like the neo-Hispanic man, the Antioqueño also, typically, has prostitutes initiate boys when they go through the rite of passage to "become men." No wonder, then, the prevalence of men who seek sexual satisfaction outside of marriage. Rosie, the Colombian sex worker who lives in Amsterdam, explains her point of view:

> Men go to prostitutes because prostitutes are more free with sex, with their own sexuality which they can express better than any other woman. Marriage ruins the relationship between a man and a woman. The wife, after some time and for innumerable reasons, gets cold and stops wanting to have sex with her husband. Or simply, the woman stops liking it, and when the husband looks for the wife, she lies there in bed without feeling anything. And husbands, well, they forget about their wives' needs. They do not make love to them. For example, they drink and want to have drunken sex; thus, wives cannot respond to the lovemaking.

And Flor gives another explanation for men going to prostitutes. "If men have a good, serious, pure girlfriend, they cannot do *anything* with her. This is why whorehouses are filled with men. There men can drink as much as they like. And an interesting thing is that men call the prostitutes "*niñas*" (girls, implying virginity).

While it would be impossible to disentangle the usually mixed tendencies of these cultures, it can be said that Esperanza, Susana, María Isabel, Manuela, and María del Carmen typify elements of the Antioqueña family pattern, and Aleja, Dora, and Soledad exemplify features of the neo-Hispanic profile.

Women as Protagonists in Colombian History

Women are infrequently mentioned in Latin American history, even though some of the countries' matriarchs participated actively in social, political, and artistic developments. In truth, women contributed to revolutionary movements and undertook acts of resistance. Rigoberta Menchu from Guatemala did so much for human rights internationally that she was awarded a Nobel Peace Prize in 1992. Centuries earlier, Sor Juana Inés de la Crúz—a Mexican nun who lived during the Spanish occupation of Mexico in the 1700s—entered a convent in order to dedicate herself to study and writing.[23] Being from the middle class and the daughter of an unwed mother, Sor Juana Inés faced only one acceptable occupation: marriage and motherhood (but not with an upper-class man because of her social status). In a subtly worded essay, "*La Respuesta*"

(1691), Sor Juana Inés de la Crúz confronted the policies toward women maintained by the Catholic Church.[24] This devout but rebellious, brilliant nun died soon after her bishop "refuted her with virulence"[25] and forbade her continuing the intellectual endeavors to which she was committed.[26] Sor Juana Inés followed the ascetic path until her death in 1695 (Arenal 1994: 14; see also Franco 1989).

At the end of the eighteenth century and beginning of the nineteenth, *La Gran Colombia*—the geographic and political entity formed by Venezuela, Colombia, and Ecuador—began its battle for independence from Spain (see Bushnell 1993). Before and during the wars, the women of *La Gran Colombia* donated homes as well as jewelry and money to support the cause of freedom (1780–1822). Later, Colombian women not only participated in fighting alongside the men but often acted as spies for the revolutionary forces.[27] Frequently, valiant women fulfilled the duties of cooks, nurses, and general caretakers for the rebels (Bermudez 1992; Castro 1995; Jaramillo Castillo 1995).[28]

Between 1809 and 1810, the fight for independence was launched through a declaration signed in Quito, Ecuador, by a group of patriots and insurgents who rose up against the authoritarian power of the Spaniards. Under the leadership of Simón Bolivar, *el libertador* (the liberator), armed conflict against royal troops—*los realistas*—began in 1813 and lasted seven years. According to Evelyn Cherpak (1995: 83–116) in her "Women of the Independence Wars 1780–1830," the fighting became so ferocious that females in Venezuela also joined the battle, calling their troops *las mujeres*—the women.[29] Bolivar referred to another battalion of female warriors in a speech delivered in front of his troops: "Even the beautiful sex, that which gives all joy to the human race, our amazons (female soldiers), have fought against the tyrants of San Carlos, with divine courage." Bolivar next described the cowardice of royal troops who dared to raise their guns against the "innocent and adorable bosoms of our female beauties" (Cherpak 1995: 94).

Occasionally, Latin American women became famous as mistresses, wives, daughters, or sisters of great men. Manuelita Saenz—Simón Bolivar's unconditional lover and friend—was well-known as the companion of the Venezuelan national independence leader.[30] In the name of love, Saenz dared to defy the strict conventions of her culture and the Catholic religion by divorcing her British husband. She further scandalized polite society by refusing to marry her lover, thus becoming a blatantly adulterous woman.[31] This revolutionary act lashed out at the upper classes of Ecuador and echoed throughout *Nueva Granada*.[32]

A few Latin American women carved out niches for themselves in traditionally male environments, like literature, poetry, and the arts. The Chilean poet Gabriela Mistral, for example, received the Nobel Prize for Literature in 1946. However, the majority of South American women remain in the role of spiritual proletariat—forgotten by history and the men who created it. On the subject of female invisibility in Latin American history, Asuncion Lavrin says in her *Latin American Women: Historical Perspectives* (1978:3–4),

> Historians of Latin America have yet to undertake the study of women either as a group or as individuals in a meaningful, thorough, and innovative manner. . . . Some individual women have escaped historical anonymity for highly personal attributes or deeds that contradicted accepted stereotypes in their own societies or ours. . . . [Thus] we have developed a "great woman syndrome" whereby only prominent females are the subject of what pretends to be the history of Latin America.

These women huddled in the shadows of the men they supported by managing households, providing ideas and encouragement, but staying unobserved within their countries.

Today—on the surface, at least—Colombian society appears to approve of women's social and political independence.[33] But as the feminist lawyer Gloria de los Ríos (1995: 423–30) affirms in her article "Condición Jurídica de las Mujeres," (The juridical condition of women) even "today, forty years after the revolutionary legal transformation of women's civic conditions, cultural traditions still bind women to concepts that consider women infants and thus submit them to their father, brother, or husband" (1995: 422).

In Colombia, women began their struggle for equal rights in 1932. (In Ecuador, female suffrage was passed in 1928.) In 1954, Esmeralda Arboleda was able to convince the Colombian Senate to accept a law granting civil rights to women. Not until 1957, however, was the right to vote actually exercised by Colombian women. Many people of both sexes in the Conservative and Liberal Parties rejected the idea of women voting. Likewise, the Roman Catholic Church vehemently opposed women's suffrage, since it wished "to preserve traditional gender constructions," no matter what was on the social agenda (Craske 1999: 6). Historians Magdala Velásquez Toro and Catalina Reyes Cardenas (1995:229–57) relate how Pope Pius XII and his Colombian bishops advised against allowing women to take part in matters that might pull them away from feminine duties as wives and mothers. Many individuals thought participating in politics would "cheapen women" (vulgarize women), or that females did not have the nature for "masculine matters." Women were presumed to be loving and caring by nature, absorbed by concern for the family's welfare, and considered ill-equipped to function as adults in the public arena. Thus, they had to be protected from such endeavours.

A Historical Perspective on Feminist Groups in Colombia

Norma Villareal Mendez's article "Camino Utópico de las Feministas en Colombia 1975–1991" (1994: 184) traces the emergence of feminist groups in that country in 1975.[34] At the time, Colombian women began openly criticizing patriarchal power, which permeated the social and political strata of the nation. Feminists demanded "the transformation of women's oppressive condition within society" and the freedom to make decisions regarding their bodies and souls[35] (see Craske 1999). Unfortunately, political upheaval in Colombia created stronger state structures that harmed women's interests. Terrorism still continues, as conflict rages between various guerrilla groups, paramilitaries, and drug dealers.[36] Female images and services are intrinsically tied to the peace process, images that the "Anotioqueña" Noemí Sanin used at large during her 1998 presidential campaign. Motherhood is used to evoke qualities associated with women: renunciation, abnegation, sacrifice, and spiritual strength. These characteristics, supposedly, are required to tame men's aggressive, chaotic behavior. The idea of "maternal instinct" is exploited to protect society and its institutions. As Nikki Craske (1999: 14) comments,

> Biology may not be destiny but it does overshadow women's lives, and motherhood seems to be remarkably resistant as a cultural identity. Changes in work patterns may be quite marked, but the commitment to the reproductive arena generally takes precedence over work and careers.

Until today, women are reputed to have supernatural qualities, like sacrifice tied to their mothering instinct—even if they are childless. Latin American women do not separate themselves from their usual role of mothers and wives. It is the *supermadre* (all powerful mother), as Elsa Chaney (1979: 161–66) labels it, who protects women in their public or political endeavors. These notions of womanhood undercut feminist attempts to fight patriarchal ideology, writes Villareal Mendez. Nevertheless, says Asuncion Lavrin (1987: 120), a group of women in Colombia, *Vamos Mujer* (Let's go, women), developed their own agenda for social change: "The list of social change is as follows: (1) true exercise of political and civil rights for Colombian women, to develop an independent and participatory personality; (2) freedom of choice and decision in personal affective matters related to love, sexuality, and fecundity; (3) construction of a new image of women transcending the traditional roles of personal dependence, abnegation, passivity, and subjection; (4) equitable working conditions with supportive services. Housework is included in the definition of work." Undoubtedly, Colombian women have been working hard to develop their visions on women's issues and what they expect to accomplish. But the struggle has been hard and often arid.

On May 30, 2000, the Colombian government issued a law requiring that 30 percent of political posts be filled by women. (And yet, in the peace process with the guerrilla group FARC [*Fuerzas Armadas Revolucionarias de Colombia* or revolutionary armed forces of Colombia], there was not one single woman either from the Colombian government or from the FARC sitting at the table where the dialogues were taking place.) The need for this ruling illustrates the real political situation of women in a society where patriarchy always has had the upper hand.[37] Despite protestations, Colombia disregards female existence by ignoring women's political capacity and human rights.[38] As noted, in May 2000, the Supreme court accepted bigamy as a normal masculine way of behavior. Such subjugation and inequality is intolerable.

Nevertheless, on August 16, 2006, the twenty-six women in the Colombian Congress decided to put aside their political and ideological differences on behalf of uniting as a solid group to fight for women's rights. Their main concern was to reach agreement with all political parties to guarantee women 50 percent participation in all political posts. Other concerns were to create laws to protect women who are heads of families and to punish any kind of violence within the family (*El Tiempo*, Bogotá, August 17, 2006). This experiment to create as many laws as needed to protect Colombian women's human rights was the first of its kind in Latin America (*Poder*, October 21, 2006: 9). The group also planned for March 2007, a worldwide forum to discuss women's issues. Another interest of these congresswomen was to work towards the election of the first Colombian female president.

On another level, many women form part of the ranks of the two groups of Marxist guerrillas and the paramilitary fighting groups. The female guerrilla warriors have given testimonies of their situation within these masculine strongholds, which are supervised and controlled with an iron grip by the men. Che Guevara, the martyred revolutionary, recommends female participation during the Cuban guerrilla warfare.

> The woman can also perform her habitual task of peacetime; it is very pleasing to a soldier subjected to the extremely hard conditions of this life to be able to look forward to a seasoned meal which tastes like something. One of the great misfortunes of the [Cuban] war was eating cold, sticky, tasteless mess. Furthermore, it is easier to keep her in those tasks; one of the problems in guerrilla bands is they [masc.] are constantly trying to get out of these tasks. (Craske 1999: 144)

As several Colombian guerrilla women have said, the women in the terrorist groups serve the men as cooks, washerwomen, and cleaning women (see Lara 2000). If allowed to fight in the war against the Colombian army, they are placed in front of the ranks, together with the youngest soldiers who are almost children. They serve as shields to protect the men from being killed first. Women are tortured more often than killed (Craske 1999: 142), because they are taken prisoner. If the women are allowed to supervise the camps, they do it at night so that the men can sleep calmly. Further, the men use female guerrillas as their "comfort" women.[39] They command who will be the mistress of whom, or organize each night who will sleep with whom. Amnesty International, in October 2004, published an in-depth report on the violence, sexual exploitation, sexual mutilation, and all kinds of atrocities the guerrillas do to women in Colombia. These terrorist tactics serve to make people leave their homes and help the insurgents to win the war. Unfortunately, says the report, women's bodies have become fields where the war is also being fought.

The Tracks of Oppression

Discrimination against Colombian women does not arrive *ex nihilo* but originates through cultural rules and ideas. History informs us how women's subjugation started with the Spanish conquest in the New World. (See a chart at the end of the chapter connecting Spanish and Islamic attitudes toward women. The religion and culture of the Moors (Islam) permeated the Iberian Peninsula for at least eight hundred years, later mixing with Catholicism.) As native cultures were absorbed or destroyed, the Spanish patriarchal structure spread, passed along from one generation to the next. Today it permeates every region and every important institution—family, church, government, private enterprise, even inside contemporary guerrilla warfare and movements.

Colombian patriarchy imposes on women its culture of female repression, including the irrational proposition that all women are potential prostitutes who have to be protected from their weak nature by men themselves. Currently, Colombian men have a legal right to bigamy.

The situation is the outcome of social, cultural, and religious beliefs. The interviewees here attest to the ways women are stifled and hurt inside this dysfunctional dynamic. As some women join with a feminist agenda to change or eradicate the system, they may expect a long, hard struggle. It can be done with *Women's Ways of Knowing* (Belenky et al. 1986) and their unified discourse.

Latin American Women

The Creation of Female Docile Bodies in Two Cultures (What they share)

Circumcised Arab Women

Women's Hymen symbol of virginity signifier of women's honor and/or shame

⟵ Born with a "lack" *difference* ⟶ Excision of Female Genitalia (Circumcision) Symbol of women's virginity

Different social construction of the body · women raised in the ideology of Shame · Masculine virility and honor

↓

Virgin Mary sublime
Model of chastity: the culmination of womanhood. Sexless Being. Myth and symbol of the perfect virginal woman, mother of Christ-wife of Christ and Church

↓

Patrilineal kinship structure. A system of proclamations and prohibitions *inserted* in marriage, modesty code, family honor, women's social roles, women's chastity /Agriculture–Pastoralism and Mediterranean culture

↓

This "Ritual" protects woman's virginity, honor, cleanliness · Preserves good reputation · *Ensures* chastity and virginity of females · gives them an identity; to be a virgin

↓

Teachings and philosophy of father's of the church . St Paul, St Augustine, St Thomas Aquinas: Sex is the root of Sin · Women promote sex and have a special connection to the dangers of the "flesh.". Women are to be kept secluded to serve their husbands who guard their sexual modesty · after fathers and brothers.

↓

Purity and Impurity of women's major cultural and social fact/issue · girls must be virgins/pure. Married women chaste/faithful
Sin ➡Flesh ➡Women
Virginity major aspect of feminine identity · Women must be protected from their own nature

↓

Women's sexual desire thought to be very powerful. It has to be controlled through body mutilation · In this way women will summit to moral, social, legal and religious constraint · GREAT infertility

↓

Results: Women's fear of men · They are turned into objects with no capacity of personal thinking, reasoning and conceptualization. Sense of shame · Dependent ON men · Domestic, social violence; unequal status · psychological "castration": confiscation of their "bodies" /Subjectivity/Right of speech
1. Penis envy
2. Tendency to hysterics

↓

Women must be punished because of their "lack." Their body is "polluted." Their body locus of male power and masculine torturing tactics. Women's sexuality considered to be evil and treacherous · Women part of men's patrimony · women are gifts

↓

Results: Great sexual problems · SEVERE psychological, psychosomatic, psychosexual and social complications. Fearful, shy, secluded in their homes and Veils, psychological and physical castration. No trace of subjectivity outside their homes

↓

Psychosocial entity = Woman is victim of her sexuality · Annihilation of her personality · Out of symbolic order · No language = Silent

Notes

1. See Asuncion Lavrin, ed., *Latin American Women—Historical Perspectives* (Westport, CT.: Greenwood Press, 1978), a pathbreaking book about the history of women's issues in Latin America before, during, and after the conquest of that part of the world by the Spaniards. Also for an excellent history of Colombia—from pre-Colombian times to the present—see Frank Safford and Marco Palacios, *Colombia: Fragmented Land, Divided Society.* (New York: Oxford University Press, 2002). And also see, David Bushnell, *The Making of Modern Colombia: A Nation in Spite of Itself* (Berkeley, CA: University of California Press, 1993). Also Alvaro Tirado Mejia academic director of *Nueva Historia de Colombia* (A New History of Colombia). Bogotá, August 16, 1989, section 6A.

2. Ann Rosalind Jones in "Writing the Body: *L'Ecriture Feminine*," in *The New Feminist Criticism*, ed., Elaine Showalter (New York: Pantheon Books, 1985: 369) is quite explicit about the importance of history in knowing who we are. She says, "We need to know how women have come to be who they are through history, which is the history of their oppression by men and male-designed institutions. Only through an analysis of the power relationships between men and women, and practices based on that analysis, will we put an end to our oppression—and only then will we discover what women are or can be."

3. Asuncion Lavrin in "Women, the Family, and Social Change in Latin America," *World Affairs* (150, no. 2, Fall 1987), 121, says about Gutiérrez de Pineda's work, "A path-breaking study of the family in Colombia by anthropologist Virginia Gutiérrez de Pineda still stands as a *heuristic* model for research" (emphasis mine).

4. These two family models, the neo-Hispanic and the Antioqueña, are a mixture of the cultural and social laws and morals received from Spain and from the Indian cultures found in Colombia by the Spaniards, that were assimilated and reorganized in specific ways by the people in the country after the European conquest. Today in Colombia, one will find these two models well delineated, and with variations depending on the region.

5. The Spanish family was molded by various intra-cultural influences that at one time or another existed within Spain itself. The Romans, Germanic tribes, and Jews were well established in Spain for many centuries, influencing its culture. The Moors enriched Spanish culture for no less than eight centuries, and also collaborated in the making of the social tapestry of Spain.

6. On the issue of metaphors or analogies that provided the scientific answers in the nineteenth century on human differences, race, and gender, see Nancy Lee Stephan, "Race and Gender: The Role of Analogy in Science," in *The Racial Economy of Science*, ed. Sandra Harding (Bloomington, IN: Indiana University Press, 1993), 359–376.

7. For an excellent historical perspective on the *conquistadores* and their conquests in the New World, see Hammond Innes, *The Conquistadors* (New York: Alfred A. Knopf, 1969).

8. On the Spanish Monarchs, see William H. Prescott, *History of the Reign of Ferdinand and Isabella: The Catholic Kings of Spain* (London: George Routledge and Sons, 1837).

9. Queen Isabel of Castile supported the Spanish Inquisition. She promoted the war against the Moors, and she gave Christopher Columbus her jewels so that he would be able to expand her reign by discovering far-away territories. See Peggy K. Liss, *Isabel The Queen: Life and Times* (New York: Oxford University Press, 1992).

10. Uta Ranke-Heinemann in *Eunuchs for the Kingdom of Heaven*, 78, 97, (New York: Doubleday, 1990) explains from where comes the dislike of sex in the Catholic Church. "Augustine was the father of a fifteen-hundred-year-long anxiety about sex and enduring hostility to it. He dramatizes the fear of sexual pleasure, equating pleasure with perdition in such a way that anyone who tries to follow his train of thought will have the sense of being trapped in a nightmare. . . . For Augustine hatred of pleasure was still more important than his emphasis on the procreative purpose of every conjugal act."

11. See Marina Warner, *Alone of All Her Sex: The Myth and the Cult of the Virgin Mary* (New York: Alfred Knopf, 1976). The author in this book tells how Mary was raised to be the mother of God, and how she was privileged to sit by God's side in heaven.

12. See Jean Franco's *Plotting Women: Gender and Representation in Mexico* (New York: Columbia University Press, 1989) to understand the different discursive positions of women in a culture violent to women, where their only mode of expression would be under the authority of the Catholic Church. The book is fascinating as it depicts women's creativity in escaping the master discourse, and how they are able to struggle for their own voice to be heard. See also Ranke-Heinemann *Eunuchs*, for a clarification of how the Catholic Church blamed/blames Eve, the first woman, for the fall of the human race and original sin.

13. On Eve, Annie Laurie Gaylor, *Woe to the Women—The Bible Tells Me So: The Bible Female Sexuality and the Law* (Madison, WI: Freedom from Religion Foundation, 1981) in Kramarae and Treichler, *A Feminist Dictionary*, 10, writes "The mythical woman of Genesis who 'showed initiative and an interest in acquiring knowledge.' Because of the results, church officials have 'used the story to deny women education, free speech, and in general, opportunity.'"

14. Maurice Hamington in his very interesting book *Hail Mary?—The Struggle for Ultimate Womanhood in Catholicism* (New York: Routledge, 1995: 132) tells how "The story of the Fall in Genesis is part of a trajectory of Judeo-Christian stories that increasingly *lay the blame for evil in the world upon women*. While the early stories are less explicit, *there is a trend toward making women responsible for the evil in humanity*" (emphasis mine). See, Gabriela Castellanos, "Eva y Maria—la mujer en la tradicion judeo cristiana" (Eve and Mary—woman in the Judeo-Chrsitian tradition). *La Cabala*, No. 8, 4–6. Cali, 1985. A pathbreaking article on how these two women represent, through Eve, the fall of the human race because of her disobedience against God. And Mary, as humanity's way to redemption by being the Virgin mother of Jesus, the son of God. The Catholic Church has Mary as the model Catholic women should follow.

15. See Michel Foucault, *The History of Sexuality: An Introduction, Volume I* (New York: Vintage Books, 1990); Mary Jacobus et al., *Body/Politics: Women and the Discourses of Science* (New York: Routledge, 1990); Sarah B. Pomeroy, *Goddesses, Whores, Wives, and Slaves* (New York: Schocken Books, 1975); Ann Snitow et al., *Power of Desire* (New York: Monthly Review Press, 1983).

16. On women's "weak nature" Saint Chrysostomo wrote, "There are in the world a great many situations that weaken the conscientiousness of the soul. First and foremost of these *dealings with women*. In his concern for the male sex, the superior man will not forget the females, who need greater care precisely because of their *ready inclination to sin*. In this situation the evil enemy can find many ways to creep in secretly. For *the eye of woman touches and disturbs our soul*" (emphasis mine). In Ranke-Heinemann, *Eunuchs*, 121, I strongly recommend the story of *Salome* in the New Testament for a clear picture of women's sinful and evil nature which is intrinsic to their femaleness.

17. On Western religions and their symbolisms, Kramarae and Treichler (1985), 389, quote Casey Miller and Kate Swift, *Words and Women: New Language in New Times* (New York: Garden City, Doubleday, 1976), 67: "While Western religions have traditionally portrayed the spiritual nature of human beings and their relations to God in male terms, sexuality is portrayed as female, the embodiment of sin, forever distracting men from godliness: sons of God but daughters of Eve. Catalysts in a cosmic struggle between evil and good, women are defined as extremes of the sexuality men experience—whore or virgin, agent of Satan or mother of God"; also, Mary Nyquist in her article "Genesis, Genesis, and the Formation of Milton's Eve" in *Cannibals, Witches, and Divorce: Estranging the Renaissance*, ed. Marjorie Gerber (Baltimore, MD, 1987) describes the two versions of the myth of Adam and Eve, and the consequences suffered by Eve for either having been created out of Adam's rib or having lost all the prerogatives that she, like he, had when each took different roles in society, because of their sin against God.

18. For sociologist Florence Thomas bigamy is "effective mistreatment of women that clearly reflects Colombian patriarchy which is resistant to change" in *El Tiempo*, June, 2001: 5.

19. Unwedded mothers in Colombia, especially unwedded young women with children, are a social phenomenon that has been growing quite rapidly while it is denied by society, specifically by families who suffer the experience of having a daughter with a child at an early age. Ana Rico De Alonso in her book, *Madres Solteras Adolescentes* (Adolescents unwedded mothers) (Bogotá: Plaza & Janes, 1986) explores the historical background of the families and the young women who have children before age twenty, plus the psychological and affective relations of and within the family.

20. See Claude Lévi-Strauss, *Tristes Tropiques*, trans. John and Doreen Weightman (New York: Pocket Books, 1973).

21. On how primitive women handle "reality" and its cultural and social network systems, see Yolanda Murphy and Robert F. Murphy, *Women of the Forest* (New York: Columbia University Press, 1985).

22. See Jean Jacques Rousseau's *An Essay on the Origin of Languages*, ed., trans. Victor Gourevitch (New York: Harper and Row, 1987) who says that human beings started to communicate first through feelings, not by reasoning. Then, they started to "sing rather than speak . . . [because] in mild climates, in fertile regions, it took all the liveliness of the agreeable passions to start men speaking. The first languages were daughters of pleasure rather than of need."

23. Sor Juana Inés de la Cruz's greatest desire since age three was to learn reading and writing. In a convent, she did so, although her "intellectually and literarily active life challenged the social, cultural, and religious mores that kept women physically and mentally confined." See Electa Arenal and Amanda Powell in *Sor Juana Inés de la Cruz: The Answer / La Respuesta* (New York: The Feminist Press, 1994), viii. Jean Franco, *Plottin*, 27, also writes about Sor Juana Inés de la Cruz's love for learning. "Sor Juana was to give many reasons for entering the convent, but all of them add up to the fact that the cell was preferable to marriage, learning a higher goal than bearing children."

24. Sor Juana Inés, says Franco in *Plottin*, 2, 6, 15, "contradicted—or deconstructed—artistic, intellectual, and religious views that would deny her and others like her the right to express themselves." The voices of these women were quite different from those of the priests and confessors who "officially controlled their lives." The works of this writer illustrate not only "women's ways of knowing" but also their understanding that "masculine culture assigned women secondary, invisible, silently reflective roles in society." See also Arenal and Powell *Sor Juana Inés*, 1994.

25. The central argument of the bishop's *amonestasión* (letter) was that "all but divine knowledge should be eschewed, especially by women." The bishop contradicted Sor Juana's view of women's participation in the creation of culture; denying the claim that the "active and creative intelligence in women was not the exception but the rule" in Arenal and Powell, *Sor Juana Inés*, 31.

26. Sor Juana Inés was a scholar, not a mystic, according to Arenal and Powell, Ibid., 22, 25, and her calling into the convent was essentially intellectual. The convent was the space she employed for reflection, study, and work. This writer's main "interest was the intellectual plight of women in her own time." She "associated motherhood with creativity and wisdom."

27. Ever since Spanish colonial times, women were enclosed in their homes, but when wars of independence began, women from all strata of society started participating in the fight against the colonizers. Two of the most renown Colombian women who died in the name of independence for *La Gran Colombia* were Policarpa Salavarrieta and Antonia Santos. See Mercedes Guhl, "Las Madres de la Patria: Antonia Santos y Policarpa Salavarrieta" in María Mercedes Jaramillo and Betty Osorio de Negret eds., *Las Desobedientes: Mujeres de Nuestra América* (Antonia Santos and Poli-

carpa Salavarrieta in the disobedient: Women of our America.) (Bogotá, Editorial Panamericana, 1997: 118–130).

28. Evelyn Cherpak wrote in "The Participation of Women in the Independence Movement in Gran Colombia 1780–1830," in Lavrin, ed., *Latin American Women*, 220, "Women contributed to the independence movement [through] participation in combat, accessory actions, and espionage. Second, women lent their support in traditional helping roles as hostesses of political *tertulias* (evening meetings) and as nurses. Third, they made significant economic contributions by donating money and supplies to the insurgents. Finally, personal sacrifices—such as the loss of loved ones, confiscation of property and personal wealth, and poverty and exile—were endured by many."

29. The essay here mentioned is chapter 4 of Evelyn Cherpak's *Women and the Independence of Gran Colombia* 1780–1830 (University of North Carolina, Chapel Hill, 1980). This dissertation was translated and has appeared in several publications in Spanish. The one I cite is from *Consejería Presidencia para la Política Social: Las Mujeres en la Historia de Colombia: Tomo I—Mujeres, Historia, y Política* (Presidencial consulting for social politics: Women in Colombian history—volume I. Women, history and politics). (Santafé de Bogotá: Editorial Norma, 1995), 76, (my translation).

30. The best biography written about Manuela Saenz, in the opinion of many critics, is by Ecuadorian anthropologist Luis Zuñiga, *Manuela: Una Novela Sobre la Vida de Manuelita Saenz* (A novel about Manuelita Saenz's life) (Bogotá, Circulo de Lectores, 2000). *Manuela* is a historical novel that received the Ecuadorian Prize Joaquin Gallegos in 1991 when it was first published.

31. In the recently published letters between Manuelita and the Venezuelan General and Liberator, Manuelita complains about Bolivar's unfaithfulness. He even had a son out of wedlock with a woman in Bolivia while Manuela was waiting for him. See *Cartas de Amor entre Bolivar y Manuelita* (Love letters between Bolivar and Manuelita), ed. Arturo Andrade (Bogotá, *Círculo de Lectores*, 2000).

32. Manuela Saenz was harshly criticized for her courage and "disobedience" in the face of social mores within a culture that forbade women from having any kind of adventures. Nevertheless, Saenz was considered to be Simón Bolivar's "liberator"; she was admired for her dedication and defense of Bolivar. See Lucia Ortiz, "Genio, Figura y Ocaso de Manuela Saenz" (Personality and disapperance of Manuela Saenz) in *Las Desobedientes* (The disobedients), 83–117.

33. Women in Colombia usually have marginalized themselves from political participation, although the presence of females in the political arena has been growing tremendously, according to Norma Villareal Mendez, "Mujeres y Espacios Políticos: Participación Política y Análisis Electoral," (Women and political spaces: political participation and elections' analysis), *Consejería Presidencial*, 319–347. In 1990, one woman was elected to the Senate, versus 114 male senators. In 1991, eight female senators were elected (7.84 percent) versus ninety-two male senators (92.16 percent). The disparity between women and men participating in the country's political life is still quite large.

34. For a complete picture of how the women's movement progressed in Latin America, see J. Jaquette, ed., *The Women's Movement in Latin America* (Boston: Unwin Hyman, 1989).

35. Miranda Davies, ed., *Third World–Second Sex* (New Jersey: Zed Books, 1983), answers many questions dealing with women's sexuality, male violence against women in Third World countries, and cooperation among women working to solve political and sexual problems.

36. See Patricia Lara, *Las Mujeres en la Guerra* (Women in the war) (Bogotá: Editorial Planeta, 2000) for a view of what women from different social classes and ethnic groups think about the war in Colombia and its impact on women. This work includes narrations by two ex-guerilla women and the companion of a high-ranking commander in the FARC, Raul Reyes. Women tend to reject war and death, irrespective of the positions they hold in society. Lara's book illustrates that female energies generally are directed toward life and love.

37. See Florence Thomas, "No! Doctora Fanny Kertzman" (No! Doctor Fanny Kertzman), in *La Mujer Tiene La Palabra* (Woman has the word) (Bogotá: Aguilar, 1999: 117) where she enumerates the many ways by which women around the world and in Colombia are discriminated against socially.

38. See Joyce Gelb, *Feminism and Politics: A Comparative Perspective* (Berkeley, CA: University of California Press, 1989).

39. According to CNN on November 21, 2001, the United Nations has reported that the two Marxist guerrilla fighting groups and the paramilitaries in Colombia tend to rape women before killing them, no matter their age. Symbolically, rape means that a man possesses the woman of another man.

CHAPTER SIX

Focus on Socioeconomic and Political Realities

When we further consider that to understand one woman is not necessarily to understand any other woman; that even if he could study many women of one rank, or of one country, he would not thereby understand women of other ranks or countries; and even if he did, they still are the women of a single period of history; we may safely assert that the knowledge that men may acquire of . . . is wretchedly imperfect and superficial and always will be so, until women themselves have told all that they have to tell.

John Stuart Mill, *The Subjection of Women* (1971: 42)

Woman is simply a help in procreation (*auditorium generationis*) and useful in housekeeping. For a man's intellectual life she has no significance (Aquinas 1274).

Uta Rainke-Heinemann,
Eunuchs for the Kingdom of Heaven (1990: 88)

Graciela: "When you first realize it, you see that you are a girl!"

Introduction
Poverty and gender discrimination show up in statistical charts in ways that tell much about the reduced status and lack of opportunities of Colombian women compared to men. Individual lives or relationships between men and women are much affected by the economic climate. In the case of seventeen-year-old

113

interviewee, African-Colombian Graciela, her father does not earn enough to support his family. To retain his masculine authority and, thus, keep his self esteem, he asserts his machismo by drinking, beating his wife, and, sometimes, his children. Predictably, he keeps another woman. Graciela is following in her mother's footsteps toward a miserable existence. Poverty keeps her from education. She runs away from her home in search of a better future with a young man who cannot support her, who abandons her when she becomes pregnant. In contrast, Graciela has a kind aunt who seems better off, married to a man who has money. At night, however, when Graciela comes to visit and sleeps at her uncle's house, he comes to the room where she sleeps with his daughters, to touch them. The aunt knows about this abuse but keeps silent. She needs a husband to support her and her children. She does not have much choice.

In many ways, these two families reflect a cycle of misery, of poverty fueling masculine violence, predatory behavior looking for power, and female powerlessness and fear.

Interview

"Graciela, tell me about your childhood, about the way you were raised. Tell me anything you wish."

"One day, suddenly, I realized I was a girl. . .and then I started behaving like one. I am the eldest. I always had to take care of my siblings, while my mother went out to work. I was seven years old. When we lived in the city, I took my brothers, I have four, to the day care center or school, depending on their age. But most of the time, we lived in the countryside. My mother didn't do any birth control, because, at the time, it was thought that children were a blessing. Both my parents told me that because I was a woman I had to wash, iron, cook, and take care of the children. They also told me that I had to sit well. I was a very helpful girl. I didn't play much. Only a little at night with my brothers, we played hide and seek. There was no way to have dolls. My father was a carpenter, and my mother washed clothes in people's homes. My mother has suffered a great deal. She is not affectionate; she keeps saying that she wants to die. She says that she has never been happy. Poverty has given her a terrible life. And my father has another woman to whom he gives money. My mother lost her mother when she was fifteen years old. Her father threw her out of the house because he wanted to live with another woman. He had twelve children. Thus, my mother thought that if she married, she would have a better life. I did the same thing at fifteen. I wanted to go to school and I couldn't because of our poverty; then, I eloped with my boyfriend. I was not allowed to go out with him alone, because my parents said that I could get pregnant, which I did!"

"When did they start telling you about taking care of yourself, your body?"

"Since I was twelve years old. I only learned about it with my own experience. I had an aunt, my mother's sister, who was very good to us. She was married to a man who had money. He was forty-seven years old. He used to buy groceries for us, and he used to give me presents. He had two daughters. When I stayed at my uncle's home, he used to come in the evenings and touch us girls . . . I told my aunt what my uncle did to my cousins and to me, but she was scared to confront him. She knew very well what was going on at night, because she saw him getting up and coming into our room. This thing happened with my uncle every time I went to visit his house to help my aunt. My father never knew about it. My father always said that men were always trying to harm women; they get them pregnant, and then they leave them. I was so frightened that I never spoke about it. I didn't even tell my mother, poor thing, who was always so sick. Until one day, I got so fed up that I decided to run away with the father of my only child. Anyway, we were so poor that we didn't have much to eat, and his family was better off than my own family. But with my boyfriend, we never spoke about money. He had his, and I had mine. I earned mine by cleaning houses. He was the only possibility I had for a better life. He left me when he knew I was pregnant. I didn't tell him either about what my uncle did to me. I was afraid that he would think that I liked it, or that it had been my fault, because in some way I made it happen. So I told no one."

"Tell me about your school years. Did you do your first Communion?"

"No. I was not even baptized, nor were my brothers and sisters either. My mother is Evangelical. She taught us children to read the bible and to sing in the church. While my father practiced that religion, he didn't drink. Actually, he had to leave the religion, because he likes to drink when he has a problem. I went to a good school for a while. The teachers were women. I learned how to read, write, add, and subtract. They also gave us religion lessons. It was a co-ed school. Inside class and in recreation, boys and girls, we were allowed to mix. Ouside, when we stood up in lines, boys were on one side, and girls on the other."

"Who told you about menstruation?"

"My mother did. She told me that girls, we grow breasts and that after having our period at thirteen, we start maturing and we become women and we can have children."

"Was there a difference between your life and your brothers'?"

"Of my four brothers, the life of the eldest is very hard. My father used to beat him, constantly. My father said that this was the way he was brought up. My father forced my brother to work, when he was merely ten years old. He helped my father with the wood work; he also sold sweets in buses. When my father and my brother came back from work, my mother and I, we served them diner. It didn't bother me at all. It was natural for my mother and me to serve the men. I always saw that women take care of the house and that, usually, it is men who go out to work. But women never rest; they are always cooking, working, taking care of the kids. Poor people have always had the same kind of family life: the parents have to work. If the father leaves the home, the mother works harder, and the eldest girl takes care of everything. There were moments, before I left my parents' house, that I didn't want to go on, but I had no other choice. I had to take care of my brothers. It was essential for my mother to work; she brought the money to buy the food. My father paid the rent. I did all the household work. Usually, my mother took the youngest child with her. Then I had to clean the house and the boys. If they got dirty, I used to hit them with a belt. I was very young and I needed them to obey me."

"Were your parents violent?"

"My father was not violent with me, with my brother, yes. And when he saw that the money he earned was not enough to maintain his household, he beat my mother. My mother said that she preferred for him to beat her and not us, her children. But my father has a terrible temper and makes life impossible for those who live near him. He says that he will never leave, because he is the man of the house. He likes to chase women. My boyfriend was also a womanizer. He is very *machista*. If men are like this, it is our fault, because we women educate them. We teach our daughters to serve men. Men think that if they drink, smoke, and have women, they are manlier. My boyfriend said that women are for men to enjoy. They are all womanizers; this is the way men are brought up."

Reflections on Women and Development

This chapter looks at the importance of women's active participation in their countries, specifically, how Colombian women have been able to participate economically and politically in Colombia. The role of Latin American women in the socioeconomic development of their respective countries has been considered essential by banking institutions and nongovernmental organizations (NGOs) for the creation of politics and development policies. After the United Nations Decade for the Advancement of Women (1975–1985), new horizons opened up. This period's forward-looking strategies and recommendations emphasized that women must become active participants in their respective nations' progress in order to help bring forth equality, development, and peace. As Amartya Sen (1999: 202) illustrates,

> Indeed, the empowerment of women is one of the central issues in the process of development for many countries in the world today. The factors involved include women's education, their ownership patterns, their employment opportunities and the workings of the labor market. . . . [T]he changing agency of women is one of the major mediators of economic and social change, and its determination as well as consequences are closely related to many of the central features of the development process.

The role of Latin American women in the socioeconomic development of their countries is considered essential, when establishing alternative politics and development policies for the advancement of Latin American countries. Socioeconomic and development research on women in this part of the world has increased since the 1960s; many studies have been done by Latin American female social scientists.[1] Available statistics report on Colombian women and on women around the world.

Statistics on Colombian Women in Relation to their Lives

Unfortunately, statistics are scarce on gender participation in the social and political agenda of Colombia. The national institute for statistics in Colombia, DANE (*Departamento Administrativo Nacional de Estadísticas*), is not thorough on women's issues. DANE's spotty statistics on female participation in the labor force, literacy and education, reproductive health services, political parties, and public life are difficult to assess. Abortion and maternal death indicators are vague. Each year, in Colombia, where abortion has been prohibited by law and remains prohibited by the Catholic Church, according to the media, 300,000 women undergo abortions. Cabal, Lemaitre, and Roa, (2001: 492) say that in Colombia "abortion is the second cause for maternal deaths . . . generating 15 percent of all maternal deaths each year . . . [and] in the years 1990–1998 there were 80 maternal deaths for each one hundred thousand births." Nevertheless, on May 9, 2006, Monica Roa, one of the authors of the groundbreaking book *Cuerpo y Derecho: Legislacion y Jurisprudencia en America Latina* (2001) (Body and legal rights: Legislation and jurisprudence in Latin America) was able to convince the Colombian Supreme Court to decriminalize abortion in three instances: when the mother's life is in danger, when the fetus has malformations, and when the woman has been raped. The Catholic Church is against the law.

Public debate on this issue began in the media in July 2001. The Catholic Church and its clergy announced, at this time, that if a woman in Colombia undergoes an abortion, she and the person who performed the medical procedure will be excommunicated—even if the woman was raped by a family member or impregnated by artificial insemination, without her consent. Abortion is the second cause of maternal mortality in Colombia (*Semana* 8, 6, 2001: 50–52). A woman who undergoes an abortion can be imprisoned from one to three years, depending on the fetal month of gestation. The law does punish the person who performs the abortion but not the father of the child (Cabal, Lemaitre, and Roa 2001: 67). Thus, whereas the church punishes both the woman and the abortionist by excommunication, the State punishes usually only the woman, as it is difficult to get the person who performed the abortion. And the man goes free.

The participation of women in Colombian politics is still very low (see Craske 1999; Wills Obregón 2007). Thus, women do not create laws to favor them (Wills Obregón 2007: 244). As the Inter-American Development Bank (IDB) affirms in *Women in the Americas: Bridging the Gender Gap* (1995: 100), even with quotas, women do not occupy many governmental posts, which are "still monopolized by men. . . . In 1992, 4 percent of ministerial posts in Latin America and the Caribbean were held by women" (IDB 1995: 101). Colombian women in 1997 obtained 12.2 percent seats in the parliament (Senate's report from the women's net, 2000). Women's posts are often restricted to female topics, such as home economics or opportunities for women in education and art. Usually and unfortunately, when women work in the government, they tend to become assimilated and complacent with patriarchal ideology. As happened with interviewee Clara, when confronted with corruption or unethical behavior, they simply step aside, unable to accept it or to change anything, as they lack power.

Women are either "co-opted or transformed by the state," rather than moved to transform the existing structure (IDB 1995: 102) or they leave politics in great disgust when they discover its tortuous, corrupted ways.[2]

Statistical material provided by the Inter-American Development Bank (1995: 199–209), after its forum on Women in the Americas in Mexico (1994), warrants examination. The bank's statistics on Colombia are the most reliable collected, to date, with regard to the distribution of women in the labor force, the percentage of women who are educated, the participation of women in public life, and female reproductive health. These data also offer some perspective on the social and political condition of Colombian women relative to men.

Following the 1990 Inter-American report, it is pertinent to know what has been the growth of women's participation in the region's work force, that is, Latin America and the Caribbean. For example, it says that it grew from 18 percent in 1950 to 26 percent in 1980. And the Colombian national institute for statistics, *Departamento Administrativo Nacional de Estadisticas* (DANE) says that it grew 27.5 percent in the year 2000.

Although the figures in the appendix seem encouraging, they must be viewed with a measure of skepticism. In the World Bank Report, for example, births per 1,000 adolescent women, ages fifteen to nineteen, are given at seventy-five. Likely, many of the reported women are married, and some may be unmarried. Can anyone say how many unmarried, very young women, poor and unserved by any licensed medical facility, would be reporting their pregnancies to an official agency?

Similarly, the World Bank shows an unmet need for contraception at only 6 percent among married women and omits again, a large number of unmarried women. Because many Colombian unions remain unrecognized by civil or church authority, the report cannot count the number of families who would not admit a need for contraceptives, (whether or not they use them), because they are Catholics. Further, many uneducated women do not know that contraception is possible.

And so it goes: pregnant women receiving prenatal care at 94 percent has to be suspect, again, because circumstances for many women are not conducive to dealing with collectors of statistics. Since women under fifteen are not considered at all, anecdotal evidence is that a considerable number of pregnant women are left out altogether (see chapter 9).

In fact, a large number of women in Colombia live in a precarious state. Colombian women's reproductive health is poor for those who do not have knowledge or financial means. The fertility rate of young women is extremely high, and the means of birth control available to large segments of the population are not reliable. Amartya Sen observes (1999: 199), "[E]ducated women tend to have greater freedom to exercise their agency in family decisions, including matters of fertility and childbirth," which suggests, that Colombian women's education is still less than satisfactory. As Robin Morgan (1997: 7) states, "Two-thirds of all illiterates are women." And illiterate women have more abortions (See Sen 1999).

An aggravating participant concerned with abortion in Colombia is the Catholic Church, which promotes abortion by condemning birth control.[3]

As noted, the government backs the Church's philosophy and punishes women who disobey religious law. Secular and religious laws are at times, intertwined.[4] On the other hand, Morgan (1997: 7) says that,

> in developing countries, less than one-third of all women have access to contraceptive information, and more than half have no trained help during pregnancy and childbirth. Complications from pregnancy, childbirth, and abortion—which kill more than half a million per year—are the leading causes of death among all women of reproductive age. With non-pregnancy-related reproductive tract infections the death toll rises to more than a million, with another hundred million maimed every year.

A report from one hundred and fifty women's groups called *Red de Mujeres* (Women's net) presented to the Colombian Senate in August 2001, shows that maternal deaths from 1991 to 1995 are 93.7 for 100,000 live births. Also, a large group of Colombian women have undergone abortions. One-fourth of all women between the ages of fifteen and fifty-five (22.9 percent) have had at least one induced abortion. Unfortunately, in Colombia, women's reproductive health seems not to be an issue of immediate concern to the government or the Catholic Church, nor are abortions and maternal deaths.

Schools and universities are filled with women, but women are still not paid the same salaries or given the same work opportunities as men, confirmed by the 1990 Inter-American Development Bank report on *Economic and Social Progress in Latin America: Working Women In Latin America* (1990: 216). It reports that "females on the average still earn less than do males and have relatively fewer financial assets and less access to remunerated work and to production resources (land, capital, technology, and the like)" (see also Cabal, Lemaitre, and Roa 2001).

Women as Managers

In March 2007, one Colombia's leading newspapers, *El Espectador* published the results of several studies, confirming that Colombian women hold more executive positions than do women anywhere else in Latin America. At the same time, their salaries fall far short of those received by men—eighty-four cents on the peso, by one account.

According to the article, women excel especially in the financial sector, because greater access to education has equalized competence between men and women. At the University of the Andes, in Bogotá, 50 percent of students in Business Administration are women. On the job, however, salary increases are structured so that women receive much less than men; their pay stays close to entry level. Over time, women in managerial positions, who start with 10 to 15 percent less than men, earn as much as 22 percent less, according to Pilar Fernandez of Los Andes, and confirmed by other researchers.

Further, women who have children earn 15 percent less than women who do not. Mothers are perceived to have less time to spend at work because of their maternal duties, visits to the doctor, or attendance at school functions. To deal with domestic contingencies, women, from almost all the social classes, hire helpers—maids, nannies, and drivers, if needed. Because Colombia has the extended family organization, typical of Mediterranean cultures, family members fill in to help when there is need, and not only on certain occasions, as is the case in Nordic cultures. Supplemental hiring generates a new level of employment, most often the price coming out of a woman's paycheck; so that, in effect, she earns even less.

Aside from women in corporate management, Colombian women entrepreneurs open their own businesses at twice the rate of the United States establishments opened by women, according to U.S Department of Labor Secretary, Elaine L. Chao.

Human resource consultant Luis Arispon says that women managers are notable for a different managerial style, one less authoritarian, less hierarchical, and more connected than the style of male managers. The most successful women, he states, "create stronger work climates fer their teams." He suggests that firms include these beneficial leadership styles as part of their regimes (Angelical Gallon Salazar, "Entre el poder y los tacones" [Amid power and high heels] El Espectador, March 17, 2007).

A Marvelous Career in Marriage

All of the women interviewed, including the eight from the focus group, agreed that the implicit and well-hidden message to females is that a woman's job is to think about marriage/union with a man, and motherhood, along with how she contributes at home to the economic well-being of the family. Work, not only for the male but also for the female, is thought to follow its course, automatically. Nothing seems to be more important for a woman than her role. Soledad, from the upper-middle income class and in her early fifties, gives an example of the role society expects from women:

> As we girls were growing up, we didn't have special dreams. Our parents, families, and teachers had in their minds only one fixed future for young women: marriage. Our future was to marry a marvelous man, and we were going to be marvelous wives, and together we would give our parents beautiful grandchildren for them to enjoy and feel proud of having.

Esperanza from the lower income class and in her late fifties confirms Soledad's words:

> My parents kept repeating to me that I had to learn to cook, clean the house, wash, and iron because I needed to know all of those things for when I grew up and had a husband. "Fine with me," I used to think, but why did I have to learn how to take care of a house at age five? How cruel.

Susana, who keeps trying husband after husband, to see if she might find a generous and affectionate one, carries the point further:

> I was raised simply to be married! I was educated to be married one day to a man who would take care of me, have children with me, and nothing else was expected of me. I had to follow my mother's example; this was my father's main concern. It was my responsibility to make four grandparents happy!

These women, from three different social classes and now between the ages of fifty and seventy, were instructed and trained from childhood in how to become good housewives and mothers. Their interviews illustrate that what has been considered essential in the education of Colombian women is preparing them to marry, to have men take care of them, and to bear children to continue a family line. The conventional message is that a woman has to end up under the same roof with a man, if she is to be acknowledged by society.

In Colombia, females and males are regarded almost as different species. The Catholic Church shares this same idea about men and women and their gender (Williams and Cooperman, *Washington Post*, August 1, 2004). Men are supposed to master the world and hide all emotions whereas women are taught to beware of the world and its perils outside the home. Inner qualities thought essential for women are not emphasized for men. So-called "feminine" characteristics—open display of sentiments—are considered a form of weakness in males (Benjamin 1988; Ehrenreich and English 2005).

In this society, the interviewees and the women from the focus group agreed that women are supposed to love and care for others. Qualities for appropriate behavior—discretion, silence, good manners and self control, along with child bearing, and child raising—are the customary form of exchange in this socio/economic model. Adults supposedly know what is best for young women. Manuela, in her mid-thirties and from the upper class, gives an example of what it means for parents to be concerned about their daughters' well-being:

> Because I was a woman I understood that I couldn't do certain things. If I wanted to be a good woman, the only way out was being a wife and mother, staying home, and not taking risks outside in the world. If a woman takes risks she is considered a prostitute.

For Manuela it was always a struggle to take "risks" or to be "adventurous" like her eldest brother, who was "not afraid of roaming around with friends and his girlfriend." Such constraints stifle a woman's ability to think creatively or grow intellectually and economically. Marriage, or having a male companion, even today, is considered the most important goal for Colombian girls. If a woman marries or lives with a man, she is considered successful, attractive, and fulfilled. A woman who does not have a male companion is scorned, even though a large percentage of Colombian women are heads of households—either because they are abandoned by their children's fathers, because they are widows, or simply because they never married, as is the case with many women from the lower economic classes.[5] To be with a man, as a wife or as a companion is not only a social instrument by which families are formed, but also an economic one, as well. A woman alone usually is socially isolated and economically insecure. Alone, without economic means, she cannot protect herself or her children. It is difficult for her to lead a decent life, and survive in freedom and well-being (see Sen 1999; Mancini Billson and Fluehr-Lobban 2005). By contrast, men are free to marry or remain single.

The Colombian historian and author Juan Gabriel Tokatlian (*El Tiempo* 1998: 6A) reports that society's discrimination against women in Colombia is a well-recognized, well-documented phenomenon. A woman in Colombia, he says in "Sexualidad y Geopolítica" (Sexuality and geopolitics), is far from being considered a valuable, autonomous subject, despite her social status. "Sexism and *machismo* are continuously reproduced by formal education and the media."[6] Tokatlian adds that the violence perpetrated against women within the family unit injures them throughout life. The alleged love and attention amid which girls are raised is actually infused with repression and violence, mischaracterized as concern. In an effort to protect women from evil, girls are restrained from freedom. Women's oppression is exposed in the media by male or female historians, sociologists, political scientists, psychologists, and Tokatlian is not the only one to do so.

Feminist Economic Critiques

Now, the economic and political lives of women are considered in relation to feminist ideas about women's economic situation in a patriarchal world. Over the centuries, social institutions have communicated what being a woman or man means in a particular culture. Gayle Rubin (1975) and Juliet Mitchell (2000), among many other feminists (see also Sacks 1975; Mies 1986; Mancini Billson and Fluehr-Lobban 2005; Wills Obregón, 2007), analyze the economic issues that help determine women's well-being and offer constructive usages of the term "gender." Undoubtedly, any attempt to reduce the influence gender exerts on human beings in a given culture will be difficult, if not impossible, to achieve, all the more so in the specific case of Colombia, where becoming human can be well-defined primarily in Freudian sexual terms.[7] Nevertheless, without deconstructing gender hierarchies for the purpose of understanding, by itself, why societies are organized as they are is unlikely to accomplish anything tangible, economically and otherwise (see Mitchell 2000).

Different approaches have been recommended. Some scholars, like the German sociologist María Mies (1986), think that concentrating on gender issues distorts women's problems by restricting them to the biological realm in a way that is artificial and unhelpful. Other writers, like British psychoanalyst and radical feminist Juliet Mitchell (1973) and historian Asuncion Lavrin (1987) consider economic aspects of the female condition too narrow a topic to expose the roots of global discrimination against women.[8] Mies (1983), however, calls also for "conscientization," awareness, with regard to gender issues, in order to understand how women have been manipulated financially, politically, legally, and religiously.[9]

Social scientists have investigated all sides of female discrimination, oppression, and exploitation that deal with the economic part of women's lives. Aspects of women's daily labor that involve food, clothes, housework, child care, health care, and managing families have been studied in minute detail by researchers interested in "women and development," "women in Third-World countries," and the "political or economic roots of female oppression." Bibliography on women's material lives is quite plentiful, especially texts on how existing modes of production and systems like capitalism and socialism intertwined with patriarchy shape political systems in ways that do not meet women's needs. Excellent economic analyses record the "misdeeds" and violence committed against women.[10] Such research has informed elaborate programs undertaken by the United Nations, World Bank, Inter-American Development Bank, Organization of American States, and nongovernmental organizations (NGOs) dealing with gender and development. These institutions have influenced states in the developing world, when the governments involved have sought financial support for various economic and political programs. These studies have also formed the basis for documents on human rights for women and challenges to the violence women endure. Some writings propose solutions and offer hope for a better world (see Sen and Grown 1987).

For example, after the United Nations Decade for the Advancement of Women (1975–1985),[11] new opportunities opened up for women. The Decade's forward-looking strategies and recommendations emphasize that women, too, have to be active participants in their progress in order to help bring forth equality, development, and peace. But women have to be educated, because "education strengthens women's agency and also tends to make it more informed and skilled. The ownership of property can also make women more powerful in family decisions" (Sen 1999: 192). For lawmakers establishing different politics and development policies for the advancement of Latin American countries, the role of women in the socioeconomic development of their countries is essential. The need for development emphasizes, for example, the importance of women as reproducers of the labor force, of rural immigrant women who offer cheap labor,[12] of peasant women who lack economic support, and of unemployed women who generate income by having home-economic business but continue to provide services for their families (Lavrin 1987).[13]

Socioeconomic researchers like Gita Sen and Caren Grown, authors of *Development, Crises, and Alternative Visions: Third World Women's Perspectives* (1987: 9), have written under the auspices of "Development Alternatives with Women for a New Era" (DAWN).[14] They explain the purpose of investigations undertaken by feminist researchers concerned with gender:

> Through our analysis and activities, we are committed to developing alternative frameworks and methods to attain the goals of economic and social justice, peace, and development free of all forms of oppression by gender, class, race, and nation.

Undoubtedly, good results have been achieved that benefit women in many ways, but much remains to be done.[15]

The Woman's Question

Feminist scholars seek to examine the women's position as producers and re-producers of use value inside the home, and, at certain times, exchange value outside the home, when participating actively in economic systems. When the industrial revolution began, relationships between men and women and those above them, such as the King or the Pope changed; the rule of the father changed, too. It was a new order of society that eradicated the Old Order (Ehrenreich and English 2005: 19). At this time, women were placed in the home, while men went into the world to work and to masculinize it, as they reorganized human society and human nature according to their own philosophy and the new market economy, capitalism. Thus, the Woman Question became an issue, as she was the organizer of the household, where "the most personal biological activities—eating, sex, sleeping, the care of small children, and birth and dying and the care of the sick and aged" (Ehrenreich and English 2005: 13) became her responsibility alone, without forgetting obedience. Barbara Ehrenreich and Deirdre English (2005: 17) specify:

> For women generally, from the hard-working women of the poorer classes to the cushioned daughters of the upper classes, the Woman Question was a matter of immediate personal experience: the consciousness of possibilities counterpoised against prohibitions, opportunities against ancient obligations, instincts against external necessities. The Woman Question was nothing less than the question of how women would survive and what would become of them in the modern world.

The Woman Question also involves female relations with men and property (Mies 1986: 178). In other words, how would women interact with men, to survive? One may say that from the beginning of human history, women and men labored together, shoulder to shoulder, on behalf of the social groups to which they belonged. Both sexes constructed the world we inhabit through culture, language, and symbolic meaning. Men and women devoted themselves to increasing life-giving resources that also improve the destiny of all creatures on earth. However, a sexual division of labor—brought about by modernization—relegated women to the home, where they were given sole responsibility for doing housework, which is not as "productive as it is private" (see Craske 1999). The value of female labor was soon ignored.[16] According to the International Labor Organization, "household work is, indeed, not equitably distributed among family members. Almost all of this work is performed by women, with the result that housewives work hard but are the group whose work is least recognized and least valued in society" (IDB 1990: 217).[17]

Because women reproduce the labor force and serve as "life-keepers and life-sustainers," women themselves have not been considered wage earners in their own right; female work has been systematically undervalued.

> Outside the formal labor force—whether as homemaker, nun, farmer, or domestic servant—women's work is regarded as unskilled, marginal, transient or simply "natural" and is invisible in the Gross Domestic Product accounting of virtually all nations. (Morgan 1997: 7)

Whenever subsistence processes that simply satisfied human needs were replaced by the accumulation of surplus value, work that fell outside the regular system of economic production was soon made invisible. Use-value that produces goods for consumption inside the household lies outside the political economy of a country.[18] Both capitalism and socialism view the use-value of labor as unimportant for the economic development and advancement of their systems, even though this source reproduces and maintains the labor force (Mies 1986).[19] The work accepted as valuable for society, ever since the organization of patriarchy (Mitchell 1973; Sacks 1975) has consisted of "economic activity," which is market production for the growth and accumulation of capital, as Marx explains in his materialistic philosophy (Beneria 1985: 128–29). Only labor that relates to an exchange of goods and services between individuals is considered "economic activity" and accredited social value. For example, "Nowhere does the work of reproduction of the species count as 'productive activity'" (Morgan 1997: 7). Although subsistence production is thought of as natural, it is not labeled "economic" and, hence, remains invisible within the great majority of societies around the world. As Lourdes Beneria notes (1982: 119–47), over the last twenty years, use-value or subsistence production has begun to be recognized as an intrinsic part of a country's economy and, therefore, a subject of interest. More needs to be done in this connection so that women are recognized and valued for their vital contributions to a healthy community.

The "woman's question" in Third World countries requires further illumination, so that female needs can be met and women's work made visible to people in power. Researchers have studied "housewifization" under both capitalism and socialism. "Housewifization" is the term María Mies (1986) gives to domestic or use-value labor performed by females.[20]

Unfortunately, the sexual division of labor in the patriarchal family system is built on "the mystification that women are basically housewives" and nothing more (Mies (1986: 112–20). Women labor, but their activity has been dismissed as an intrinsic part of being a female. As it turns out, "women in the work force put in two full work shifts—one at home and one on the job. . . . [T]he male family members have not increased their participation in the household accordingly" (IDB 1990: 217).

In Colombia, interviewees from the poorer classes repeatedly emphasize how woman's work is taken for granted. Flor, like several others, speaks of how she helped her mother, at an early age:

> I had to help my mother with the household and with my brothers and sisters (I was the eldest of ten). At the age of six, I helped to cook, make *arepas* [cornbread], fetch lumber for the stove and water for household consumption, and wash our clothes. We didn't have electricity. . . . Life was difficult, and we had to work to help our parents.

Esperanza continues her narration of her own experience with housework

> At the age of five, my parents forced me to do housework. I was very little, and I didn't know how to do anything. I had no idea how to cook, wash, iron clothes, sweep the floors, etc. Because my mother was constantly having asthma attacks, my father made me do housework to help her. He used to put two or three bricks in front of the stove for me to stand on so I could reach pots and pans and cook the food. Sometimes I was forced to peel a whole bunch of green plantains! My age didn't matter. I also had to wash the clothes for my father and brothers. The dirty blue-jeans were the worst, I remember.

The attitude in the developing world presumes that women's work is an obligation that females bear for the rest of humanity. Craske (1999: 90) comments on how women's work inside the home is a way by which society undervalues "women's work, and therefore women themselves [because] it has been seen in a persistent way . . . as secondary and complementary to the 'real' work carried out by men." Housework is not marketed or rewarded; labor done to "help" the head of the family is not considered "economic" activity but is viewed instead as "unpaid family work." Home-based chores (such as fetching lumber or water for domestic consumption) are viewed as "natural" jobs, with no surplus value attached to them, simply because such work isn't remunerated (Beneria 1985: 122).

Juana stresses how such an attitude defines a girl's future. "Girls' destiny is to stay home to help their mothers and later get married and have children. . . . I had to help in the kitchen, clean the house, wash clothes, and make the beds. . . . [After selling bread every morning] I had to help with house chores." And Graciela recounts how a family structures itself according to these norms. When she was merely five years old, she had to help her mother take care of her younger siblings and do the housework, while her mother went to her job. They could not count on her father's salary, since he was not a reliable person.

Mies describes how this marginalization of women's labor, according to the International Division of Labor (ILO), is the result of the economic systems, in this case capitalism, that exploit women so they can serve as an extra labor force[21] whose low wages are conveniently justified.[22] Aleja describes the sexual division of labor between parents and how the mother's work is considered normal, while the father's labor makes him "busy":

> I was raised in the country. . . . We lived on a beautiful farm. My parents were the *administradores* (caretakers) of the farm. My mother was in charge of the workers' food, my father of weighing and collecting crops—corn, cotton, etc.—and of *aguardiente* (distilled liquor fermented from the sugar cane). My mother directed the women in the kitchen and dining room. My father spent much time away from the *hacienda*. He had to go to other villages and talk to other people, buy goods for the farm, and sell crops, honey, and *aguardiente* . . . There was little time for conversations. We all had to work. . . . My father, well my poor father never said anything to us. We left him alone and didn't bother him since he was always so busy.

Under such rules, females accustomed to working without wages will not organize into labor unions. Women are reduced to mere housewives while men are honored as the "breadwinners" quite independently of what either party is actually doing. By reinforcing the myth that woman's work is unworthy of remuneration, says Craske (1999: 91), women's identities as workers are "undermined":

> There is the notion, firstly, that only single and/or childless women work and they cease to be involved in marriage/childbirth, and secondly, that women's income is private "pin"money rather than an integral part of the family income. Women's work is neither secondary nor complementary; rather it is essential and central to the household's well-being. Nevertheless, this image

persists despite the fact that women contribute more of their income to the family expenditure than men.

Increasingly, more and more people in a global economy know that this myth of men being the only breadwinner is not true.[23] Further, "Women and children comprise . . . eighty per cent of all poverty populations. One-third of all families on earth are women-headed" (Morgan 1997: 7).

Moreover, the 1990 Inter-American Bank's report on *Working Women in the Americas* (1990: 217–18) tells how the myth is exposed:

> It has been calculated that performance of household maintenance and other non-remunerated work can total around sixty hours per week. . . . In Colombia for women who engage in remunerated work, the workday is longer than eight hours, because they also perform household chores before and after their formal workday. In addition, they use week-ends as time to "catch up on the housekeeping" and to take care of the other members of the family, who are *resting* (emphasis mine) . . . One of the highest costs of the contradictory situation in which women function and of the way in which women's work is perceived by society has to do with the widespread undervaluation of this work. . . . Lack of understanding of the complexity of the household work performed by women has often led society to ignore or discount such work.

The report by the *Red de Mujeres* for the Colombian Senate (August 2001) tells that among the traditional roles in rural areas, cooking is 100 percent women's labor, whereas, men's participation is 0 percent. For domestic activities in general, women's participation is 95.6 percent and men's, 4.4 percent.

Women in the Americas: Bridging the Gender Gap

No longer the passive recipients of welfare-enhancing help, women are increasingly seen, by men as well as women, as active agents of change: the dynamic promoters of social transformations that can alter the lives of *both* women and men (Sen 1999:189).

In April 1994, the Inter-American Development Bank (IDB), whose most pressing issue is economic and social development in Latin America, organized a forum in Guadalajara, Mexico, on women's active participation in the sociopolitical life of the Americas. The Bank issued a statement that Latin America cannot succeed in combating poverty "unless both women and men are able to participate freely in all spheres of life, unhindered by discrimination" (1995: v).[24] Women have to be taken seriously in formulating development strategies, and policies must change the endless invisibility to which females have been subjected, says the forum's report titled "Agenda for Action" (1995: v). Women are usually the "backbone" of the household and, therefore, must not be ignored. The reproduction of the family and the welfare of all its members depend primarily on women.[25]

Many people believe that in Latin America, and Colombia, specifically, cultural norms affecting women's lives in the twenty-first century have changed radically to benefit women. This sophism diverts attention from the social problems that still permeate women's lives in that part of the world (see Cabal, Lemaitre, and Roa 2001). The "Agenda for Action" (1995: 1–16) reiterates that if women are not empowered, social, economic, and political progress in the region will not continue. "Understanding gender differences is vital to development planning," because women and men have different needs, incentives, experiences, health problems, access to resources, education based on cultural values, work, gender interests, and the like. These are "the hidden barriers" that prevent women from having their human rights honored and their personal well-being improved. The report advocates the elimination of gender discrimination in the Americas and identifies the barriers to freedom for women as principally cultural, economic, social, and legal (IDB, 1995: 50–51, 93, 117).

At the end of their book, *Cuerpo y Derecho* (Body and rights), Luisa Cabal, Julieta Lemaitre, and Monica Roa (2001: 484), in which they analyze five Latin American countries (Argentina, Colombia, Chile, Perú, and Mexico) and their laws on the rights women have over their bodies, the authors conclude that

> Women's bodies have to stop being the territory on which states, creeds and individuals impose their wills and instead become spaces where women themselves can decide the meaning and the destiny of their own existences.

The Bank's report emphasizes that development projects and policies initiated by the bank's borrower countries do not benefit men and women equally. Even though issues of class, ethnicity, work, and education separate women among themselves, gender is definitely *the* most important variable to be studied before any equitable development strategies can be designed.

> [T]he concept of gender [is] a system of socially ascribed roles and relationships between men and women, which are determined not by biology but by the social, political and economic context. Gender roles are learned, and they can change over time. It is the analysis of these roles and relationships which shows the imbalances in power, wealth, and workload between women and men, and

it is this analysis which may then lead to the possibilities and necessities of change. (IDB 1995: 60)

Generalizations about women are likely to be misleading when analyzing projects. Nevertheless, women are united by "the invisibility of several important aspects of their lives" (IDB 1995: 10–11). One of the principal recommendations of the IDB forum was that policy makers must realize that women are actors both "collectively and individually" on all levels of society. To reach a level playing field for women and men in development, stereotypes about gender roles must be rejected. "*Gender roles* are still distributed in such a way that women are at a *disadvantage when it comes to reaping the benefits of their efforts*" (IDB, 1995: 19) (my emphasis). Women's secondary place in the sociocultural strata in Latin America is a result of "the traditional division of labor" and the ideology of *machismo* and *marianismo* that permeates both the Catholic Church, military ideologies, and the political, social, and cultural arenas (IDB 1995: 48, 90–93).

Generally speaking, and depending on the social class and the economic needs of the family, women in Colombia have been separated from the outside world—the field where men act—and more often than not, depending on whether they are married or have a companion, have been prevented from making decisions about their lives. As seen, with reference to critical issues like abortion, divorce, and economic income, women have little input. On the rare occasions when a woman enters politics, she usually does so under the protective wing of a man.[26] If the female candidate wishes to remain independent from a political party (as occurred in October 2000 when María Emma Mejia ran for mayor in Bogotá), she must receive support from male politicians who will assist her in achieving strategic appointments that may prove useful to them both.[27] If a woman decides to run for the presidency, she surely requires the help of old political foxes who, in the end, will wink to let the public know whether to approve or disapprove of the female candidate.[28] This process occurred in 1998 when Noemí Sanin[29] was an independent candidate for president. Women need to win the trust of other females who will believe that both sexes have the capacity to govern. Usually, women do not think that other women have the capacity to be good politicians, doctors, economists, or lawyers. Unfortunately, women do not trust women. And more often than not, those females who are in power, those who have well-being because of their social position, or because they participate actively in politics, do not treat other women well. Or simply, they do not believe that a woman is capable of any kind of accomplishment. In Colombia there is a cruel saying that depicts this mistrust: "The worst enemy a woman has is another woman."

Traditional wisdom aside, in December 2007, Senator Marta Lucia Ramirez addressed President Alvaro Uribe by means of a letter, made public, exhorting him to take action in filling the quotas, established by law, for female participation in the government. Although the quota for cabinet ministers is 30 percent, the actual figure in the Uribe administration "comes to scarcely 23 percent," she wrote. (When he assumed office, women occupied 46 percent.) The current three female ministers, among thirteen positions, hold posts in Education, Communications, and Culture. If Uribe had kept the promise he made in his electoral campaign, six of those ministries would have been headed by women.

Senator Ramirez, in the same letter, requested that the president fortify the Council for the Equality of Women, giving them necessary resources to advance political leadership and equal rights of women. Sexual equality, she reminded him, is "fundamental for the development of the country."

In reply, a presidential advisor remarked that female participation under Uribe has been "ample and one of great quality," that women occupy their positions not because of their gender but because of their qualities. Nor should one look only at the president's cabinet, but also in other areas of government, such as family planning. He also cited the president's female secretary for having great influence. "*Senadora le pide al Presidente ampliar la cuota femenina*" (Senator asks the president to enlarge the female quota) (*El Tiempo*, Bogotá, December 22, 2007).

Women Outside Traditional Family Structures

Today in Colombia, divorce is common but discouraged within most Catholic families. Couples in the lower economic classes tend not to marry. When they do, separation and a new relationship starts outside the church, with no hesitation. The working classes do not rely as much on religion as do people from the other classes in Colombia, for whom the Catholic Church is an overwhelming force. Middle- and upper-class women in Colombia who assume active roles outside the family can be targets of contempt. In particular, older women and matriarchs often view them as less than "feminine" compared to the self-sacrificing wife and mother waiting patiently at home. The woman who assumes an active role in society—as do ordinary males— is, overtly or covertly, feared and ridiculed as different. Also they can be accused of ruining their family lives on behalf of their work in the outside arena. Silvana Paternostro (1998: 220) describes a normal conversation between upper-class wives (during lunch or tea) as dealing with "their families, their diets, the latest painting on the wall, and their clothes." These *señoras* are married to men who "strongly believe that there are good girls and there are bad girls, that there are mothers and wives at home and prostitutes outside, and that they as men are entitled to have both while we as women, we are one or the other." Both Spanish and Arabic ancestry contributed to this attitude. Many people still ask, "What good can a woman do alone in the world if she is single and divorced?" Strangely enough, widows have a different status and have an aura of respect. Straightforward answers to the question above are avoided.[30] Although some flexibility is accepted concerning women's work inside the home, no active behavior aside from the traditional roles of wife and mother is accepted openly and normally, unless the woman has no husband or companion or her family is extremely poor.

Juana, another interviewee, makes special emphasis on this issue.

"If a woman marries and has a good job she might be made to leave her job. This situation has brought about a lot of divorces or separations among young people today. Men are such *machistas* that they think if their wives work, the women might find other men!"

Middle- and lower-class Colombian women do have more autonomy than their counterparts in the upper classes, usually because the former exert a more influential financial role in the family. With both husband and wife working, this mutuality of experience can create a stronger bond. Still, women are not granted adequate respect for their contribution to household income. Subordinated on the basis of gender, poor women are among the more oppressed human beings in Colombia. Discriminated against because of social class, they are also some of the poorest citizens (Bonilla 1985: 26).

Mayra Buvinic, in her article "Women in Poverty: A New Global Underclass" (1997: 38–53), defines poverty in more than quantitative terms: "Poverty has many dimensions and is difficult to measure. Calculated in dollars and cents, it is inadequacy of income; but measured in terms of the human condition, it is inadequacy of health and nutrition, education, and other components of well-being, including leisure time" (1997: 39). Buvinic (1997: 40) goes on to say that the total number of poor people suffering worldwide is 1.6 *billion*, of which 900 *million* are "income poor" and "most of the 'remaining' 700 million poor are women." Poverty entails many different variables, one of which involves violence perpetrated against individuals or groups.

A married woman in Colombia is quite often subject to her husband's decisions concerning financial matters, which automatically places her at a disadvantage economically. Sister María Luisa gives her own interpretation of women's economic situation:

> The economic power is [an] enormous obstacle for women's liberation in the twenty-first century. Even if a woman has grown in her self-esteem, even if she is aware of her rights and belongs to feminist groups, if *she still depends economically on men*, there is no way for her to reach equilibrium in their woman-husband-companion relationship at home, or woman-boss relationship in the working place. If a woman is the wife/companion of an important man, she is expected to follow him, make him feel superior, act as the jewel to enhance his made-up personality, and act as his pet. Many women have to endure a relationship with their bosses or are in a relationship that is tremendously damaging and violent. This is done for only one main reason: economic support. A woman fears losing her job or being left alone with a home to support and children to raise and educate. Many women decide to live under the grip put down by *machismo* and even endure aberrations in their personal lives so that they have, instead, economic support for themselves and their families.

Because of inequality, a woman is unlikely to become her mate's companion or friend. Women from the privileged classes usually know little about the world outside their social circles. Upper-class women are ignorant of political and social realities just beyond their grasp.[31] They tend to be immature, unrealistic, superstitious, naïve, and conservative. Their primary task is to represent a man, a name, and a family. Usually, women who do not have to work become prisoners of their social class and leisure time. Living empty lives, they often stay wherever they are—even if unhappily—because it is easier for them to do so or because most of the time they do not know other possibilities. Soledad's mother portrays well such a woman who has given up her life to please a man:

> My mother was a quiet woman, although strong in spirit, but she accepted everything that came from my father. She loved him very much, and as a wife she thought she had to please her husband, no matter what. My mother followed the role of the good self-abnegating wife; she was a considerate wife and mother. I think this is the case with all wives and mothers, even today, no matter where they come from. By giving in to my father's whims, my mother was able to maintain her marriage. My father was extremely selfish. . . . If there was an avocado for dinner it was sliced into six pieces; my father served himself one whole half. He was arbitrary. . . . He didn't like to come home, for example, and not find my mother waiting for him. Thus, my mother had a "curfew." . . . This was the atmosphere where I grew up. When my father died, I thought: "How sad that he's gone, but finally my mother will have a life of her own!" My mother didn't have control over anything: her life, her money, or her

thoughts. A woman who has no material needs accepts manipulation by a man more easily. She is comfortable and, thus, forgets her misery.

Some analysts have harshly labeled such wives another breed of bought women. In fact, they are closer to *geishas* whose only chore is satisfying the needs and caprices of their masters.[32] "Good little girls" until the end of their days, such wives are children who never grow up.[33]

Furthermore, there is a general belief that women of the upper classes do not suffer discrimination, intra-family violence or rape, and are free from reproductive problems. The assumption is that if they are well educated, they will receive pay equal to that of their male colleagues. Material comfort is thought to solve any problem an individual faces in her lifetime, so women in Colombia from the bourgeoisie are assumed to be free from hardships. These fallacies must be acknowledged, analyzed, and interpreted. The entrapment and discrimination a bourgeois woman suffers are real and must be corrected. Social class, ethnicity, and religion drastically separate women from each other and diminish the chances of achieving positive action through solidarity.

When some of these women finally decide to improve their lives along with their minds, nothing short of a social revolution is involved.[34] Kristeva (1981: 141) reminds us that "[t]here can be no socio-political transformation without a transformation of subjects: in other words, in our relationship to social constraints, to pleasure, and more deeply, to language." Changing the rules may alter Colombia, improving the relationships between men and women, men and men, women and women, and encompassing the way women influence children, parents, and other women. However, fixed atavistic phenomena are hard to modify. The struggle will be difficult and must first be initiated by constructing consensus among women.[35] Ultimately, it must be revolutionary. As Marilyn French (in Brock-Utne 1989: 497) says, "Feminism is a revolutionary moral movement, intending to use political power to transform society, to feminize it. For such a movement assimilation is death." Mitchell (2000: 414) affirms, "Women have to organize themselves as a group to affect a change in the basic ideology of human society. . . . A cultural revolution needs theory and political practice."

For Sister María Luisa, feminism is also applicable as a moral movement that may influence the Catholic Church on behalf of women:

If we Colombian women were capable of holding the positions we are entitled to before the Catholic Church, we would be able to be part of the decision-making process of the church, to be heard, to stop our being invisible, and to help other women of our society to rise from the ashes, work towards a very much needed change and become valuable citizens. We have been preparing ourselves to reach this goal for many years. We are now ready to participate actively in the church![36]

One can envision a cohesive group of women who, with their own individual characteristics, will be enthusiastic to create a dissident team that comes together only to disrupt the rules established by patriarchal law that oversees women's needs, wishes, and desires.[37] As Cixous says (1981: 245), "Woman must put herself into the text—as into the world and into history—by her own movement," that is, by her actions, thoughts, desires, and sexual subjectivity.

Furthermore, in an interview written by Elaine Hoffman Baruch titled "Psychoanalysis and Feminism" (Guberman 1996: 117), Kristeva declares, "There have to be 'I's' (individuals) and women have to become authors, actors, not to hypostatize or overvalue those particular kinds of work, but so that this perspective will push each one of us to find her own individual language." Kristeva hopes all women—irrespective of social class or ethnic identity—will be able to express themselves and grasp their destinies without fear. The only way women can lead more fulfilling lives is to speak up, calmly and with certainty, about their material and spiritual needs, in a society that will listen to all of its members.

Writing in *El Tiempo*, Florence Thomas, coordinator of the group Women and Society (*Mujer y Sociedad*) from the University of the Andes spoke out calmly and with certainty that in the year 2008, three major cities and one department (equivalent to a state in the U.S.) would begin with major institutional advances to respond to the needs and demands by women and their organizations. Bogotá's Public Policy Plan for Women's Equal Opportunity consolidated several organizations for women's rights. It created a city department for women's issues, with concentration on the right to freedom from violence, and seven *casas*, houses, in the neighborhoods, to teach their objectives. By appointing a Secretariat for Women, Medellin, too, expanded its women's rights campaign. Pasto, in the South of Colombia, opened an Office of Gender and Human Rights, with emphasis on economic empowerment. And the State of el Valle del Cauca installed a Secretary of Equality of Gender, for social and Political participation and recognition of sexual and reproductive rights. "Democracy without women doesn't work," Ms. Thomas asserted, as she directed herself to women who would assume new roles, building on their achievement.

Ladies, you will have to govern for all the citizenry, without failing to represent the interests of women. Your inclusion in policy making—certainly difficult and slow—cannot be remote from a critical conscience of what it means to be a female political leader in a culture still profoundly patriarchal . . . The exercise of power in your hands must challenge you to build feminine authority and, with it, to transform the old political practices that so often reproduce violence and exclusion. . . certainly you have to prepare yourselves, because, without a doubt, you are going to find multiple obstacles and resistance on the way. Politics is still an extremely masculine exercise that seeks to maintain itself at all costs, obstructing with subtlety any attempt to make policy in other ways. But I suppose, you already know that. (*Politicas publicas con Rostro de Mujeres* [Public policies with feminine face], Bogotá, *El Tiempo*, December 26, 2007)

Notes

1. For studies of gender and development in Third World countries, see Susan C. Bourque and Kay Barbara Warren, *Women of the Andes* (Ann Arbor, MI: University of Michigan Press, 1979); Lourdes Beneria and Gita Sen, "Class and Gender Inequalities and Women's Roles in Economic Development—Theoretical and Practical Implications," *Feminist Studies* 8, no. 1 (Spring 1982), 157–176; Lourdes Beneria, ed., *Women and Development: The Sexual Division of Gender in Rural Societies* (Praeger Special Studies, 1985); Sue Ellen M. Charlton, *Women in Third World Development* (London: Westview Press, 1984); Miranda Davies, *Third World/Second Sex* (London: Zed Books, 1987). Davies' book is most important for understanding women's struggles in developing countries. It speaks about how gender is used for mobilizing poor women to their disadvantage and also shows how female networking can help women resist discrimination and violence within the family, workplace, and elsewhere in society. See also *Regional Programs Banking the Unbankable* (London: The Panos Institute, 1989); Luisella Goldsmith-Clermont, "Economic Evaluation of Unpaid Household Work: Africa, Asia, Latin America and Oceania" (Geneva: UNFPA, 1987); María Mies, *Patriarchy and Accumulation: Women in the International Division of Labor* (London: Zed Books, 1987); Gita Sen and Caren Grown, *Development, Crises, and Alternative Visisons: Third World Women's Perspectives* (New York: Monthly Review Press, 1987); Janet Henshall Momsen, *Women and Development in the Third World* (New York: Routledge, 1991); Barbara Rogers, *The Domestication of Women* (New York: Tavistock Publications, 1980).

2. See the *Washington Post* (November 9, 1998): A29, and the *Economist* (March 11, 2000): 116.

3. On Colombian women and the issue of abortion and how it affects their lives see Florence Thomas' *La Mujer Tiene la Palabra* (Woman owns the word) (Bogotá: Aguilar, 2001). See also Cabal, Lemaire, and Roa, *Cuerpo y Derecho* (Body and legal rights) 2001.

4. Amartya Sen, *Development as Freedom* (New York: Afred A. Knopf, 1999), 199, explains that "[t]he negative linkage between female literacy and fertility appears to be, on the whole, empirically well founded," because "the unwillingness of educated women to be shackled to continuous child rearing clearly plays a role bringing about this change."

5. Lavrin, "Women, the Family, and Social Change," 113, mentions that "among the lower income population, the percentage of female-headed households could rise to 37 percent of the total," in *World Affairs*.

6. See an article published in *El Tiempo*, August 5, 2001, speaking about a research project on co-ed schools. The results show the adverse situation of girls versus boys in school.

7. On the idea of eradicating gender from society, see Rubin, "The Traffic in Women," 157–210. Rubin also provides an excellent explanation of how children become "human"—that is, female or male—through the Oedipus complex and by evading the incest taboo through the kinship system that circulates women within social groups, benefiting and empowering men at the expense of the independence and appreciation of women as subjects in their own right.

8. Lavrin, "Women, the Family, and Social Change," 109–28, who does not use psychoanalysis in her discussion of women's historical situation, simply says that the economic realm cannot be the sole perspective for visions that will help bring about social change. Cultural elements like "patriarchalism" are important tools for "analysis of persistent socio-cultural patterns of gender subordination for women." Lavrin says women are thinking human beings, creators of our lives, and, thus, financial analysis is insufficient for providing solutions to complex problems.

9. See Roberta Rubinstein, *Boundaries of the Self, Gender, Culture, and Fiction* (Urbana, IL: University of Illinois, 1987). Rubinstein uses literary criticism, psychological and anthropological methodologies, and feminists theories to examine cultural boundaries and given identities. Her work also focuses on the "silencing" of women through sexual and cultural roles inside patriarchal and female boundaries.

10. Esther Boserup, in *Women's Role in Economic Development* (New York: St. Martin's Press, 1970) analyzes the situation of women in developed and undeveloped Third World countries. She finds that with development policies, women's status deteriorated tremendously not only economically but also politically, legally, educationally, and physically because of health systems.

11. Arvone S. Fraser, *The U.N Decade for Women: Documents and Dialogue* (London: Westview Press, 1987), 25, says, "The integration of women into the development process embraces all aspects of life—social, economic, political, and cultural—and requires that women are active as decision-makers and recognized as contributors to, as well as beneficiaries of, development." Lucille Mathurin Mair, "Women: A Decade Is Time Enough," in *Third World Quarterly* (8–2 April, 1986): 583–593, writes, "The ideology of female domesticity has been so well manipulated by tightly bonded male bureaucracy as to make the United Nations its decade's most visible monument to patriarchy."

12. The pathbreaking book on women's role in the economies of underdeveloped and developing countries like those in Africa, South and East Asia, Arab countries, and Latin America, is Boserup's *Women's Role*; see also Juliet Mitchell, *Women's Estate* (New York: Columbia University Press, 1973).

13. See Carmen Diana Deere and Magdalena Leon de Leal, "Peasant Production, Proletarization, and the Sexual Division of Labor in the Andes," *Signs: Journal of Women in Culture and Society* 7, no. 2 (1981): 338–359. These two scholars, to the date, are still being studied in the Latin American Continents, and in the United States, too.

14. DAWN is a network of activists who, through research, are trying to improve women's lives in underdeveloped countries where female existence is curtailed by economic and political systems. See Gita Sen and Karen Grown *Development, Crises, and Alternative Visions: Third World Women's Perspectives* (New York: Monthly Review Press, 1987).

15. Kathleen Staudt and Kristen Timothy, "Strategies for the Future," *Women, International Development and Politics: The Bureaucratic Mire* (Philadelphia: Temple University Press, 1997), 339, describe how bureaucratization in the most renowned institutions for the organization of women, gender justice, and development lacks the power or mechanisms to eradicate a devastating attitude by getting rid of "uninterested staff and government officials who snicker when women are mentioned. Gendered bureaucratic resistance is sometimes worse in Western international or bilateral assistance agencies."

16. See Boserup 1970. Even if women are part of the workforce, female work in the home has been "housewifized" and thus rendered unimportant. See also Mitchell 1973; Rubin 1975; Beneria 1982; Mies, 1986; Craske 1999; Cabal, Lemaitre, and Roa 2001.

17. See Alice Hoschild, *The Second Shift* (New York: Avon Books, 1989); Barbara Reskin and Patricia Ross, *Job Queues, Gender Queues* (Philadelphia: Temple University Press, 1990).

18. Beneria, "Accounting for Women's Work," in, Beneria, ed., *Women and Development*, 130, explains that household production "reduces labor costs in commodity production" and thus has "a direct effect on the accumulation process."

19. Beneria notes that labor that is not "commoditized" and produces "goods and services for exchange" is regarded as an important "economic activity." "Accounting for Women's Work," María Mies, *Patriarchy and Accumulation on a World Scale* (London: Zed Books, 1986), 128, also explains how both capitalism and socialism devalue labor that doesn't produce surplus or accumulation of capital and goods either for the "market" or the "state." Mies cites Russia, China, and Vietnam as examples of socialist systems that have changed economically but still discriminate against women and exploit them in similar ways.

20. Gita Sen and Caren Grown, *Development, Crisis, and Alternative Visions: Third World Perspectives* (New York: Monthly Review Press, 1987), 75, write, "The attempt to drive women back to their 'proper' roles is sharply at odds with the reality

that many women *have* to seek employment in order to feed their children and themselves."

21. Sen and Grown, *Development, Crisis*, 75, say that women around the world are "held responsible for unemployment." Women are blamed for whatever goes wrong in their communities, such as "not taking proper care of the children, cultural decadence, or Western influences, etc."

22. Sen and Grown, ibid., 75, write, "The creation of an ideological climate against women working outside the home makes it easier for the government to cut back on child-care or health services and for employers to justify paying even lower wages to women or ignoring statutory benefits like maternity pay."

23. As Mies, *Patriarchy*, 121, affirms, women in rich industrialized countries "are increasingly thrown out of the 'formal sector' and are increasingly reminded that work for husband and children and consumption work is their 'natural' destiny. Third World women as consumers and procreators are considered highly undesirable." Beneria, "Accounting," 76, adds that in "industrialized societies where subsistence depends predominantly on wages, the function of domestic work is to 'transform' family income into consumable goods and services, only a small part of which is produced within the household. Domestic labor tends to concentrate on the transformation of market goods for household consumption."

24. To understand the importance of women's participation in the economies of underdeveloped and developing countries and how without women's help in agricultural settings, in economic settings of all kinds, and in industrialized urban areas, not much could be accomplished. See Boserup, *Woman's Role*.

25. Maxine Molineux in *Feminisms in Development* (2007: 228–40), affirms that NGOs today think that differences between men and women have been redressed which, she says, is not the case. Policies are not followed, kept or thought to be of importance. There is an enormous void that has to be redressed on issues dealing with gender and development policies.

26. On this subject, Norma Villareal Méndez writes an enlightening essay, "Mujeres y Espacios Políticos, Participación Política y Análisis Electoral" (Women and political spaces, political participation, and electoral analysis), in *Consejería Presidencial*, 319–347. See also Alvaro Tirado Mejia, scientific and academic director, assisted by Jorge Orlando Melo and Jesús Antonio Bejarano, *Nueva Historia de Colombia: IV Educacion y Ciencia Luchas de la Mujer Vida Diaria* (New history of Colombia: IV— Science and education: Women's daily struggle) (Bogotá: Editorial Planeta, 1989).

27. María Emma Mejia was considered the perfect candidate from the Liberal Party to become mayor of Bogotá. Her mentor and protector, Horacio Serpa, occupied a strong position in Ernesto Samper's government (1994–1998), which was stained by having received money from drug cartels. María Emma Mejia declared herself independent of all political parties. Nevertheless, her friendship with Serpa curtailed her success in Colombia's political arena. At the same time ex-president Ernesto Samper rebuffed Ingrid Betancourt as liberal candidate for the Senate, as she recounts in her book *Rabia en el Corazón* (Until death do us part) (Bogotá: Grijaldo,

2001), 244. Further, twice ex-minister, ex-ambassador, and renown economist Cecilia López who wanted to participate as liberal presidential candidate for the 2002–2006 elections, told me in a private conversation we had here in Washington, how she was ignored and humiliated by her own party. She resigned from the liberal party and declared herself independent just as Ingrid Betancourt and Noemí Sanin did before her. I heard Ingrid Betancourt, who has been kidnapped by the FARC guerrilla group since 2003, declare publicly that she had never been discriminated by men which made her remain at the margin of any feminist movement as she did not considered it important and even thought it harmful for her political career to be signaled "feminist."

28. In December 2000, I conducted a personal conversation with Claudia Blum—one of six female senators in Colombia. Senator Blum confirmed that the political field for women in Colombia is still terribly difficult. Women do not get elected as easily as men. Today, Colombia has one hundred and fifty male senators, and only six female senators (Wills Obregón 2007).

29. In Noemí Sanin's case, former president Alfonso Lopez Michelsen commanded the Liberal Party to vote for Noemí first and later Andres Pastrana, the Conservative candidate, thus leaving the Liberal candidate forgotten by her own party. Mr. Pastrana won the election, and Noemí received 26.6 percent of the votes out of a 10.7 million total. See Barbara Frechette, *El Poder Compartido* (Shared power) (Bogotá: Editorial Norma, 1999), 258.

30. Florence Thomas, a French/Colombian psychologist, writes in her book *Los Estragos del Amor: El Discurso Amoroso en los Medios de Comunicación* (Love's ravages: Amorous discourse in the media) (Bogotá: Universidad Nacional, 1999) that love in Colombia is considered the responsibility of women while female identity ultimately depends on male narcissism.

31. Elsy Bonilla, in the introduction to a book she edited, *Mujer y Familia en Colombia* (Woman and the family in Colombia) (Bogotá: Plaza and Janes, 1985), 28, says that irrespective of social class, women have been barred from all spheres that are not domestic. Such exclusion is culturally determined and has nothing to do with biology or gender.

32. Silvana Paternostro, *In the Land of God and Man: Confronting Our Sexual Culture in Latin America* (New York: Dutton, 1998), 218, tells how twenty-three-year-old Shakira—a Colombian popsinger who won MTV prizes three times and a Grammy Award in September 2000 and is now the girlfriend of the son of Argentina's president—sings songs that picture women being more in contact with everyday life. Nevertheless, the image of what is expected of a woman has changed little: the Colombian singer said in a newspaper interview that she firmly believed that a woman should only give "herself in body and soul on the day of her wedding."

33. Paternostro, ibid., 220, writes that a woman (from upper and middle upper classes) must "conquer a man to marry." To help achieve this goal, suitable young women are educated abroad but are "rarely encouraged to get an education to become financially independent" because the goal is to find a husband who will "decide the

laws of his home and those of his country." A woman's success in life is still measured by the one whom she marries. Of course, there are exceptions. Manuela speaks about this issue before chapter 5 of this text.

34. One of Colombia's greatest female thinkers and activists, María de los Angeles Cano (1887–1967), came from an affluent family and was extremely well educated. She fought to help change sexual roles in society and free women from the prison of gender. A writer and a political agitator, she helped unionize workers in her hometown of Medellín, Antioquia. See Isabel Vergara, "María de los Angeles Cano Marquez: del Sindicalismo al Socialimso Subvirtiendo las Reglas del Padre (María de los Angeles Cano: From sindicalism to socialism; subverting the father's rules), *Las Desobedientes* (The disobedients), 230–253.

35. Suzanne Horer and Jeanne Socquet elaborate on women's vision for feminist politics and activism. "We think that women must offer other forms of social systems, other forms of creation, other goals, other directions, and by 'other' we mean 'better': we mean those that stress the values of human beings as a whole, that truly liberate them; that is to say, those that put them directly in front of themselves instead of in *front of a double, a shadow, an image, a golem*" (emphasis mine). Marks and de Courtivron eds., *New French Feminisms.* (Boston: Massachusetts University Press, 1981), 243.

36. Ranke-Heinemann in *Eunuchs*, 127, writes about women's history within the church: "The history of Christianity is likewise a history of how women were silenced and deprived of their rights. And if this process no longer goes on in the Christian West, which is not thanks to but in spite of the Church, it certainly has not stopped in the Church itself."

37. See especially Kristeva's article "Women's Time," in *Signs*, 13–35, as it is pertinent at this time.

CHAPTER SEVEN

Female Socialization
and Stages of Life in Colombia

Marriage was the only profession open to her. . . . The daughter of the educated man.

Virginia Woolf, *Three Guineas* (1974: 38).

The cowardice of woman is a distinctly home product. It is born of weakness and ignorance; weakness and ignorance are by no means essential feminine attributes but strictly domestic attributes. Keep a man from birth wrapped in much cloth, shut away from sky and sun, wind and rain, continually exhausting his nervous energy by incessant activity in monotonous little things, and never developing his muscular strength and skill by suitable exercise of a large and varied nature, and he would be weak. Savage women are not weak. Fishwives are not weak. The home-bound woman is weak, as would be a home-bound man. Also, she is ignorant—not, at least nowadays, ignorant necessarily of books but ignorant of general life.

Charlotte Perkins Gilman, *The Home: Its Work and Influence* (1903: 43)

Susana: "On Top of my Life!"

Introduction

As social historian Asuncion Lavrin advises, observing socialization of women inside the Colombian family is important to understand how their identity is structured. Often, mothers are compliant and follow strictly the rules given by cultural, social, and religious laws. While fathers, openly or covertly, make the rules,

145

mothers enforce them. There are exceptions but generally women convey the fa-
ther's orders. Fathers can be unreasonable and tough when their ideas and rules are
not carried out. In school, teachers take care that rules and cultural traditions are
transmitted clearly to students. Most of the women interviewed believed with cer-
tainty that because of gender differences, the world belongs to men, whereas
women's domain is the home.

Susana begins her interview by reflecting on her life, the experiences of which de-
note the familiar pattern. Her stern father rules the household through a mother who
announces and carries out his wishes. At the same time, Susana is instructed by her
submissive mother to do whatever she wants behind her irascible father's back. Su-
sana is taught by that same mother that she could be apparently obedient.

Often, cultural and social rules are intertwined with the rules of the Catholic
Church, as we see in this specific case. But, cultural and religious rules differ, al-
though not openly, depending on whether the recipient is a boy or a girl.

Interview
"Tell me Susana, what do you remember of your childhood? Tell me the way they
educated you as a girl. Tell me anything you like."

"I was raised simply to be married! If we compare my education to that of
my brothers, it was completely different. I was educated to be married one
day to a man who would take care of me, have children with, and nothing
else. I had to follow my mother's example; this was my father's main concern.
Also, it was my responsibility to make four grandparents happy! My brothers,
instead, had to have a good intellectual education. At an early age they were
sent to a very good boarding school in the States. They had to be prepared
to attend the best universities. Also, my father said that boys could not be
tied to their mother's 'skirts.' Personally, I think that this early separation of
my brothers from my mother affected them in a negative way. My father totally ignored me and my studies; instead he was very concerned with my
brothers, but mainly, as I mentioned, with their education. The result was
that I did not like school, nor was I interested in learning anything. I was
treated as a female; I was considered fragile. Thus, I had to be taken care of
very carefully. My brothers were allowed to do as they pleased. They went out
alone, without a chaperone, whereas, I was chaperoned up until I was eighteen years old. I married simply to stop hearing my father stamping his feet,
because he did not agree with me.

"I never had any interesting conversations or any kind of communication,
with my parents. I always felt ignored by them. I was very much afraid of my
father, who completely ignored me, and who had a quick temper. Whenever
I asked my mother about anything concerning sex or the functioning of our

bodies, she answered that I was too young to know about "those things." My mother never answered any of the questions I asked her. Never. But I do think that both my mother and my father gave me good values. On the other hand, my father, who apparently was unconcerned about our intimate lives, my brothers' and mine, indirectly, he continuously supervised us. He *sent* his orders through my mother. He never said anything personally; she spoke for him. From an early age, I heard my mother mentioning my father's bad temper, his indirect supervision over our lives, and his iron will over our obedience to his law. Simultaneously, my mother told me that I could do anything I wished if my father did not know! Thus, I grew up learning how to keep secrets away from my father, to spare his bad temper! In a way, my mother was teaching me to be independent and do my own will. Also, I think she was telling me not to let any man, not even my father, mistreat me. My mother's advice was that I had to be 'secretive,' and then, I could act according to my wishes. Probably, through me she was vindicating herself. At the same time she advised me not to answer back at men, because they did not like it. And this was what I saw in my house: my mother always obeying my father without questioning his orders! So, I grew up with the idea that women had to obey men. But, behind their backs, we could do whatever we liked. My mother always reminded me that I could not let a man touch or kiss me. If I did, he would reject me and would not marry me. She said that men, if they had an opportunity, were going to sexually abuse me. Thus, I had to be careful. My brothers were men, they had none of these issues to worry about.

"About my school years and the nuns, I only remember bad things! I was terrified of the nuns! I didn't like their education. Everything was horrible! I felt like in a prison, plus the only thing they told us, the students, was the way we had to behave: ballet lessons were forbidden; they were sinful. We could not go swimming with men; if we did, our swimming suits had to be very discreet. We were not supposed to look at our bodies when we were taking a shower. We had to be careful in the way we dressed, as not to tempt men with our bodies. We were responsible if men sinned. We had to be aware of our bodies, for they could be a cause of trouble and sin to others. They told us St. Paul's teachings: that we human beings had to marry to bring forth children, not to satisfy any other desire. When I married the first time, the priest told me that my husband and I, we could only be together whenever we were going to have a baby, that sexual pleasure should not be our main concern. My first husband had never been with a woman before me, so our honeymoon was very difficult. My education was filled with violence, yes. I was afraid of my father, of the nuns, of men. My father was on top of my life;

I had no privacy. Adults around me ignored me. Worse, my word was not valued. At school we had to be silent no matter what. Thus, I had to be unseen and silent in my home and at school. All of what I am telling you is concealed violence! My second and my third husbands did not beat me physically, but verbally. My third husband did hurt me physically, whenever he had a drink. My second husband, who was a university professor and wanted me to study, didn't let me continue my education after I had our first child. And, my third husband was worse. He did not let me go out of my house; I had to stay in with the children at all times. He thought that if I studied or did volunteer work I was going to go out looking for a man!

"I always tell my daughters that before anything else, they must finish their university studies. That before marrying they have to have a profession, so that they may earn their living and not depend on a husband or companion. I tell them that, no matter what, they have to make men respect them. They must not let men humiliate them, as my three husbands did to me. I feel guilty with the failure of my marriages. I am a sack of guilt feelings! My father says that because I am impossible, and have always been so, this is why my marriages have never worked. I still think that one day I shall find a man who will love and respect me. But probably it would be better if I don't marry again and have an open and free relationship with a man I fantasize and who I am sure exists."

❧

The Latin American historian Asuncion Lavrin in "Women, the Family, and Social Change in Latin America" (1987: 110–11) speaks of the necessity for further investigation of Latin American families as the primary locus of socialization in terms of gender role models. But, the range of situations adversely affecting women is vast. It includes relationships with men; political, legal, and religious laws; cultural values; and socioeconomic conditions for survival and decent living. This chapter concentrates on the circumstances surrounding the stages in Colombian women's development from childhood to young adulthood. Females acquire identity as *women* during this period. In these years, feminine and masculine sexual roles are assigned differentially by the society they belong to; an associated range of behavior patterns is organized, taught, and learned by individuals (see Butler 1990; Dinnerstein 1975). Gender roles are learned, above all, through socialization. This chapter shows how socialization works to construct Colombian female identity from childhood to marriage, and as it continues to be reinforced by older colluding women who abide by the system and the ideology of patriarchy and/or *machismo*.

In order to understand male supremacy and female dependency, subjugation, and the defilement of all which is *feminine* in Colombia, Asuncion Lavrin's (1987: 113) idea works well: to conduct research on the origins of gender construction in particular historical and cultural contexts. Lavrin firmly believes that such analyses are necessary to create politics and elaborate public policy on behalf of women, while assessing "all the obstacles now barring a large number of women from satisfactory personal and social life." By analyzing gender roles, it becomes evident that these roles provide strength to patriarchy's organization of men's and women's lives, and that society continues to protect these roles on behalf of men's interests. According to Lavrin (1987: 110–12), the responsibility women have for "themselves" entitles them to "an exploration of the ideology of male supremacy and female subordination. . . . We must understand the nature of cultural roots of gender role models if we wish to dismantle what has been going on in society against women's well-being."[1]

This chapter, then, explores socialization in the family. For as Andrea Dworkin (1974: 190) indicates,

> the nuclear family is the school of values in a sexist, sexually repressed society. The socialization process is an excellent perpetuator of gender stereotypes and patriarchal beliefs. One learns what one must know: the rules, rituals, and behaviors appropriate to male-female polarity and the internalized mechanisms of sexual oppression.

Thus, the deepest roots of the family must be uncovered in order to see the origins of its structure.[2] Socialization is an abstract concept that some people have difficulty discussing, particularly if they have thought little about their lives in the past. No wonder that the interviews conducted for this research were sometimes painful and laborious. The subjects had difficulty remembering and analyzing experiences that were shaped within a patriarchal, *machista* framework.

Patriarchal Ideology and *Machismo*

As shown in chapters 5 and 6, no matter the cultural milieu, no matter the worldview of the family, Colombian cultural norms have been firmly established on patriarchal ideology, in one way or another, from the time indigenous peoples met the Spaniards who "discovered" their "New World." Women have been the recipients of this ideology to their great disadvantage. And men have benefited from patriarchy, no matter what social class the actors have been born into, maintaining male power throughout Colombian history. Luce Irigaray (1985: 186–87) analyzes what patriarchy does to women.[3]

> Mother, virgin, prostitute: these are the social roles imposed on women. . . . [V]alorization of reproduction and nursing, faithfulness, modesty, ignorance of and lack of interest in sexual pleasure; a passive acceptance of men's activity; seductiveness. . . . [N]either as mother, nor as virgin, nor as prostitute has woman a right to her pleasure.

Asuncion Lavrin emphasizes that the "personal aspects of family formation and forms of bonding, such as marriage and its historical patterns" which organize gender role models for society (1987: 110), are most relevant in structuring women's lives. The intimate experiences of women have to be deconstructed extensively and profoundly to better understand women's problems and bring forth improvement. According to Lavrin, traditional relations between the sexes deeply affect female existence within the social, political, and private spheres.[4]

Variations according to religion and social class have impact on the divergence in education between girls versus boys. The social codes are clear and must be followed, or the offending child will be punished. "Our culture accepts terrible rules on behalf of maintaining the family . . . [and] the father's word is sacrosanct" (Lavrin 1987: 110).

Not only Lavrin but many other contemporary social scientists and historians write that women's lives in the Latin American countries, but specifically in Colombia, are, even today, manipulated by gender role asymmetry. From an early age, the differences between boys and girls are accentuated through games, household chores (or lack thereof), freedom to socialize unsupervised outside the home, and other forms of socialization. Subtle patterns of behavior prescribed by parents help establish gender identity, when children are quite young. María del Socorro, another interviewee, tells how she remembers her mother being very *machista* in favor of men. "When I was a little girl and we finished eating, my mother always made me pick up the dishes, for example. My brothers never had to do anything in the house because they were considered very special." What the interviews show is that rules and codes that women and men follow are culturally dictated and enforced by society, and all its institutions, but principally by the family (see Mitchell 2000).

Hierarchy and stratification—the result of patriarchal ideology—are blended with another male philosophy based on honor and shame:

machismo.[5] Jane Schneider (1971: 1) tells how these cultural codes—honor and shame—encompass the entire Mediterranean region in which "honor . . . depends upon reward and sanctions characteristic of face-to-face communities . . . [and] shame [concerns] related practices governing family integrity and the virginity of young girls." [6] And Pitt-Rivers (1966: 45) goes a bit further, explaining that *Machismo,* a legacy left by eight hundred years of Moorish cultural influence in Spain, came to the New World with the Spanish *conquistadores.* Evelyn Stevens (1973: 90), who has written extensively on this subject, defines *machismo* as "the cult of virility." The chief characteristics of this cult are "exaggerated aggressiveness and intransigence in male-to-male interpersonal relationships and arrogance and sexual aggression in male-to-female relationships." *Machismo* is defined by Chris Kramarae and Paula A. Treichler in *A Feminist Dictionary* (1985: 239) as the "Latin American word for the mystic of 'manliness.' It denotes a configuration of attitudes, values, and behaviors." It includes breaking the rules, violence, sexual potency, and contempt for women. And Julian Pitt-Rivers says about honor, "Honor is the value of a person in his own eyes, but also in the eyes of his society. It is the estimation of one's worth, his *claim* to pride, but it is also the acknowledgement of that claim, his excellence recognized by society, his *right* to pride" (original emphasis).[7]

On the other hand, *machismo* has its counterpart in *marianismo.* Evelyn Stevens (1973: 91–92) in her article "*Marianismo:* The Other Face of *Machismo*" defines this trait as follows:

> *Marianismo* is as prevalent as *machismo.* . . . [I]t is the cult of feminine spiritual superiority, which teaches that women are semidivine, morally superior to and spiritually stronger than men. . . . Far from being an oppressive norm dictated by tyrannical males, *marianismo* has received considerable impetus from women themselves. This fact makes it possible to regard *marianismo* as part of a reciprocal arrangement, the other half of which is *machismo.*

On women being semidivine (see Schneider 1971), Maurice Hamington (1995: 35) says that the division of women into those who are the good and bad, Mary and Eve, has helped to objectify woman as "other," making them "less than human" and increasing sexism. Christianity, thus, helps to create social beliefs that give "cultural permission for the physical abuse of women by men."

Marianismo also has had its cultural monuments. At the end of the nineteenth century, the Colombian writer Jorge Isaacs wrote one of the country's most loved classics, declared to be the Colombian national novel, *María.* It is the story of a perfect young woman, pure and virginal, who falls in love with a young medical student, Efraín. Their love story takes place in the Cauca Valley, in the *hacienda* (ranch) *El Paraíso* (Paradise) owned by the author, which still exists and is visited by tourists from around the country. But María dies before her love is consummated in the spousal bed. It could be said that, with her transparent name, María represents a role model for any young woman of her times, and maybe she still does, since she recreates the image of the Virgin mother (see Sommer 1993).

Among the interviewees, María Isabel best contradicts the rules set by *marianismo*. María Isabel had terrible confrontations with her parents while growing up, since they considered her "different" and too difficult to handle. "I had the capacity to reason and make decisions by myself . . . they thought I was crazy," she says. "My mother [thought] that because at age twelve I could understand different things from the usual ones young girls at that age would know, she considered me bad and dirty." Her parents tried to control her through strict rules that María Isabel did not follow. And when she did not follow their commands, they declared her "dirty and unbearable." Later this young woman married a man twenty years her senior. She says,

> My ex-husband . . . offered me what I truly lacked: a good father and mother. Of course he felt my sadness—my lack of love—and later took advantage of it to perpetuate his sexual perversions. His game was ambiguous; he said that he wanted what was most outstanding in me: my virginity! He kept telling me about his love affairs with women who were able to give him what I could not because of my "purity." For him I was pure, for my parents I was dirty. They represented two sides of the same coin.

For her husband Fernando, María Isabel's most striking characteristic was her innocence on sexual matters. Her being able to reason, make decisions about her life, or have a good job was unimportant. She had to be uncontaminated, a virgin, which she was, for his future sexual plans. Instead, for her parents the simple fact that she had a mind of her own was dangerous, since it could lead her to lose her purity and become contaminated.

Growing Up Female: Purity and Sexuality

Gabriel García Márquez's (1981) novel *Crónica de una Muerte Anunciada* (Chronicle of a Death Foretold) is about the issue of women's virginity in Colombia. Based on a real story that happened in a small village in the northern part of the country in the twentieth century, this author depicts how women in Colombia belong, body and soul, to the men of their families. The main female character of the story loses her virginity before marrying. This transgression gives her two brothers the moral authority to kill her presumed lover, a Muslim who has intruded into the community and allegedly deflowered the maiden, something not permitted and condemned by the social group. Most typically, however, moral authority relies on the father. As Pitt-Rivers (1966: 45) explains, "The honor of a man is involved, therefore, in the sexual purity of his mother, wife and daughters, and sisters, not in his own. (*La mujer honrada la pierna quebrada y en casa.* The good woman: locked in the house with a broken leg. A Spanish saying.)

Within the family[8] of each woman interviewed, the father's word was Law. His decisions were followed without question, even when the father was absent. The *machista* ideology, fortified by Catholicism, was the dominant patriarchal philosophy. Thus, interviewee Susana can speak about her father's orders:

My mother was afraid of my father; she kept reminding me that all members of the household had to obey my father's orders. But if I was wise enough, she said, I could do what I wanted to do—if my father didn't know. Today, after three divorces, I'm still doing things behind my father's back!

María Isabel also describes how her mother transmitted the father's orders to the children, while he himself never uttered a word or a command. "Mother was in charge of having things done according to my father's desires and whims." She obeyed his law unconditionally and transmitted it to the rest of the family members.

Even Dora, who grew up with no father and had only her mother and grandmother, experienced the same control:

My father abandoned our household when my sister and I were six and five years old. We didn't have a man in the house, but my mother was very religious, and my sister and I had to follow strict rules. We never went out alone. We had to be very careful of men who were bad and peopled the streets, showing their penises to young girls. We also had to take good care of our bodies, which could be soiled easily and thus we could lose our virginity without noticing. For example, it was dangerous if we went bicycling because such exercise could make us lose our virginity.

The stories told by the interviewees reveal the same patterns, irrespective of social class or the woman's age. As children, these women had been trained to respect the wishes of a powerful, feared father, whether or not he was physically present. His word was respected, said Clara, as if it were the pronouncement of "the Holy Ghost."

For females, the father's rules were wrapped more tightly around them than was the case for the boys with whom they were raised. Girls were expected to be obedient—not only because they were children but because of their gender. Being female equaled a prison sentence in that girls were under "house arrest," secluded within the walls of their homes. "You see," said Juana, "my parents never allowed me to go out. My life was so sad: I could never leave home unaccompanied until I married at seventeen; then, things began to change for me. My husband and I have had a wonderful relationship. We are very good friends, we respect each other, etc."

Juana never knew the reason she wasn't allowed out; when she did leave the house, she had to be accompanied by her brother. Juana feared, in her adolescent years, that something might happen to her "body" outside, but she couldn't understand why her brother faced no such restrictions. His body did not seem to be endangered. Juana concluded that "because men are different, life is different for them; it's better"; the problem of protecting her virginity took away from her the freedom to move at her ease. Flor was more emphatic in her understanding that girls were forbidden from going out alone, lest they lose their virginity. "It was very clear," she said, "that the world was for boys to enjoy. We girls had to think about the home, cooking, cleaning, and our virginity. This last issue was never specified; girls were simply told that they had to 'take care' of their bodies." Whereas these two women from the lower economic classes were free to discuss openly these issues, women from the upper economic class would be too genteel to discuss such intimate matters. To some of the interviewees, the concept of purity was more difficult for them to explain, so they brushed off the topic.

Similarly, Nora agrees with the others, that forced enclosure is related to virginity. For Nora, however, reality was more complicated. She had been given up for adoption, and her new parents feared that she might have inherited sinful traits that would cause her to follow in the footsteps of her unmarried biological mother. Consequently, Nora believed the rules were enforced upon her more strictly than for other girls. She was not even allowed to have friends. (Her parents were agnostic and still they believed that she could "fall.") "These were abnormal rules to be imposed upon a child," she repeated throughout her interview. These limitations stifled Nora and helped suppress her intellectual development. Nora feels resentful and has never forgiven her parents for this deprivation. She always loved music and has a beautiful soprano voice, but when she asked her parents if she could take opera lessons, her father responded that only "bad women were opera singers." Like many other women I interviewed, Nora recalls her early life as sad, boring, and empty.

Among the interviewees from the upper economic class, Manuela said that she had a happy childhood. But as soon as she entered adolescence, the rules became much stricter for her than for her brothers, who were also youths. For Juliana, treatment in school and with her male companions started to change when "my body started developing into the body of a woman." Her life came to a complete turn. She stopped being outspoken and minding about her studies. She stopped playing boys' games, such as soccer. She began to care for her clothing, her hairdo, and being attractive to the boys in school. Clara had much the same experience. As a child, she was as "free as the wind," but she and her nine sisters faced harsh regulations as soon as they reached puberty, whereas her brothers' lives did not change at all. She says,

> My father was a hard, strict person who didn't have a good way to impose his orders upon us [girls]. Whenever one of us broke his terrible rules, my mother pretended she hadn't noticed our disobedience. It was very difficult to control or change girls who have been allowed to roam free around the farm and suddenly, because of their age and gender, were harnessed and curbed. . . . I was a rebel all my life and therefore had terrible confrontations with my father.

Most of the interviewees, regardless of economic class, attribute their home imprisonment to gender and its physical manifestations. Their lives were surrounded by a void.

Each of the women said that while growing up, she learned that virginity was a female responsibility and burden. "We have to maintain tradition; this is our responsibility . . . to keep our virginity till the day we marry . . . to keep our virginities for our husbands," affirms Juliana at age eighteen. Most of the women interviewed were told in one way or another that a woman's *only* asset is her virginity, which she must protect from men's predatory acts. Most of the women were told, in an open or covert way, that men are bad and that when it comes to women, their intentions are not good.

Girls are required to protect their purity with help from the rest of the family. All subjects who spoke to me—regardless of age—agreed that not being sexually pure by the canons of the church and society, or liking sex, would cause them to be rejected by the father, brothers, and boyfriends. Society would label them as persons with "light morals," explains Dora. A girl's whole life revolves around the issue of losing or not losing her most important asset: the purity of her body. Female identity is based on not being promiscuous.

But sexual purity is explained with reference to virginity as María del Carmen comments,

> My father still thinks, today, that a woman has to be a virgin when she marries. He doesn't agree that a couple should have sex before marriage. To this day my father expects me to marry the man with whom I have sex. He is afraid that I'll become promiscuous. . . . My mother instead . . . when I went to secondary school . . . she advised me to be careful and not get pregnant.

A woman should not know too much about sexual activity, and not mind too much about sexual issues. When a woman is linked in some way to sexuality, her sexuality will be intrinsically connected to prostitution, she may even be labeled a prostitute. Such was the case with Manuela when she was an adolescent and her father called her "bitch" the day he found her watching a porno film that her brothers and cousins watched for fun. Manuela further tells how when she went to a co-ed American high school in her hometown, some of her friends had sex, "but it was understood that 'good girls' didn't do it!" In this same vain, Juliana says that "today, young women who have sex with their boyfriends are not expected to know too much about its logistics." It must be understood that the notion that there are two clearly defined groups of women, good and bad— depending on whether they are sexually active or not—pervades the entire society and, hence, the consciousness of young and old alike. Even today, says Juliana, girls who engage in sexual intercourse before the "accepted time" are categorized as "whores," unless they marry or go and live with the man in question. "Good girls" will become wives and mothers whereas "bad girls" are the ones with whom men have fun. Instead, heterosexual men who are labeled "womanizers" are considered manly and have the right to prove their masculinity (see Pitt-Rivers 1966). Young women who respect themselves have to prove that, sexually speaking, they are "innocent" and, indirectly, "pure." The same was said by the eight women from *Aguablanca*, the poorest section of Cali, whose ages varied between thirty-five and forty. The husbands or companions of these women did not like them to know "too much about sex," since it would mean either that they had another man, that they would sooner or later be unfaithful to their partners, or simply that they were prostitutes. These women said that a way for the husbands or companions to prove that their women were faithful to them was by not using contraceptives. Sexuality has a connotation of dirtiness and indecency.

School Years

Forty years ago, most people in Colombia saw no need for girls to finish high school.[9] Soledad, from the upper economic class, says, "My parents were totally uninterested in their four daughters' education. They said that girls could go to school until tenth grade; afterwards, high school was considered unnecessary. Young women were told to take courses in cooking and variations in home economics, including embroidery and child care." Since her mother never contradicted her father, her parents never encouraged Soledad to finish her studies. Flor, twenty years younger and from the lower economic class, describes a similar situation, "Our father said that girls didn't have to study because they were supposed to get married, have children, and take care of the house. Boys were sent to school and had all the liberty in the world." Twenty years ago, going to college was not considered important for women. However, many female members of the solid middle class, who began to flourish in the country, did attend universities.[10] Prior to that time, some women had fought their way through school and formal education, but these were rare exceptions. Among the women interviewed by Barbara Frechette in her book *El Poder Compartido* (Shared power) (1999: 38–40) was Esmeralda Arboleda, who told how her mother decided that all four daughters were to finish high school and then go to universities. Consequently, the mother made Esmeralda attend an all-boys school so she could get a high school degree, since the town where they lived had no secondary schools for girls. Esmeralda's mother was excommunicated by the Catholic Church for having done such an outrageous thing until a large group of women stopped going to church, after which the bishop forgave Mrs. Arboleda. According to Colombian historian and feminist Magdala Velásquez Toro, in 1932, during the liberal government of Enrique Olaya Herrera, women were granted permission to share the same rights as men regarding secondary-school attendance (1995: 210). In 1933, Colombian women were given the legal right to go to universities (Velásquez Toro 1995: 210; De Los Ríos 1995: 422). Eleven years later, Velásquez Toro reports that seventeen women graduated from colleges in the country while six hundred and seventy-eight males completed university education during the same period (1938–1944).

Today, intellectual education for girls is rarely neglected. Depending on social class, women generally attend secondary schools and universities, as do their brothers. If family resources are limited, however, male children may be chosen to complete both primary school and higher education, while the girls are left behind. Juana spoke about this issue: "There wasn't enough money to send José and me to a good private school. But we did go to a mediocre public school. Generally, boys go to school, and girls don't. Girls' destiny is to stay home and help their mothers and later get married and have children." Flor corroborates Juana's words: "Usually, poor girls don't go to secondary school. I only did three years of grammar school. Poor boys finish high school only if they don't have to help their families." And Clara, who became a senator, goes still further in her consternation at not having been able to finish her studies as her brothers did. She says,

> My father was all for education. . . . But during the depression he chose his three sons to study in Europe even though the only one who really cared about education was me. . . . I started questioning my father's decision. His answer was that only my brother was going to college in Europe because *he was a man!* The priority of going to Europe was reserved for boys—not girls. Here began the enormous difference between men and women in my family. Women were expected to get married while men could accomplish great things!

If a woman does go to college and subsequently marries a man with sufficient economic means, she won't need to work outside the home and might be prohibited from doing so. The roles women are theoretically permitted to fill and the implicit expectations of their families and the wider community differ significantly. More often than not, married women are pressured into bearing children and dedicating themselves to the same domestic labor their mothers and grandmothers undertook.[11]

Not too long ago, religious convents were thought to provide the best education for Catholic girls, regardless of social class.[12] For generations, these schools run by religious communities devised the methods of instruction for a large percentage of Colombian women. Above all, girls were trained to become suitable wives and mothers who would thereby serve society and remain worthy to enter heaven after death. Silence, obedience, and purity were considered important requirements for young women, whereas all pleasure was thought to be evil and, thus, avoided. Body and mind were strictly controlled through a series of rules rarely questioned. Analytical thinking and creativity were generally stifled. Rich personal lives were not sought by young women nor valued by the people in charge of their development.

Indeed, most of the women interviewed recalled their school years as extensions of family upbringing, concerned with purity. The process was applied more subtly at school, where girls, like boys, learned reading, writing, and arithmetic. Behavior expected of females was reinforced in a more coherent way than it was within the family.

Six of the nine middle- and upper-class women (included) who were interviewed studied in schools run by nuns. Nora, whose parents were agnostic, attended a school with male teachers who were intellectually sharp and quite strict in terms of discipline. Nora preferred school to her home life. In class, she had contact with other children where she could share a passion for learning and books. At school, she also experienced freedom from the "torture" that Nora says she lived at home.[13] Dora, who lived at a religious boarding school from age eight until graduation, talked about her school years in an apathetic way. At school, she said, girls "learned to be organized and received an excellent moral and intellectual education." On the other hand, Clara, Susana, Soledad, and I look back on school years with consternation or dislike.

Aleja remembers how her teacher, Abigail, used to beat the students with a ruler or made them stand by the door with a brick on their head. Rosalia commented "that the male teachers were more violent than the female teachers. The men used to beat us with a ruler." Clara also received a violent discipline by the nuns, who were German. "We were tightly constricted by the Germanic rules of the nuns since we were all 'rebellious' country girls who were free as the wind." And in her home the rules were imposed by her father, who always had the last word. She says,

> I didn't obey when my "*whys*" were not answered. I stood my ground against him. . . . I wasn't afraid of him. . . . My father annoyed me with all his ideas that he wanted to impose on me. . . . What really bothered me was having limitations on my beliefs, wishes, and thoughts. Such restrictions I could not accept or understand. I felt violated by my father in terms of my human integrity, and for this affront I deeply resented him.

On the other hand, Susana remembers being afraid of the nuns and feeling persecuted by them. She considered the school a second prison, the first being her home. The nuns educated her, says Susana, to forget about earthly endeavors. The main subject of interest at school was virginity and obstacles that might interrupt the normal flow of the body's purity. For example, ballet lessons were forbidden; also, bathing in the shower without covering the body was discouraged; bathing in swimming pools with men was out of the question; any kind of friendship with boys was discouraged; dressing in an immodest manner—in tight blouses, for example—was forbidden. The list grew and grew. Susana choked while enumerating all the issues the nuns thought could endanger a woman's purity.

Soledad's recollections are similar to Susana's. She was required to memorize endless lists of rules to help her in the practice of purity, and she constantly endured a lack of respect from her teachers. Soledad always felt "violated" in her human integrity, in the privacy of her body and mind, by both her mother and the nuns at school.

> The nuns used to look into my personal things—drawers, handbags, the pockets of my uniform—to see if I had letters from my boyfriends. For me this was a terrible violation of my privacy. The nuns preached respect for the other, but no one respected me. I felt persecuted by the nuns. Their conduct was an affront to my integrity. . . . My mother, too, supervised me like the nuns. She was equally terrible. I was tortured by everybody: by my parents, the nuns, the priests, and later, by my husband. . . . I felt that I was spiritually raped by everybody around me.

Dora searches deeply into her memories and recalls,

> [O]ur youthful world was very structured and happy. We didn't ask for more. But as children, we had no intimacy with ourselves. We were like an open book for those who educated us. We had to be because, in any case they would "search" into our souls.

Dora, Soledad, Susana, and I remembered the lack or privacy and how the nuns reminded the students not to go around in two's; students had to be always alone or in groups of three or more. The purpose of this rule probably was to avoid too close a relationship that could lead to homosexuality.

María Isabel, who was an excellent student, also recalls that her parents did not care whether or not she did well in school. She felt rejected by both her parents, who only gave her strict rules and orders. She notes further that her unhappiness was based on the *lack* she had that differentiated her from her brothers. The women mentioned here suffered from a sophisticated violence that was difficult to detect, and, therefore, to eradicate.

For working class women, school was considered a more normal process than it was by the middle- and upper-class interviewees. Children were expected to attend school and learn to read and write, provided the family had enough money to educate both males and females. Several interviewees went to co-ed schools where boys and girls attended classes together but were segregated for recreation. "Although classes were mixed and there were no separate rules for boys and girls during classroom time, at the end of each class we had to separate; boys played together, and girls played together," says Rosalia. The reason for separating females and males at this time was unknown to the interviewees. None of them could guess why this procedure was followed. The interviewees thought there was no difference in education between males and females at school.

Segregation during recreation was not considered important to the women with whom I spoke. Aleja, my former nanny, thinks that separating girls and boys during recess was normal in grammar school. "That was the way it was organized. It was like that." María del Carmen, who attended an all-girls grammar school in a small town near a large city, remarks: "It was better to have girls apart from boys, so this was the way public schools in that town functioned: each group had their own school. Boys and girls separately; it worked very well." Probably the separation of children according to their gender had to do with keeping boys and girls away from opportunities to interrelate in a physical way that could lead them to inappropriate intimate relationships.

None of the women's parents encouraged them to pursue intellectual endeavors or professional careers, except for María del Carmen, whose mother helped her overcome obstacles in order to study accounting; and María del Socorro received her bachelor's degree as a result of her mother's insistence. Rather, as Susana says, "My father ignored me and my studies. Instead, he was concerned with my brother's education." María Isabel and Manuela earned master's degrees for which they themselves paid; Gloria completed two years of pre-med education and is now studying computer science. Clara has actualized herself impressively—was a senator, founded an art museum—achieving marvelous accomplishments without having received a formal education. She is intellectually and politically a self-made woman. Juliana has different perspectives before her, as she belongs to a much younger generation and she comes from a well-to-do family who supports her desire to go from a bachelor's degree to a master's degree as something normal for her to do. Nevertheless, she remembers how one of her female teachers "thought that girls didn't have to be as intelligent [learned] as boys." Thus, she did not expect much from them.

Whereas none of the working-class women received any specific religious instruction, Aleja, Soledad, and I are practicing Catholics. Aleja, for example, explained that her mother had taught her from an early age to be pious and to pray every day. Just before first communion, a priest, nun, or teacher prepared both boys and girls to receive the sacrament. Aleja remained a devout and practicing Catholic to the end of her life. Juliana, if she can, goes to church, every Sunday. Three of the women practice their religion from time to time; and the rest never think about going to church or receiving the sacraments of penance and communion. Occasionally, some of them pray; Rosie, the sex worker in Amsterdam, does. Lower-class women are more skeptical and pragmatic about handling dogmatic religion and other forms of instruction.

Issues of Purity and Virginity in the Education of a Girl

In the education of children, the subject of sexual purity is mentioned as one of God's commandments until marriage, which then demands faithfulness to the partner. But the implicit message has been that only women—not men—should pay attention to the sixth commandment. Clara elucidates, "No one told us in a straightforward way that girls shouldn't permit men to touch them, but we understood what had to be: we *needed* to be virgins when we married." Also, for a girl to maintain and care for her virginity is an issue of importance, even in the twenty-first century. The working class women agreed that purity of body was not a concern for boys. Flor, who is thirty five, explains quite clearly what the issue of purity of the body implies in this cultural context:

> The pattern of behavior for a man and a woman is different. A woman has to be a virgin until she marries. Boys are taken to prostitutes by their fathers at the age of twelve or thirteen; this is their manhood initiation. Men drink, have lots of women, and do not do household chores; if they do any of these, they would be labeled *maricón* [gay]. We were very poor, but men always had the money to drink and go to the "women." This is how men show that they are *machos*. Women keep quiet and if they don't, they are beaten up. Girls have to be careful not to lose their virginity. Bicycling and horse back riding are dangerous exercises, which can make them lose it. A girl is different from a boy. It's boring to be a girl. . . . We only work and work. Women have few distractions to make them relax and be happy.

Flor's understanding is that no matter what happens to a young woman, even if she is raped, virginity "is a woman's problem, not a man's." She further says,

> They told us that if a man raped a woman, he had to marry her because nobody else would marry her. It was also the way a man could be forgiven for his violent act. And my grandmother kept telling me that if we stopped being *señoritas* [maidens], the man who would marry me wouldn't love me. But I didn't really understand what "virginity" really meant. In some way, I would be soiled, I thought.

A woman's body is, thus, covertly considered an object of sin because of religious beliefs reinforced by cultural mores. As mentioned, in the words of Rosalia and Flor, when "Eve gave the apple to Adam, they sinned and evil in the world began." Thus, the fall of the human race is considered to have occurred through a woman, Eve, and with her, the beginning of deserved female suffering and the ideas of virginity and of the purity of a woman's body. Juliana, too, said that for Catholic girls, it is a sin to have sex with their boyfriends, unless they know that sooner or later they will get married; then, they will not worry too much about the transgression. But she says,

> For boys things are different; they don't worry about sin . . . [and if needed] they go to the prostitutes. . . . Men think that they are more of a man when they have sex with many women and they talk about it between them. They like to boast about it! The best way for you not to have such an experience—of being talked about or dropped by your boyfriend (which usually happens after you have sex with them)—is by not doing it! You see, for men everything is a "seduction and a conquest," nothing more. Also, girls who have had the experience say that what is normal is for the man to be on top and the woman at the bottom. This is more normal, they say. If you know too much about sex you are considered dirty, like a prostitute.

The women interviewed have had the notions ingrained in their minds that the female body is somehow "polluted" and that it, therefore, contaminates men, although this subject is not discussed forthrightly.[14] The implication is that women are weaker than men on a corporeal level,[15] which is why girls must be secluded, silenced, manipulated, used, and abused. The legal and religious ideologies in Latin America more or less reiterate this belief. Such societies believe that the female body must be tamed, just like nature was tamed, by man, and cleansed by patriarchal codes.[16]

Men are thought to be made of "different stuff"—all evidence to the contrary. Hence their lives are "different." Men are expected to be free while women are not. "We knew all the time, since childhood, that men could do anything they wanted!" exclaims Flor. Almost every one of the women interviewed accept the myth that men are ruled by sexual impulses they cannot control. Several of the interviewees expressed the opinion that, for men, sexuality resembles animal behavior, which is thought to be devoid of emotion but also represents male strength. Thus, these women think that male power resides in the penis, which also symbolizes political dominance.[17]

The Body, Solitude, Privacy, and Sex

Although it is believed, today, that girls and boys have the same upbringing, young females from all social classes in Colombia tend to be treated differently when young, within homes, families, and schools.

The seclusion of girls is related to cultural, religious, and symbolic notions about the female body. Colombian culture perpetuates the myth that "a female's body has to be trained to be pure and virginal so that it may not harm the woman who owns it. One day, this body may be acquired by a man who will make it his," says Nora. Susana is specific: "A woman will be a wife to a husband and the mother of his children. We were objects."[18] Because the female body is considered problematic, girls can be socialized in seclusion and trained to be sweet, submissive, modest, silent, and pure. Finally, it has been mentioned all along in this work, the objective is for the woman to marry and have children. Many of the women interviewed agreed with the following statement by Soledad:

> Girls in Colombia are raised to be objects. They are taught to please others. They have to be vain, coquettish, and superficial. Even today, if a girl has a university degree or a job, the prevailing idea is that some day a man will come along to protect her! Marriage and motherhood are women's real destiny and roles; everything else is a façade to hide this tremendous reality.[19] (see De Beauvoir 1952)

Women in Colombia are often treated like delicate objects that could be harmed easily. Several of the subjects interviewed mentioned that, when young, they were protected like "porcelain" or some "semi-precious object" that could be damaged by accident. Dora, like Flor, says, "We had to be very feminine, the way to protect our virginity." All the interviewees say that while they were growing up, it was understood openly or covertly that if women were marred physically or spiritually, no man would want them. Manuela, age thirty-five, speaks of her own experience with sports: "My brothers and cousins liked to play soccer, but they discriminated against me in this area. They wouldn't accept me as a participant in this game. 'You are a girl, and you cannot play soccer,' they reminded me." Juliana also mentions that she had competed with boys in masculine fields: sports, mathematics, and or outspokenness. When she entered her adolescent years, she was made to change. She had to become "feminine" and acquire the approved female characteristics. Thus, she lost her interest in her studies; she stopped playing soccer with her friends; her math grades declined; and her forthright personality and way of speaking were silenced.

Meddling in a woman's private life by planting seeds of fear and malaise is an injustice that is violent in a psychological sense. Such intrusions can later prove as damaging as physical attacks. For example, in confession, a priest might ask a girl whether she has "touched anything private with her hands."

Soledad was interrogated in this way several times before she decided to stop confessing to priests. Likewise, when Rosie was ten years old, a priest who was supposed to be blessing her started to molest her sexually. Personally, I remember when a priest who was directing spiritual retreats preached that "half the sins of the world are committed on account of women's bodies and immodest behavior."[20] Indeed, Gloria, thirty years old, who attended a Franciscan school, was quick to blame women for men's behavior.

> Women cannot behave like men. Men are free to lose their virginity. This is the proof they can give to show that they are not *maricones* [gay]. Instead, girls, no: they have to be virgins up to the day they get married in church. They have to maintain their place; they must make others respect them. If a man loses respect for a woman, it's considered her fault, not his. For example, if a woman wears a miniskirt and a man looks at her, he may very well think that she is provoking him, even if she is not. It is *her* responsibility if he rapes her.

Gloria accepted what her religious instructors wanted her to believe, making her merciless in her judgment of women's actions or experiences.

With the exception of the sex worker and a few others, I interpret that the women interviewed for this study considered the subject of sex to be taboo. When the subjects speak about sexual activity—and few do—they objectify sex and address it as something apart from themselves. "I did not know what that *thing* was," says one. "If I had known what it was all about, I would not have married," says Dora. Flor notes that all her suffering began when she knew a man intimately. She says, "A woman's suffering really starts with *it*; it's normal. You see, a man can do what he wishes; a woman may not. She can only be with the man she loves." Gloria insists that "sex is not needed for one to be happy!" Gloria does not connect sexuality with love. Soledad mentions that her husband was quite passionate and asked to have sex every day. "He wanted to be on top of me all the time, something that for me was insufferable!" Aleja does not even utter the word "sex." She claims total ignorance whenever I bring up questions related to the subject, such as "Who told you about how babies are made?" or, "Did they tell you anything about virginity and purity of the body?" When the topic is raised, she opens her big, dark-brown eyes widely and answers seriously with a straight face: "No. Nobody said anything. I don't know." Sex is generally termed "*it*" or "*that thing*," and the women separate it from emotion, intellect, and all other aspects of life. Mind, heart or love, and sex are considered unrelated domains. Further, for those women who do not know what a sexual relationship implies, its realization is hard. Juana remembers,

When I married I didn't know how babies were made! I was very innocent or ignorant, about how our bodies function. . . . I didn't know what was happening to me when I menstruated the first time; I didn't know that men went to prostitutes. It was a terrible shock when I learned about all those things. . . . When my son was born I cried all the time. I wanted to go back home because the child didn't stop crying. I thought that what had happened to me was a punishment. You see, sexual relations and having a baby were two terrible things for me.

And Rosalia, who is thirty years old and from the lower economic class, says,

I was only seventeen years old when I went away with a man. . . . I didn't know anything about sexual relationships between a man and a woman. I thought (when I experienced it) that what happened between the man I went away with and myself was perfectly horrendous! [And] I only learned about "prostitutes" when I lived with that man I went away with and who was my first companion.

The training young women receive on how to be virgins and maintain the purity of their bodies conceals the truth about sexual experience, leaving them open to disillusion and mental health issues.

By contrast, the sex worker's discourse differentiated and integrated mind, heart or love, and sex very well. Rosie distinguishes between "having sex" and "making love." She considers her work an art, a serious profession that may teach men who come to benefit from her skills to help them in their intimate personal lives. Rosie works toward goals that she hopes will bring peace of mind, including financial help for her mother, siblings, and the children she loves above all else; she prides herself for having always been an excellent mother. She makes sense of her life, reflects about its meaning, plans for the future, and she considers herself independent.

Definitely I consider myself a free woman. I am free to do what I wish. I work if I need to do so. I go out with whom I choose. I choose my clients. I made enough money to educate my children very well. I have my own house, and I can think of retiring quite soon, after being here in Amsterdam for seventeen years. No one tells me what to do or where to go. I am an independent woman.

Ironically, among most of the interviewees, Rosie seems to be freer with herself, and better able to speak about her body and her sexuality. She has extricated herself from a brutal marriage. She has raised her children to be successful in their professional and personal lives. She enjoys a satisfying relationship with a man. Yet, after commenting about her accomplishments, she acknowledges that she has not told her children of her "career." "Life punished me," she laments. "My family life is a shambles." As she spends her days in a showcase window, waiting for clients, some of whom are "rough and disagreeable" (some call her "old"), she admits, "I feel sad and nervous . . . afraid I can't earn enough to pay my debts and send money to my children." She wishes she could live close to her children, to open a small business. In other words, she wishes for another kind of work.

At the same time, the women from Aguablanca, like Rosie, differentiated drastically between "raw sex" and "making love." Undoubtedly, for these women the perspectives on sex had to be well delineated in order to fit into an intimate relationship, in which they consider "love" to be the main ingredient.[21]

Many of the women also thought that sexuality turns a woman into a man's possession. Soledad gives details on this subject: "A woman becomes a man's property as soon as she marries him. He and everyone else feels that he, the husband, owns her." Furthermore, she continues, wives, sexually speaking, have to please their husbands.

> One marries and gets used to the idea that a husband has to be satisfied. Sexually my ex-husband never understood my needs, which were completely different from his; our minds didn't meet in our lovemaking. He was not tender. All expression of affection had to end in sexual activity. It didn't matter if I was tired or ill. He simply wanted to be on top of me all the time. With my husband I relived my life with my parents: I had to please others and forget about myself!

Similarly, Flor, who did not "believe in marriage," found that marriage brought women's suffering to clarity: "It is then [with marriage] that the real suffering for the woman begins."

Clara's mother, on the other hand, advised her daughter not to marry because she said that marriage only brought a hard life. Yet when the mother understood that Clara had no other way out from the prison where she lived, the father being the sole authority who kept his family under with the rule of his thumb, she realized that the only horizon for her daughter was to get out and marry. Clara did, at nineteen. Several of the women from the poorer classes did not like the idea of marriage, since it took away from them the only bit of freedom they could have in respect to their companions. Many of the women's discourses reflect that marriage, sex, suffering, and violence are interrelated parts of one whole subject.

Unfortunately, few of these women's mothers helped them resist the violence to which they were subjected. María Isabel remembers,

> My mother could not love me because she did not want competition for my father's love. My father could not love me because of his *machista* and religious upbringing; loving his daughter was a dilemma for him. Love and sex are intertwined for him! He can't differentiate between love, sex, desire, sexual desire and passion, incest, etc.

Nevertheless, the mothers of Clara, Manuela, Soledad, and María del Socorro, when their daughters' situations got very bad, did their best to help. They encouraged them to seek better lives free of violence and enclosure. Rosie and Juliana mentioned that they had, and still have, excellent relationships with their mothers. So did Clara, Dora, and I, when our mothers were alive.

The majority of women interviewed received no sexual instruction. Nora, for example, shaved her pubic hair for quite a long time, believing its appearance was abnormal. None of the women were told beforehand about menstruation, except for Clara, Manuela, and Juliana, whose mothers did explain this aspect of maturation. Usually friends, older sisters, and cousins discuss sex and motherhood with younger girls.

Transmissions of Cruelty

Unfortunately, older women in Colombia—including mothers and teachers—help sustain stifling patriarchal values that oppress females in the next generation. During the early socialization of children, women transmit cultural expectations. Women may not have created this system, but they are active collaborators in its perpetuation.[22] Older women are the gatekeepers of a biased regime from which they gain a modicum of power by perpetuating its destructive process (Gadant 1986: 1).[23] Socialized to uphold and transmit patriarchal ideology, women unwittingly collaborate in a system that enslaves them. Margaret Atwood, in her grisly novel *The Handmaid's Tale* (1998), gives an excellent example when she fictionalizes the transmission of cruelty from older to younger women on behalf of society in an imaginary country ruled by a patriarchal, military authoritarian government. The police in this fictitious nation, who serve as guards for the young women, are drawn from the ranks of the society's older women. Women safeguard the family institution even as it victimizes them.[24] The novel's premise brings to life a hypothesis evidenced by many of the interviewees—Aleja, Esperanza, Juana,

Dora, Nora, María Isabel, Manuela, María del Carmen, and María del Socorro, just to name a few—that in male-run societies, older women are the caretakers of the "Law of the Father" and transmitters of the cultural rules in the making of "a docile body that may be subjected, used, transformed and improved" (Foucault 1979: 198). Irrespective of the society, men operate as a law unto themselves—as they do in Colombia. Gender differentiates males from females in a way that is exaggerated by Colombian culture. Mothers frequently support the laws that make men special at the expense of the women. Discriminatory rituals that symbolically differentiate females from males are often observed by mothers. María del Carmen recalls, "When my mother prepares food, she always serves the men before the women." As instanced in anecdotes told about the mothers of Esperanza, Nora, Soledad, Susana, Manuela, María del Carmen, and María del Socorro, in supervising younger women, older women help perpetuate the violence and oppression they themselves undoubtedly endured when they too were young.

Furthermore, because of the ideology of the family that is enforced by legal and religious laws, women, generally speaking, accept any kind of intra-familial violence and mistreatment that affects them and their children, and many, to the end of their lives, say that no matter what happens in the family milieu, they love and respect their husbands. Aleja, for example, says in earnest, "My mother was extremely respectful of my father." A woman is to accept quietly and with resignation what the husband decides is best for the family and its members; and the church backs up this ideology, labeling it a sin not to follow what has been accepted by society. Flor's mother presents a case in point:

> Even though my father was nice—and gave all the money he earned to my mother and didn't have another woman—he was extremely *machista* and used to beat my mother a lot. He drank a lot, but he didn't abuse us children. . . . I suffered tremendously when I saw my father beating my mother. I asked her why she allowed him to do this to her, and she only answered that she had to accept it on behalf of her children whom she couldn't leave. If our father left us, we were going to be hungry. It is well known that in our social class, men beat women. I am convinced that a woman shouldn't allow a man to beat her, but a woman puts up with such treatment because of her children or because she is in love with her man or because she was educated to respect and obey her husband's wishes.

Women do keep quiet about their husbands' or companions abuse, on behalf of the family or because they simply have no other way out; but they become ill, bitter, frustrated, or depressed, like Clara's mother:

My mother was an exceptional being—free in her way of thinking. She was intelligent, courageous, and very well read. Full of desires and dreams she
couldn't carry out. My mother was thoroughly frustrated. Even as a child I felt
her yearnings. She was obliged to have child after child, and all my life I saw
my mother crying. Every time she had a baby, she cried. She was advanced for
her times. She was a "2000 woman."

Depicting similar strains, Esperanza said with no hesitation, she knew that
neither her father nor her mother loved her because of the abusive treatment
she received all her life from both of them. She understood from her mother
that the abuse originated from her mother's wanting to follow the father's
rules and not disobey his orders and wishes.

On the other hand, daughters might accept the mistreatment their mothers receive from their husbands simply because the abuser is the father a
daughter loves dearly. This was the case with Aleja, who adored her father.
What is most impressive in Aleja's narrative is how she continuously speaks
about her father's warmth, love, affection, and gentleness for his children, in
contrast to her mother's bitterness and violence. María del Carmen, likewise,
forgave her father's drinking and constant womanizing, simply because he always brought home his salary to supply his family's needs, generously bought
the food once a week, and cooked whenever he was around. In contrast, she
complains of her mother's being closed up, not talkative, strange, and cold,
and showing affection only for her two sons.

Hence, one concludes that no matter the social class, the age of the
women, or the education they have, sooner or later they come to the rescue of the men around them, be they father, husband, companion, or son.
Women find good reasons to excuse any responsibility from a man's behavior, or they come to his rescue and say simply, "That's the way things
are."[25]

The Law of the Mother

It may seem that that is the way things are, but that is not the way things
have to be. In exploring the possibilities of a friendly discourse, by interviewing women, one observes what the women interviewed think about life
in general and what their thoughts are on the ways women can empower
themselves, their daughters or other younger women, and each other; and
which actions will help to surmount the obstacles that obstruct a large number of women from "having [a] satisfactory personal and social life," such as
Asuncion Lavrin (1987: 113) invokes. The question about what they would

say to younger women to help them envision a better life was especially pertinent in stimulating thinking about such issues.

For the inteviewees, reaching for a better life entails caring for their daughters and sons, advising them to cherish their bodies, and, as Maria del Carmen affirms, to "love themselves." Manuela, a young, upper-class woman expresses that idea, too.

> I would say that the most important thing is for a woman to trust her desires and wishes. To a daughter I would tell her not to be afraid to explore, to take risks, to experiment with life. Doing so is part of living. It is important for a woman to follow her heart and live consciously. By experimenting, she will learn what she likes and dislikes. To be autonomous will help her not to be influenced by the wishes of others. She should strive for as much education as possible. Education will give her freedom, especially economic freedom, and she won't need to marry a rich man in order to survive! A woman who depends economically on a man will be under his grip. I would tell my daughter or another young woman that having a man at her side isn't very important compared to having valuable experiences to enrich her life. If she lives with someone, she shouldn't let that person mistreat her. Instead, that person should understand her and be a companion and a friend.

Being in control of themselves by living consciously and being ethical, honest, independent, and responsible, and having high ideals and goals is mentioned throughout the interviews. Some also stress the importance of teaching other women to love their families, their work, and not to be violent or aggressive with others. Women should "not allow husbands or companions to humiliate them."

Several of the interviewees also express the idea that men do not wish women well, that women, therefore, have to protect themselves from men's antagonistic acts. Women have to think of ways that will help them evade suffering. For many, this taking care means not permitting anyone to mistreat or harm them, in any way.

The interviewees agree on the need for women to have a good education in order for others to respect them, and to make them independent and capable of a better future. Susana says, "I always tell my daughters that, before anything else, they must finish their university studies. Before marrying, they must have a profession so they can earn a living without depending on a husband or a companion." Women should rely on themselves and not on others for success.

The women mention the importance of teaching younger women to have their minds open to the realities of what a woman's destiny is in a man-made world. Maintaining ongoing conversations with younger women will help spread the idea that women, like men, also have the right to enjoy pleasurable lives. In short, many of the interviewees mention that mothers should be friends of their daughters, establish good communication with them, and be available when they need help. Nora explains,

> To a young woman I would offer the same advice I give my son. I talk to him honestly because I don't want the same thing that happened to me to happen to another woman (or him). I would tell her the truth without hiding anything. You can't paint a rosy picture of life. You have to give a girl self-confidence and love. Possessions do not convey confidence. Girls must be allowed to make decisions on their own while receiving approval and guidance. I would discuss with a girl the changes in her life, in the world, in values, etc. In other words, I would have a constant dialogue with her.

Several of the women say that to teach young women about sex is important, as part of helping them to realize the importance of knowing their boyfriends, before thinking of a serious commitment. Another idea is that older women can teach younger women to develop good communication with husbands or companions.

Notes

1. See also Sherry Ortner and Harriet Whitehead, *Sexual Meanings: The Cultural Construction of Gender and Sexuality* (New York: Cambridge University Press, 1981); Rayna R. Reiter, ed., *Toward an Anthropology of Women* (New York: Monthly Review Press, 1975); Rosaldo and Lamphere, *Women.*

2. For a good explanation of how gender has influenced women's roles in western cultures, see Monique Wittig, "The Mark of Gender," in *The Poetics of Gender*, ed. Nancy K. Miller (New York: Columbia University Press, 1986); on using biology as a base for constructing "gender," see Simone de Beauvoir, *The Second Sex* (New York: Vintage Books, 1952).

3. In Mediterranean cultures, according to Jane Schneider, "An unmarried girl's loss of virginity brings unbearable shame to her family or lineage which, if they are to recover their honor, must first kill the girl and then her lover or seducer." See her "Of Vigilance of Virgins: Honor, Shame and Access to Resources in Mediterranean Societies," *Ethnology*, no. 3 (July 1971):1–23.

4. Asuncion Lavrin, "Women, the Family, and Social Change," 112, deliberately repeats that, "if we assume that female roles are shaped within the family as part of the education of children of both sexes, and are later translated into practical forms of subordination in social life, we must understand the nature of the cultural roots of gender role models."

5. See on this subject Jean Peristriany, ed., *Honor and Shame: The Values of Mediterranean Society* (Chicago: University of Chicago Press, 1966); Julian Pitt-Rivers, *Mediterranean Countrymen: Essays in the Social Anthropology of the Mediterranean* (Paris: Mouton, 1963); Jane Flax "Political Philosophy and the Patriarchal Unconscious: A Psychoanalytic Perspective on Epistemology and Metaphysics," *Discovering Reality* (Boston: D. Reidel Publishing Company, 1983).

6. Monique Gadan writes in the introduction of the book she edits, *Women of the Mediterranean* (London: Zed Books, 1986), 1, "The family structures . . . of the Mediterranean . . . are characterized by the power of the extended family over individuals, with its greater weight falling on women for whom motherhood is defined as the sole means of fulfillment; by the power of the mother who obtains social recognition for her function as reproducer (not only of the lineage but also the patriarchal ideology) by the power of men over women who are excluded from the political arena and confined to domestic matters; by the position of women as stakes of power for men, eternally objects and means, never (or rarely) subjects except to be subjected, deprived of *speech* (emphasis mine) save to gossip . . . women of whom men are suspicious and whom they dare not love too much."

7. Jane Schneider, "Of Vigilance and Virgins," 19, in *Ethnology* vol. 10, no. 3 (1971), contrasts the Islamic and Christian religions practiced by Mediterranean societies, in Northern Africa and Middle Eastern pastoralists, and in southern Italy, Western Sicily, and Southern Spain in their treatment of women who are considered an intrinsic part of men's patrimony and thus "the repository of family lineage and honor." Schneider writes, Islam "dignifies women by shrouding them in veils, Christianity removes the veils and offers the Virgin Mary as a model of feminine virtue. . . . [Further,] Mediterranean pastoralists (and cultivators) they do not ritually avoid their wives, but they find many occasions to express a lack of trust in them. Indeed, there is a spread assumption that women—specially in the role of wife—are victims of their sexuality and potential traitors to the household—'Cows of Satan' or 'devil's net' . . . The Sarakatsani men identify themselves with sheep, which are descended from God, while women are identified with goats, descended from the devil."

8. About the family as "the first form of social organization," Mitchell, *Woman's Estate*, 156, says that even though "the family *has changed* since its first appearance, it *has also remained* (my emphasis)—not just an idealist concept but as crucial ideological and economic unit with a certain rigidity and autonomy despite all its adaptations." On the other hand, the ideology of the family, as Mitchell, ibid., signals, is "individualism, freedom and equality; while the social and economic reality can be very much at odds with such a concept."

9. Magdala Velásquez Toro, "Condición Jurídica y Social de la Mujer" (Women's social and legal conditions), in Mejia, ed., *Nueva Historia*, 9–66, explains that well into the twentieth century, education for Colombian women was expected to deal only with issues relevant to the female functions of mothers and wives. The few women who were able to attend school learned religion, reading, writing, a little geography and history, and everything possible about cooking, sewing, and home

economics. The spheres pertaining to men's and women's education were very well differentiated.

10. See Frechette, *El Poder Compartido* (1999), 231–60. In this exciting book, the author interviews outstanding Colombian women of the 1990s. Noemí Sanin, the woman who almost won the 1998 presidential election, describes being the third child among fifteen offspring, all of whom went to college after finishing high school. Their mother was a teacher who considered the education of her daughters and sons the most important issue in the family's life.

11. On the topic of what is expected of Colombian women, see Paternostro, *In the Land of Man and God*; see also Rosa María Gil and Carmen Inoa Vazquez, *The María Paradox: How Latinas Can Merge Old World Traditions with New World Self-Esteem* (New York: Perigee Press, 1996).

12. My father's driver, who is forty-five years old, has two daughters, sixteen and seven years old, who go to a nun's school since there, he says, "they will be taken good care of against the dangers they face in the outside world." And my father's accountant, age thirty-eight, also has his sixteen-year-old daughter in a nun's school because he thinks "girls are taken care of there and are better disciplined."

13. Mitchell, *Woman's Estate*, 100, considers the family a cultural creation and thinks that its image is one of "peace and plenty, but which, just like the 'image of the true woman,' the image of the true family can be deceptive and in actuality both [images] may be sites of violence and despair."

14. On this subject, Paternostro, *In the Land of Man and God,* passim, discusses the issues of women's bodies and virginity as constraints for women's well-being; also, on the same subject, see Thomas, *Los Estragos.*

15. Mary Douglas writes on women's so-called polluting powers, especially in connection with menstruation, in *Purity and Danger* (London: Routledge and Kegan, 1966). "Pollution" is defined as anything that is different, out of order, or alien.

16. On the fear Mediterranean men have of women and their bodies, see Stanley Brandes, "Like Wounded Stags: Male Sexual Ideology in an Andalucian Town," in Sherry Ortner and Harriet Whitehead, eds., *Sexual Meanings* (New York: Cambridge University Press, 1981), P; on the taming of female gender as nature, see Sherry Ortner, "Is Female to Male as Nature is to Culture?" in Rosaldo and Lamphere, eds., *Woman, Culture and Society,* 67–87.

17. See Mitchell, *Psychoanalysis*, ibid., 395–96. On the symbolic power of the penis, Brandes, ibid., 230, says, "The locus of power and will, of emotions and strength, lies within the male genitalia. Men speak as if they are impelled to act according to opinions and desires that originate in their testicles or penis."

18. See Luce Irigaray, *This Sex Which Is Not One* (Ithaca: Cornell University Press, 1985); Alev Lytle Croutier, *Harem: The World Behind the Veil* (New York: Abbeville Publishers, 1989).

19. Women have been considered symbolically as objects to be exchanged between clans. On this subject, Irigaray, *This Sex,* 176, writes, "As commodities, women

are thus two things at once: utilitarian objects and bearers of value. . . . Woman thus has value only in that she can be exchanged." See Rubin, "Traffic"; Marcel Mauss, *The Gift* (New York: W. W. Norton and Company, 1967).

20. See James Joyce, *Portrait of the Artist as a Young Man* (New York: Bantam Books, 1992), chapter 3, to understand how Catholic spiritual retreats are structured, what their goals are, and how they discipline Catholics; see also Uta Ranke-Heinemann, *Eunuchs for the Kingdom of Heaven: Women, Sexuality and the Catholic Church* (New York: Doubleday, 1990); Joanne Carlson Brown and Carol Bohn, "For God So Loved the World?" in Brown and Bohn, eds., *Christianity, Patriarchy and Abuse: A Feminist Critique* (Ann Arbor, MI: UMI Research, 1987), 3. These authors write about women's inferior status in patriarchal society: "Our full personhood as well as our rights have been denied us. We have been labeled the sinful ones, the other; and even when we are led in, so to speak, we are constantly reminded of our inferior status through language, theological concepts of original sin, and perpetual virginity—all of which relate to sex, for which, of course, women are responsible."

21. I must note that these eight participants who kindly participated in the focus group are extraordinary. They are human scientists in their own right. Apart from the Sisters having educated them with talks and conferences, she also had them finish their high school, and they were to do a short term project at the university on social services. Each of these women is instructing sixteen other women.

22. Daly in *Gyn/Ecology*, 39, speaks about the usefulness of radical feminism as it "affirms our original birth, our original source, movement, surge of living. . . . Radical feminism releases the inherit dynamic in the mother-daughter relationship toward *friendship*, which is *strangled* in the male-mastered system (emphasis mine). Radical feminism means that mothers do *not* demand the Self-sacrifice of daughters, and that daughters do not demand this of their mothers (emphasis in the original). . . . What both demand of each other is courageous which is mythic in its depths, which is spell-breaking and myth-making process."

23. The technology of bio-power or power over the body, says Foucault, can be applied to older women as they are "surveillants" of younger women, but also surveillants of themselves as they are located in a special space, the "panopticon," where guardians observe the prisoners, but also observe themselves on behalf of maintaining the political patriarchal power of the society. See *Discipline and Punish*, 198–200.

24. Of the "diabolical aspect" of control and power over human beings (bodies), Foucault writes, "In this form of management, power is not totally entrusted to someone who would exercise it alone, over others, in an absolute fashion; rather, this machine [the panopticon] is one in which everyone is caught, those who exercise the power as well as those who are subjected to it." In *The Foucault Reader*. Paul Rubinow, ed. (New York: Pantheon Books, 1984), 156.

25. Jana Svehlova on the issue of women accepting and forgiving their "wardens" relates it to the Stockholm syndrome. The dictionary of Political Sciences

explains this syndrome as the "[e]motional bond between hostages and their captors when hostages are held by long periods of time under emotionally straining circumstances." I am very grateful to Jana for this insightful and provoking commentary as it fits quite well with what I have been describing in the last section of this chapter.

CHAPTER EIGHT

Oppression, Violence, and Discrimination Against Women in Colombia

[I]t . . . bears witness to women's desire to lift the weight of what is sacrificial in the social contract from their shoulders, to nourish our societies with a more flexible and free discourse, one able to name what has thus far never been an object of circulation in the community: the enigmas of the body, the dreams, secret joys, shames, hatreds of the second sex.

Julia Kristeva, "Women's Time" (1981: 32)

Maria Isabel: "Tied Together in a Knot"

Introduction

Violence, physical, psychological, and emotional, starts in the family. Set expectations and rigid rules regarding propriety and what a young woman may think, plus rejection by her parents, lead interviewee Maria Isabel into a disastrous marriage. Her husband, twenty years her senior, exploits her vulnerability for his own perversions. Virginal purity, an issue for both her parents and spouse, creates psychological havoc for the young woman. Eventually, she escapes through psychoanalysis, her studies, and a network of friends.

Chapter 7 marks and encapsulates what has been seen in all circumstances throughout this study, that what happens in the family—a woman's socialization—sets her up for a life of oppression, a life without respect or self-respect, and illness. Patriarchal violence against women is global. It impacts women in their health, marriages, employment, education, economic advancement, as well as in the religious and legal systems, with repercussion in the woman's general well-being. It amounts to a major human rights crime.

Interview

"Let's start from the time when you were a little girl. What do you remember of your family life from childhood?"

"My parents complained—and more so, my mother—that I, with the help of nobody, had 'ruined myself.' These were the words she used on my twelfth birthday. It was the day on which I told myself that I now was able to reason and make decisions by myself. My mother's answer was simple: that I was bad and dirty because of my ability to understand different things from the usual ones young girls my age would know. Thus, declaring that I had the capacity to think meant, for my mother and father, that I was crazy, strange, unreasonable, and different. My mother thought I had ruined myself with strange ideas. Certainly, I agree that there is nothing more difficult than being responsible for one's actions. In other words, consciousness has consequences. There is nothing crazier than this idea, because responsibility entails loneliness. The result of self-awareness and liking to think was that I didn't belong in the context of my family. I did not fit in my parent's milieu because I never did what they wanted me to do—even though my parents didn't know what they wanted me to be or do! Furthermore, they didn't know what to do with me! I was like a thorn in their side, an obstacle in their lives.

"The problem that arose when I came into their lives made them reject me. They didn't reject my three brothers. If I had been a boy, things undoubtedly would have been different for me. The ideas my parents had of what I needed to be to satisfy them kept changing. My parents had one approach to handling me: discipline. Rules for them covered everything—even love. Because I was a girl, my mother thought subconsciously that she had to share my father with me, which she didn't want to do. And because I was a girl, my father was afraid of expressing love for me. He feared his own feelings, his normal incestuous drives that he thought would become uncontrollable. Because of this fear of loving me, my father abandoned me. His Catholic, *machista* education prevented him from seeing the different kinds of love that exist. Love and sexuality were tightly interconnected for my father; they were tied together in a knot. He couldn't differentiate between the two. This issue frightened him terribly and turned him into a spiritual cripple."

"How is what you just told me, Maria Isabel, related to violence?"

"I was left alone by my parents and my brothers. It was as if I had been thrown out of the family, because I was different. My only wish was to receive approval and affection from my father and mother. I told my parents in many different ways: 'Please love me! Look at ME! I am nice!' My brothers, who never asked for love or approval, received all they needed to grow up happily. Perhaps I also represented a threat to both my parents, although in different ways. For my father, I was another women for him to love. For my mother, I was competition in terms of sharing my father's love. I simply disturbed their peace of mind. Because I was conscious of all these feelings, I spoke daringly and clearly about everything. My voice was different from that of my parents. Because they treated me like a stranger, I did not love them. The only means they had for controlling me were strict rules, and they also declared that I was 'dirty' and 'unbearable' because I failed to follow their rules. I had a *lack* in me that disturbed the family tranquility. I didn't follow rules, it was understood, simply because I was different because of this *lack*. From an early age, I knew that I disliked my family life."

"Can you relate your childhood to the life you led as a married woman?"

"Yes. My ex-husband, who was forty-three years old at the time we married, while I was twenty-three, offered me what I truly lacked: a good father and mother. Of course, he felt my sadness—the absence of love—and later took advantage of it to perpetuate his perversions. His game was ambiguous; he said he wanted to protect what was most outstanding in me: my virginity! But at the same time, he kept telling me about his love affairs with women who were able to give him what I could not, precisely because of my 'purity.' For him I was pure; for my parents, I was dirty. They represented two sides of the same coin. For a year, this man worked on me psychologically. Little by little, he subdued my spirit and made me believe I was his slave and he, my master. I was his confidant in regard to sexual activities he performed with other women. He told me about those experiences in great detail. He made me believe that if others (like my parents) knew about the things he told me, I would lose face in front of them.

"Finally, he asked me to marry him. He said he wanted me to be all his. By this time, I thought that he owned me and that I was lost. I made a good target for him. He wanted me to have sex with other women while he watched, because he was impotent and could only become aroused by watching women perform. This situation is very difficult to explain to someone who hasn't gone through something similar. This man manipulated my mind in such a way that I believed all the things he kept saying. I believed, for example, that because I listened to him, I became really dirty. Finally, my mother's spoken augury, and my father's silent one, turned out to be true.

"After we married, I had three experiences of the kind I just mentioned: sexual activity with women while he watched and masturbated. My husband forced me to do so and threatened that he would tell other people if I didn't do as he wished. He also argued that everything is permitted between husband and wife and because the holy sacrament of marriage encompasses everything that occurs in that relationship, nothing can be judged wrong or bad. On several occasions I thought of killing myself. I felt lost and filthy. At times, I also fantasized about killing him. How? By simply pushing him out of a window. My ex-husband was spiritually crippled, but in a much worse way than my father, since this man was a pervert and my father was not. Fernando, my ex-husband, was never satisfied with what I did for him, be it sexual or otherwise, just like my parents weren't satisfied with the way I was as a person. The more I did to please him, the more he demanded."

"How did you survive, as a child and as your ex-husband's wife?"

"As a child, I survived with the help of my studies. I was always excellent in school. Nevertheless, my parents didn't show any interest in my accomplishments. They paid no attention when I showed them my grades. They simply didn't care. When I was married to Fernando, I helped myself by concentrating on being an excellent wife and a good mother to his two children (who had lost their mother). Those roles helped me go on living with some kind of dignity. By proving I could do things well, even though the people whose love I wanted would not give it to me, I tried to demonstrate, through accomplishments, that I was good, intelligent, and deserving of love. This attitude saved me, because I developed my mind through thinking, analyzing, learning, and finding a network of supportive friends, as well as listening to my inner voice. When I was a girl, the parents of a friend kind of adopted me. They always listened to what I had to say and approved of me, no matter what I did. They applauded when I got good marks and recognized my talents. In short, they loved me for what I was. Later on, I met you and your sister. Both of you respected me as a human being. You were older, but you gave me recognition as a person who had something to say, whose word you considered valuable, and who was worthy of love. I always looked around for help. Later, when I was married to that man, I knew that only someone who treated mental illness could help me. I went to see a psychoanalyst, who, in four months, helped me to get out of my catatonic state, leave my husband, and start restructuring my life in a different way. I was able to understand that I was *not* dirty and had a right to live and be happy.

"My parents and ex-husband were similar in the way they guarded the family context and established rules to be followed in the home. Everything that went on within the family milieu was considered sublime and had to be protected. My mother was the gatekeeper of my father's sacred chamber, of his word and law. The rules were his. She spoke for him; he was silent. She was in charge of having things done the way he wanted them. Our home was an altar, a holy place where I didn't have a place. Because my mother belonged to 'god' (my father), she had access to the heaven from which he ruled. Later, Fernando—who was also like a god in that he was much older, more powerful, and, presumably, wiser than I—became the divine authority figure in my life. I had to call him *senor* [sir]. He had the power to dominate my life the way my father did, but my father exercised his will through my mother as an intermediary. In the eye of these three people, my parents and my ex-husband, I was just a slave. My mother, with whom I shared gender, had a different position. She had access to him, because her responsibility was to protect his word. She also had power over me, because she was my mother. By comparison, I was nothing much. In the name of the family or of marriage, nothing was considered unlawful. Violence diluted by sacred rules was permissible.

"Sometimes it is still hard for me to believe that I will be successful in any job I do. I no longer worry about love or relationships. I finally understand that I can be loved because of what I am as a human being, but at times I remain insecure and I don't have sufficient confidence. The difference is that now I am conscious of the problem and know the time has come for me to change my life. We have the power in our own hands to make things change. Nothing is impossible to reach! I am a survivor; yes, I am! As a child, I had good friends who loved me, and I had my studies. As an adult, I had the luck to meet women like you who listened to me; I had my psychoanalyst, who rescued me from madness and death. I always tried to speak about my fears, because I lived in terror. By speaking out, I was able to face what I was experiencing. Today, when I see violence approaching, I get away immediately. Now, I am in control. I can handle my parents, even though I won't be able to change their minds. Our relationship has changed and is now quite good. My life is different, because instead of fear and hate, it is filled with pleasure and love. I am happy. I know that what I received as a child was bad. Our culture accepts terrible rules on behalf of maintaining the family. For a woman, many such rules and codes are terribly unfair. I don't think things have changed much for women in our country."

Without equality and peace to enable personal development and well-being,[1] society is unhealthy and underdeveloped; its members find themselves in calamitous conditions.

The Abandoned Rights of Women

Discrimination brings unhappiness, illness, and underdevelopment. Development is not only economic—it includes every aspect of human reproductive life. Arvon Fraser (1987: 94) states that "total development [means the] political, economic, social, cultural—and also the physical, moral, intellectual, and educational growth of the human person." Development is nothing more than a state of harmony and equilibrium in the life of human beings, within their culture and society: "Health is by no means only a question of curing disease . . . it also means physical, emotional and mental well-being" (Cottingham 1983: 143). Discrimination is simply an obstacle to health, since it promotes stress and its consequences, with the resulting mental and physical illness (Fraser 1987; PAHO 1998) and concomitant inequality with disruption of peace. And peace, as Jocelyn Scutt (1996–1997:110) says, "is not a destination. It is a way of traveling."[2]

Recent reports from the World Bank (1999) and the Organization of the American States (1997–1998) demonstrate precisely that violence, discrimination, and the general mistreatment of women in Latin American countries is so lamentable that women suffer chronic lack of respect, ill health, depression, and anxiety.[3] The 1999 report from the OAS is distressing in this regard, as it reveals a lack of human rights for women in Latin America. Although documents have been issued by international organizations such as the World Bank and the Organization of American States to advise governments on the problems women face, they are signed by people in power and little has been done to tackle the problems. Such detailed documents have not resulted in actions against these abuses. Unfortunately, not even education has helped to improve the deplorable situation women endure on a daily basis in this part of the world. States lack agendas with political visions of how to create strong or radical public policies on behalf of women's rights that will end oppression and violence against women. As Charlotte Bunch (1995: 12) says in her article "Transforming Human Rights from a Feminist Perspective," "The lack of understanding of women's rights as human rights is reflected in the fact that few governments are committed, in domestic or foreign policy, to women's equality as a basic human right." The issue of women's rights and needs is still kept in the shadow by governments, and is not considered important for legislating in their favor (Bunch 1995).

Violence against Women as a Health and Human Rights Issue

Lori Heise, who directs the Center for Health and Gender Equity (CHANGE), is a member of the Health and Development Policy Project (HDPP); she has dedicated many years to international research on women's health. Also noted for her extensive work in the area of gender-based violence[4] (Peters and Wolper 1995: 362), Heisi (1989: 1) says that violence against women "has recently been recognized as a legitimate human rights issue by the United Nations and by some governments." Despite the fact that oppression against women and girls is known to threaten high-quality public health, scant effort has been concentrated on this concern as a "public health issue, and even less to tackling its underlying causes." In 1993, according to Heisi (1989: 1), the United Nations Commission on the Status of Women gave out an official declaration of what violence against women included:

> The definition [of violence should] encompass, but not to be limited to, physical, sexual, and psychological violence occurring within the family and the community, including battering, sexual abuse of the female children, dowry-related violence, marital rape, female genital mutilation and other traditional practices harmful to women, non-spousal violence, violence related to exploitation, sexual harassment, and intimidation at work, in educational institutions, and elsewhere, trafficking in women, forced prostitution, and violence perpetrated or condoned by the state. (Stamatopoulou 1995: 40)

It is obvious that oppression and violence complement each other, and that they are, unfortunately, prevalent throughout the world. Women's human rights are based on women's right to enjoy a happy and fruitful life, free from "inhuman and degrading treatment concerning the high percentage of maternal mortality" caused by abortion and/or sexual and reproductive health, and any other kind of violent or inhuman treatment that threatens their human, and psychological integrity (Cabal, Lemaitre, Roa 2001: 22–43, 472–84).

The lives of those subjected to the punishments mentioned above are severely and irrevocably damaged. Nevertheless, oppression and violence continue to be perpetrated by men against women and against men, as well. "Violence against women is global, cross cultural, and epidemic . . . by fundamentalists of all patriarchal religions" (Morgan 1997: 7). Why, one asks, do men oppress women? Why do they enjoy pornography and prostitution, which degrade women's integrity? Why does patriarchy focus desire towards hatred, killing, and harming others, instead of encouraging love, life, and peace? What is it within the patriarchal system that allows this violent human behavior? Are there other patriarchal "roots" that are disguised and have not yet been uncovered?

Heisi (1989: 2) reiterates a long-standing point: "Violence against women has evolved in part from a system of gender relations that posits that men are superior to women." She goes on to say, "The idea of male dominance—even male ownership—is present in most societies and is reflected in their laws and customs." The interviewees reinforce this point. Esperanza, for example, relates how she was told from an early age that her "roles [in life] and work were related to being a woman. Female duties are not male duties. Woman's place is the home. "When I rebelled and cried, my mother's only words were that I had to learn how to cook for a man!" Discrimination starts in the heart of the family. Esperanza continues her saga and contrasts herself with her brothers:

> My brothers didn't have to cook, clean, or help my mother do household chores. They never gave us a hand. They didn't have to do anything. Of course not! They were males! For example, I used to get up at three in the morning to help my mother make the *arepas* [cornbread] for breakfast. At four o'clock, the brother who followed me in age, and I, we went to fetch the milk. . . . I was ten years old, he was eight. Apart from fetching the milk, Pedro had nothing else to do in the house. After we finished breakfast at six o'clock, I had to help clean the house, make the beds, cook for the family, help feed the animals— my mother and I we did all of these jobs together.

This interviewee gives a detailed account of how the sexual division of labor in the family works: what is expected of girls and what is expected of boys. Further, even when boys have to work at an early age, to help support the family, they are held in high regard, waited on by mothers and sisters, and allowed to enjoy leisure time—none of which is the case for mothers and daughters. "Female duties are not male duties," says Esperanza.

As all have attested, girls are taught to serve men, and being under a form of "house arrest" is a facet of such training. Girls are excluded from the outside world that men can explore at will. Also, boys, like adult males, supervise the whereabouts of young and/or adult females. Girls, preferably, should not go out alone. Unlike girls, boys are free to move at their ease with little supervision. Usually, certain places are forbidden to females. Young women might go out at night but they are expected to be accompanied by an adult or a male member of the family. Juana is also explicit on this point: "Married women cannot go out alone, especially to social meetings. A woman usually goes out with another woman. If she has an invitation to a party and the husband isn't invited, the wife goes with her mother or any other adult woman."

María del Carmen, age thirty, who had a fine education, tells in further detail why and how she and her two sisters were secluded within their home when they entered adolescence.

> What we had to be or do was implicit in the rules we were given. For example, girls couldn't go anywhere alone. We always had to be chaperoned. My father didn't like us to go roaming outside the home. . . . When it comes to women, my father is a hard, inflexible person. We had to be chaperoned by our broth-

ers. Until I was twenty-one years old, I couldn't go out alone. My brothers were as strict as my father. We were never unsupervised. At fifteen years of age, I had a boyfriend who occasionally came to visit me in the evening. By nine o'clock, they would tell him to leave! Usually I had to receive male friends in the garden behind the gate that separated the garden from the street. We conversed there; that was all we did. By contrast, my brothers could go and come as they pleased. They went out alone, beginning at an early age.

These interviewees portray what it is to be male or female, and the type of menaced life a female child or a young or adult woman might have to endure in Colombia. Heisi (1989: 2) maintains that such social violence is the result of gender roles that construct power relations between the sexes, based on the belief that men have the right to "control women's behavior." She affirms that gender roles and power relations have to be challenged in order to alter them, so that damage to women's physical and mental health created by oppression and suffering, may be eliminated.

Diane Bell and Renate Klein (1996: xx) give a definition of a healthy woman who fits well with the assertion that violence and oppression destroy the health of the individual who suffers them. A healthy woman "is physically safe, economically secure, and is able to enjoy her human rights to the full." Manuela's story, a case in point, shows how this young woman met with physical violence in her own household. Manuela's mother worked, which gave her opportunities to look for other perspectives in life. But her husband did not agree to her not being a full-time housewife and mother. Also, he considered that it was a bad example for Manuela and her sister. Thus, Manuela's father tried to awaken his daughter's "maternal instincts" each time he had the opportunity. Once, in a terrible argument, Manuela told her father that she was too young at fifteen to consider motherhood. Indeed, she told him to keep quiet because she did not respect his word, since she knew that he was a womanizer.

> I made it clear to him that I knew that he went out with prostitutes or other women who were not my mother. . . . Thus, I decided to pack my suitcase and leave my home. When my father saw what I was doing, he took a broomstick and started running after me. When he caught me, he hit me very hard with the broom. This violent episode marked me tremendously. It marked my relationship with my father for the worse. I realized my father could be very violent and I felt rejected by him.

How brave for a young girl to confront her father, as Manuela did, and absurd for a father to coerce a fifteen-year-old to desire to have babies. In reality, he objected to his daughter's self-expression and determination—and her telling the truth.

As was stressed earlier, the differences between boys and girls are accentuated, from an early age, through household chores (or lack thereof), freedom to socialize unsupervised outside the home, religious guidance and other forms of socialization. Subtle patterns of behavior prescribed by parents help establish gender identity when children are quite young. Religion does not necessarily promote such conduct, although it may reinforce the gender dichotomy. Religion influences, naturally, all practicing Catholics. Rules and codes that women and men follow are culturally dictated and enforced by society and all its related institutions, but principally by the family and the Catholic Church.

Important to keep in mind, "violence against women is not an inherent part of 'maleness' but a function of socially constructed norms of acceptable behavior" (Heisi 1989: 29). Thus, the roots of men's attitudes and chaotic behavior can be analyzed, criticized, and understood in order to enable modification of destructive behaviors. Simultaneously, women can be empowered by education, by raising awareness, by increasing their economic rights and power, and by allowing them to make decisions regarding their lives and their persons. In other words, women will attain complete autonomy only when they are able to enjoy human rights and respect for themselves and their lives.[5] The personal boundaries of any human being are sacred; they must be honored.

Women have been, and still are, violated in their bodies, in their sexual integrity, and their autonomy. Patriarchal culture has misused women's bodies and continues to commit violence against women through pornography, prostitution, rape, incest, and battering. Esperanza tells of the violence she constantly received from her father. She cries as she speaks.

My father never stopped screaming at me. He always found a reason to yell. Even today I don't know why he shouted at me continuously and was unable to address me in a nice way. He treated me in a hateful, violent way. This is what I remember: my father always screamed at me. I always thought—and still do—that my father didn't love me. I grew up wondering and worrying about this sad fact. Was there anything wrong with me? . . . Father treated my brothers differently. Perhaps because I was a girl and the eldest, he treated me with indifference and harshness; his behavior toward my brothers was different. He cared for them; he didn't care for me. On the contrary he despised me. No matter what happened in our home and irrespective of what I did, my father found an excuse to be against me and favor my brothers. He preferred them. I told myself that probably the problem was because I was female. I considered my-self Cinderella.

This testimony clearly depicts the violence and ineradicable hurt to which fe-male children may be exposed in many families. They are accorded little re-spect, consideration, and appreciation simply because they were born females. Says Esperanza, "When I was fifteen, I kept repeating to myself: 'Why the hell wasn't I born a boy?'" The circumstances within the family can become so vi-olent that young women often consider suicide, as was the case with Esperanza. "One day my father was so terrible to me that I decided to kill myself. Thanks to my mother I didn't. I was going to swallow a bottle of aspirins."

Some women experience more limitations than others. Their testimony witnesses much violence, mistreatment, and discrimination. Once more, we have Esperanza's narration of the continuous mistreatment she received from her father:

> He started beating me up when I was hardly five years old. He beat me with anything at hand: a *machete*, a stick, his hands. When I was small, he beat me because I had to help my mother in the kitchen. Later, he beat me because he said I was a "bad woman" and he wanted me to marry a friend of his, whom I considered an old man; I refused. My mother *never* protected me from my fa-ther. It makes one wonder how women can resist such treatment and how they have accepted such roles to begin with.

Rosalia speaks of the miserable time she had with the first man she knew: "I was very unhappy . . . because he used to drink a lot, and then, he used to beat me. This man thought I was unfaithful to him." And Dora is still more explicit about her mistreatment by her husband:

> I wasn't prepared for married life; I didn't know anything about raising babies or being a housewife. I didn't know anything about men. People had told me that men were bad, but this statement had sexual connotations for me. I never enjoyed our intimate relations. My husband didn't know how to please me. How can a man go directly to the physical act without a kiss or a caress? This process was terrible for me—like a violation of my body, of my intimacy. . . . My husband beat me. He was wild, a savage. He used to attack me for the smallest incidents . . . he hit me all over my body and face. The bruises lasted up to a month. I was just eighteen years old (and my mother was dead).

Of the women interviewed, all had been beaten or verbally abused by their fathers, mothers, husbands, or all—with the exception of María del

Carmen and Juliana, who enjoy a close relationship with their fathers, and Dora and Gloria, who didn't have a father when they were growing up. And Juana tells how her mother, like Aleja's, used to beat her with a leather whip they used to harness the cattle.

Also, several of the women, as children, saw fathers physically abusing mothers; nine of the women said their mothers were always frightened and humbly obeyed the husband's orders. Several of the women were present when their parents had terrible fights. Almost all of the interviewees feared their fathers in one way or another; all, with the exception of Juliana, were told that men were evil and women needed to protect themselves.

As mentioned, girls were taught to grow up in fear of men who want to take advantage of women and harm them. The nature of the danger is rarely specified, but the unspoken idea of rape is ever-present. Flor recalled that girls "were responsible for not allowing our boyfriends to touch us." Most of the women were told that women's bodies must be cared for, because if a girl lost her purity or became pregnant, she would be rejected and ostracized by her family and community.[6]

When investigating actions and events that have afflicted Colombian women and their human integrity, one must keep in mind that everything personal is political.[7] In order to discover the ways in which the lives and well-being of women in Colombia are affected by the oppression, discrimination, and violence they experience, it is important to uncover the issues that bring violence against women. It then becomes necessary to define the kind of power[8] Colombian men have over women: by law, religion, and practice within the family.

As shown above, one such basic mode of power is *machismo*, which is compounded with patriarchy and intertwined with *marianismo*. In Birgit Brock-Utne's article, "Women and Third World Countries—What Do We Have in Common?" (1989: 500), she emphasizes that patriarchy is a worldwide system uniting men with all kinds of privileges: "Patriarchy can be defined as a set of social relations between men, which have material base, and which, through hierarchy, establish or create interdependence or solidarity among men that enables them to dominate women." Patriarchal ideology is simply "a universal value system," write Rowland and Klein (1997: 14). Thus, the oppression of women is a universal fact that has its own particular cultural variations, and is sometimes well camouflaged and quite invisible. It can be invisible not only to those who study cultural issues such as health and education to develop public policies, but also to those who suffer mistreatment (see Morgan 1984). Ruth Bleir defines patriarchy as "the historic system of male dominance; a system committed to the maintenance and reinforcement of male hegemony in all aspects of life—personal and private privilege and power as well as public privilege and power" (cited in Rowland and Klein 1997: 14). It can be said that men's narcissistic desire for omnipotence or might is satisfied through patriarchal ideology, which accomplishes its control through social institutions, politics, and legal and religious laws. Control is also achieved by manipulation of the economic political strata of society, the marginalization of women from the public sector, and making women responsible for the private sphere of the family.[9] Women's bodies are also convenient objects of control, using such vehicles as health issues, prostitution, and pornography (see Rowland and Klein 1997).

Ideas about Origin

Patriarchy, which rules with the Father's Law—organized by the incest taboo—thus organizes society (Rubin 1975).[10] Nevertheless, "The Oedipus complex. . .which fashions the appropriate forms of sexual individuals," giving to men "full control over the sexual destinies of their female kinswomen," subordinating and oppressing them, makes women ill (Rubin 1975: 184–85, 189, 196). For Lacan (1977: 67), this idea is clear and simple: the Father prescribes the Law that defines the origin of culture and language into which the person is born. Woman, because of the symbolic "lack" that patriarchal culture defines, is controlled through her sexuality, and is taught to repress her human nature (Butler 1990).[11]

María Isabel makes this point herself: "I had a *lack* in me that disturbed the family tranquility. I didn't follow the rules, it was understood, simply because I was different because of this *lack*. Undoubtedly, I was different from my brothers: I did not have a 'penis.'"[12] And María Isabel continues,

> I was left alone by my parents and my brothers. It was as if I had been thrown out of the family because I was different. . . . My parents didn't reject my three brothers. If I had been a boy, things undoubtedly would have been different for me. . . . My parents had one approach to handling me: discipline. Rules for them covered everything—even love.

Her much older husband abused her human integrity by making her have sex with other women, as he watched, for his own sexual satisfaction. This man mistreated her as much as her parents did when she was a child. When María Isabel thought of killing him, she realized how mentally disturbed she was and asked for help from a psychoanalyst. She underwent psychoanalytic therapy until she was able to separate from the man who had replaced her parents in a torturing relationship.

Male Supremacy, Female Subordination, and Socialization

As many social and human scientists acknowledge, society is greatly influenced by gender ideology, which directly affects human behavior, role stratification, the division of labor and/or the relations between the sexes through the socialization of children. These analyses have shown how culture helps to establish male supremacy and female subordination in society. Therefore, it is important to understand how the microstrata of society (i.e., the "private sphere") functions; specifically, how the institution of the family influences women's lives. The aim is to understand what prevents Colombian women from leading "a satisfactory personal life" (Lavrin 1987: 114), and what can enable the raising of such women's consciousness, which has been in the feminist agenda for a long time (Lavrin, 1987: 120), a solid foundation from which social cultural change can begin to take place.[13]

Every civilization imposes its own rules and systems for interpreting life. Universally, the family is the single most important unit of a society, within which cultural codes are applied and individuals educated, according to specified conventions. The French philosopher and psychoanalyst Hélène Cixous (1981: 44) works from this premise, arguing in "Castration or Decapitation?" that one needs to work "on the couple if we are to deconstruct and transform culture." For Cixous, it is within the female/male pair that the cultural struggle begins and persists. It is the binary opposition woman/man that implies that the female is the incoherent, the hysterical, the natural, chaotic one whereas the male is the intelligent, reasonable human being. Furthermore, woman is labeled as "passivity," and the male as "activity" (Moi 1997: 110). Since the couple is symbolically the terrain and the space of cultural struggle, it is also the "space demanding, insisting, on a complete transformation in the relation of the other" (Cixous 1981: 44).

Of course, in Colombia too, the family has, for centuries, served as the "crucible of identity" and gender socialization, as we have seen. Women have occupied a primary role within the family and, thus, have been primary socializers. In the Forum of the Americas in Guadalajara (IDB 1995: 215–18), there was a consensus that in Latin American cultures, girls are taught, at a very young age, that they will one day become the nerve center of a household. As shown, little girls in Colombia learn that because they are precious and delicate, they are constantly guarded. Girls realize that they are different; life will never be the same for them as it is for boys. The safest place for female children, generally speaking, is inside the home with mothers and other women, as the women interviewed have testified.

Submissiveness, passivity, docility, and dependency have been the preferred feminine traits. Noemí Sanin, in her presidential campaign of 1998, claimed that those feminine qualities would appeal to the public, as a sure way for her to win the elections. Thus, she used them continuously, as a reminder of what a woman is. In the 2002 presidential campaign, for some reason, Ms. Sanin did not mention those appealing female characteristics.

The features of femininity, as an invention by men, are imagined inherent qualities. The notion of what constitutes attractive behavior is used to limit female potential. In keeping with the theory, modesty, virginity, and abnegation were praised, and they still are today.[14] Becoming "feminine," a woman is expected to obey and be quiet, sweet and delicate, well-groomed, and careful in her use of language—all of which rests on her silence. And as Barbara Ehrenreich and Deirdre English explain (2005: 29),

> The romantic construction of woman is as artificial as the sixteen-inch waists and three-foot-wide hooped skirts popular in the mid-nineteenth century. Economic man is rational; therefore romantic woman is intuitive, emotional, and incapable of quantitative reasoning. Economic man is self-interested; she is self-effacing, even masochistic . . .a creature who was supposed to be all that is "human" (as opposed to "economic") and ends up being subhuman, more like a puppy than a priestess.

Dora, another of the interviewees remembers, "My mother's main concern was to teach us, her daughters, about all those delicate things that would make us become the desired woman. . . . We simply copied her." In the fourth part of Simone de Beauvoir's *The Second Sex* (1952: 267–424), the author explains the process used to turn little girls into docile adults. Similarly, in South America, females have typically been treated like intermediate beings, somewhere between males and eunuchs, thought to be naturally inferior to men.[15] Women are not encouraged to develop the traits beneficial for men—autonomy, transcendence, and power. Soledad was allowed to do men's activities, such as driving a truck. She attended meetings with her father and her father's male friends. But, she had to be silent.

So-called "female qualities" actually inhibit vibrant living and exalt women as ethereal beings.[16] Women have been approached as objects to be manipulated by others, rather than as subjects with ideas of their own. Because a "decent woman" is taught that "she must try to please," girls do not search for personal identity: they have "renounced autonomy." A desirable woman is called "doll," *muñeca*—in other words, something inanimate, immature, inhuman, and insubstantial to be toyed with, cuddled, or consumed—not a serious, grown-up "worthy of liberty" (De Beauvoir 1952: 280).[17]

Colombian girls are taught to flaunt "feminine wiles" as weapons for trapping men; tears, flirting, illness, sensuousness, and ingenuity have been part of the repertoire used against men.[18] Women employ deceptive practices to bolster themselves in the struggle between the sexes. Soap operas, commercial ads, and beauty contests depict how Colombian women should behave, to comply with what is expected of them. Soledad describes well what is expected of women by society in general:

> I see the idea of a woman being like a "pure" object, which cannot be stained, bringing her a bad future. In the end, the idea is that women are only good for procreation, keeping the house clean for husbands and children, and serving them unconditionally. *We could be compared to a chair!* Yes, they give us everything that fulfills our material needs, like dresses, shoes, jewelry, and comfort. They keep telling us how beautiful we are, how well-dressed and elegant we look, but at the same time they take away what is substantial for our existence. They teach us to be superficial and make us believe, while growing up, that we are wonderful, that we own the world and that we can conquer that world. But when we try to do so, they stop us and say, "Yes, you are beautiful; you may have all the dresses and shoes you want; you can have all the dolls you wish to have, but that's all. Don't get other ideas: for that is all you have." They tell us all these things precisely because they don't consider we own a "thinking mind" to help us act in our behalf or allow us to express our opinions. We don't even have the right to feel.

The patriarchal philosophy does invade every part of a woman's existence. It invalidates her as a necessary contributor of her country's economy and development, and vital reproducers of other men and women who will benefit society. It subjugates her as a human being without rights of her own. Therefore, as her self-confidence is undermined, she is vulnerable. Within the home, where life should be respected and valued, a repetitive cycle of abuses, psychological and/or physical eradicates self-esteem bringing multiple kinds of illnesses. The cultural ideology holds a belief that all women, as daughters of Eve, are born potential prostitutes, who require protection from their natures. Unfortunately, the church furthers the demeaning patriarchal beliefs in its Catholic teachings; the law, in its biases. All of the above leaves women unprotected and abandoned by society and its laws. St. Augustine who once did love a woman with all his might, writes in his *Confessions*

(2002: 302) "so in the bodily realm woman is made for man. In mental power she has an equal capacity of rational intelligence, but by the sex of her body she is submissive to the masculine sex."

The culture's philosophical and ideological stranglehold on women has implications for national as well as the personal development of 52 percent the population of Colombia. How can a nation grow and thrive if half its population is held (to use Nora's words) in "forced enclosure?" For that matter, how can families prosper when husbands and wives start out on a basis of mistrust, fear, and disrespect?

As demonstrated, violence, abuse, discrimination, or any kind of inequity that women receive from their families or society in general, can be experienced in different ways. But the results will always be the same: fear, distress, nervousness, sadness, trauma, lack of self-esteem, desperation, anxiety, and covert or overt suffering, which harm women's lives and health (Cabal, Lemaitre, and Roa et al. 2001). Oppression, violence, and discrimination in Colombia take on innumerable facets. At times, mistreatment is obvious; other times, it may be concealed by care, affection, love, and an apparent protective interest on the part of a parent, the state or the church. Susana still complains of her father's indifference towards her and her life; Aleja, Clara, Rosie, Esperanza, Nora, Juana, and Manuela tell of the abuse, physical or otherwise, they received from father, mother, or both; and Soledad, Susana, Dora, and Rosalia from their husbands. In all cases, if the situation is analyzed, it is straightforward violence, lack of respect, and manipulation that work to the detriment of the women concerned, in the form of physical and psychological injury to them.

Notes

1. Scutt in "The Personal is Political" says about peace, "Without concern for the environment of the hearth, there can be no concern at all. Without peace on the home front, there can be no peace at all." In *Radically Speaking*, 109.

2. See H.B. Schopp-Shilling and C. Flitterman, *The Circle of Empowerment* (New York: The Feminist Press, 2007), in which they explain how the United Nations for the last twenty-five years has incessantly worked to eradicate all forms of discrimination against women through the adoption of the Universal Declaration of Women's Human Rights which was adopted at the General Assembly of the UN in 1982 and adopted the Convention on the Elimination of All Forms of Discrimination against Women, CEDAW. The book explains how the CEDAW Committee has worked incessantly on the elimination of all kinds of discrimination against women since 1982. The United States is still the only industrialized country that has not ratified CEDAW's Convention.

3. See R. Emerson Dobash and Russell Dobash, *Violence Against Wives* (New York: Free Press, 1979), for a sociological study of violence against women within the family nucleus.

4. In a document that Lori L. Heise prepared for the World Bank on "Violence Against Women: The Hidden Health Burden" (Washington, D.C.: The World Bank, 1994), ix, she says that "[g]ender-based violence—including rape, domestic violence, mutilation, murder, and sexual abuse—is a profound health problem for women across the globe. . . . Recent World Bank estimates of the global burden of disease indicate that in established market economies gender-based victimization is responsible for one out of every five healthy days of life lost to women of reproductive age . . . female-focused violence also represents a hidden obstacle to economic and social development."

5. See Mitchell, *Woman's Estate*; Susan Secheter, *Women and Male Violence* (Boston: South End Press, 1982); and Heisse, "The Global War Against Women," published in the *Washington Post* (Sunday, April 9, 1989: B4), where she writes, "Violence against women—including assault, mutilation, murder, infanticide, rape, and cruel neglect—is perhaps the most pervasive yet least recognized human-rights issue in the world . . . also a profound health problem sapping women's physical and emotional vitality."

6. Humm, *Dictionary of Feminist Theory*, 26–27, writes that "[t]heories about the sexuality of the body, power, and the Political control of women's bodies by patriarchy are central to feminism. In contemporary society, a woman is usually represented *only* as her body. Accurate information about the body is withheld from women, whose bodies are regarded in functional terms. . . . A feminist theory of the body is based on concepts of sexual self-determination."

7. See Kate Millet, *Sexual Politics* (New York: Avon Books, 1971), in which the idea of the "private is politics" was developed, a breaking point in the women's movement.

8. Ann Oakley defines power as "a daily presence in the asymmetrical nuclear family" in Kramarae and Treichler, *A Feminist Dictionary*, 351. Also, Humm's *Dictionary of Feminist Theory*, 217, says that theories of power for radical feminism are not adequate if they "do not take women's domination as a central theme and do not see this model for all forms of interpersonal domination. [For example,] the psychology of male power is expressed in cultural artifacts like pornography and in the sexual violation of women."

9. Frederick Engels, *The Origin of the Family, Private Property and the State*, Eleanor Burke Leacock, ed. (New York: International Publishers, 1985).

10. To understand Freud's theory of the Oedipus Complex and how it constructs gender, see Benjamin, *Bonds of Love* (1988); Mitchell, *Psychoanalysis and Feminism* (2000); Chodorow, *The Reproduction of Mothering* (1978); and Weedon, *Feminist Practice & Poststructuralist Theory*, 1987.

11. Pitt-Rivers, *Mediterranean Countrymen*, 45, explains in an anthropological way how females in Mediterranean cultures are sexually constricted. "[F]emale honor is

not entirely without a physiological basis . . . in that sexual purity relates to the maidenhead (hymen). . . . The male . . . lacks the physiological basis of sexual purity and risks the implication that his masculinity is in doubt if he maintains it." Purity in the male, as mentioned, means "castration" which does not "honor" him. Thus, "[t]he natural qualities of sexual potency or purity and the moral qualities associated with them provide the conceptual famework on which the system [of honor and shame] is constructed."

12. Mitchell, *Psychoanalysis and Feminism*, 320, explains the meaning Lacan gives to the phallus: "The phallus is the very mark of human desire; it is the expression of the wish for what is absent, for reunion (initially with the mother)." Through this desire the human individual becomes a speaking subject.

13. See Eisenstein, ed., *Capitalist Patriarchy*, for an understanding of how Socialist and Marxist feminism focus women's economic problems.

14. Hamington, *Hail Mary?* 149, reflects on how, in Western civilization the uneven socialization of females and males brings forth an idea of power relationships creating two different sites, one for the *weak* (females), and one for the *strong* (males). "Many suggest that such unequal socializations may contribute to the presence of the widespread violence perpetrated against women in *today's society*" (my emphasis).

15. See on this subject of female "mental castration" Ranke-Heineman, *Eunuchs for the Kingdom of Heaven* (1990).

16. These qualities relate to Mary as the model women in Latin America must follow. See Gil and Vasquez, *The María Paradox*.

17. Mitchell, *Woman's Estate*, 110, mentions how women "have been appropriated as sexual objects, as much as progenitors or producers." As she says, "contemporary sexual vocabulary bears eloquent witness to this—it is a comprehensive lexicon of reification—'bird, fruit, chick. . . .'" The later Marx, says Mitchell, was well aware of this habit, as he pointed out how marriage is incontestably a form "of *exclusive private property*" (my emphasis).

18. Mitchell, ibid., 162, offers an explanation of how oppression generally conditions women: "[I]t produces a tendency to small-mindedness, petty jealousy, irrational emotionality and random violence, dependency, competitive selfishness and possessions, passivity, a lack of vision and conservatism. . . . These qualities . . . are the result of the woman's objective conditions within the family itself embedded in a sexist society."

CHAPTER NINE

The Church: A New Virgin Mary for the Prelates and the Colombian People

On Women: Words of the Church Fathers

A tenet of Catholic theology is that human misery is caused by Eve's sin, disobedience to God, by eating the apple of the forbidden tree, and her urging Adam to do the same. Women, sly and cunning, tempt men to sin. To counter Eve, to advocate a decent place for women in the divine plan, the church elevated the Virgin Mary, the mother of Jesus, who gives milk with love and suffers in silence. This image of the Virgin not only defines the role of women allowed by the church, it serves also as a means to censure women, through the centuries, in the name of Eve. Here are statements representative of what the Fathers of the Church have said about woman and her feeble nature, excerpted from *Eunuchs for the Kingdom of Heaven* (Uta Ranke-Heinemann 1990).

St. Jerome

"[A] woman ceases to be a woman. . .[and may be called a man] when she wishes to serve Christ more than the world." (190)

"[T] he begetting of children is allowed in marriage, but feelings of sensual pleasure such as those had in the embraces of a harlot are damnable in a wife." (*On Ephesians 5:25*) (62)

"I do not deny that holy women are to be found among the wives, but only when they have stopped being mates, when they imitate virginal chastity

even in the constraining position that the married state brings with it."
(62–63)

St. Chrisostom

"There are in the world a great many situations that weaken the conscientiousness of the soul. First and foremost of these is dealings with women. In his concern for the male sex, the superior may not forget the females, who need greater care precisely because of their readiness to sin.

In this situation the evil enemy can find many ways to creep in secretly."
(*On Priesthood*) (121)

"For the eye of woman touches and disturbs our soul, and not only the eye of the unbridled woman, but that of the decent woman as well." (*On Priesthood*) (121)

"The whole (female) sex is weak and flighty." Further, "What then, is there no salvation for them? Yes, there is. What kind? Salvation through children." (*Ninth Homily* on 1*Timothy* 2:15) (130)

St. Augustine

(On why the serpent spoke to Eve, not to Adam) "We cannot believe that the man was led astray . . . because he believed that the woman spoke the truth, but that he fell in with her suggestions because they were so closely bound in partnership . . . Eve accepted the serpent's statements as truth, while Adam refused to be separated from his only companion, even if it involved sharing her sin." (*The City of God XI*) (11)

Against the rhythm method of contraception he wrote, "I am convinced . . . that nothing turns the spirit of man away from the heights more than the caresses of woman and those movements of the body, without which a man cannot possess his wife." (*Siloloquies* 1, 10) (86)

"The birth of children is most abhorred in marriage, and thus you turn your 'hearers' into adulterers of their own wives, when they are on the alert to see that their wives do not conceive. . .they wish to have no children, for whose sake alone marriages are contracted. Why then aren't you the sort of people who forbid marriage in the first place? For if that is taken away, husbands are shameful lovers, wives are harlots, marriage beds are bordellos, and fathers-in-law are pimps." (*Against Faustus* 15, 7) (83)

"It is impermissible and shameful to practice intercourse with one's wife while preventing the conception of children." (*The Adulterous Relations* 2, 12) (85)

Thomas Aquinas following Agustine wrote on women's roles as men's "handmaids": "I don't see what sort of help woman was created to provide man with, if one excludes the purpose of procreation. If woman is not given to man for help in bearing children, for what help could she be? To till the earth together? If help were needed for that, man would have been a better help for man. The same goes for the comfort of solitude. How much more pleasure is it for life and conversation when two friends live together than when a man and a woman cohabitate." (*De genesi ad literatum* 9, 5–9) (88)

Clement of Alexandria

"The very nature of their own nature must evoke feelings of shame." And, "Women should be completely veiled, except when they are in the house. Veiling their faces assures that they will lure no one into sin." (*Paedagogus*) (128)

Clement of Alexandria discussing sports for young men emphasizes what should be women's sports, "Women too should not be excluded from physical training. They should not be called upon to wrestle and race, but they should be made to practice spinning wool and weaving, and helping with the baking of bread, when necessary. Women should also fetch from the pantry the things we need." (*Paeddagogus*) (130)

Pope Pius XI (1930)

"God pursues," with the highest of degree of hatred, "those who practice contraception." (85)

Pope John XXIII (1948)

"After more than forty years I still warmly recall the edifying conversations that I had in the Episcopal palace in Bergamo with my revered bishop Monsignor Radini Tedeschi. About persons in the Vatican, from the Holy Father downwards, there was never an expression that was not respectful, no never. But as for women or their shape or what concerned them, no word was ever spoken. It was as if there were no women in the world. This absolute silence, this lack of any familiarity with regard to the other sex, was one of the most powerful and profound lessons of my young life as a priest, and even today. I thankfully keep the excellent and beneficial memory of that man who raised me in this discipline." (323)

A Pastor (1966)

"Actually we were left almost entirely without guidance on the subject of celibacy; for the most part we were advised that the best way to conduct ourselves was to run away from women." (Waltermann, ed.) (131–2)

Cardinal Ratzinger (on "Marriage and Family" 1980)

"Precisely from this point of departure {women's experience}, purely from the experiential standpoint, something becomes convincingly clear that our previous theological argumentation failed to show: that in the case of the alternative between natural methods and contraception will not end, but that there is an anthropological gulf between them, which for that very reason is a moral gulf. But how am I to indicate this door to understanding?" . . . "With the pill a woman's own sort of time and thus her own sort of being has been made continually 'utilizable.'" (283–4)

Pope John Paul II ("A Priceless Gift," 1980)

"Women are not allowed the functions of a mass-server." (134)

Christa Meves (1976, in the essay "Does Christian Catholic Marriage Still Have a Future?")

"Owing to the increased life expectancy for women, who in the nineteenth century lived for an average of only 35 years, often dying after being weakened by childbirth, often dying of childbed itself, there was also an increase in the number of people who live together for thirty, fifty, even sixty years. This length of time means an additional trial, especially for the husband. For while earlier he could, after the death of his (often still young wife), remarry a (usually younger) wife, today he is forced to put up with a wife who often ages more quickly than he does." (283)

∾

Rosie: "I Always Believed I Belonged to Men"

Introduction

Born and raised in Cali, Rosie, in her mid-forties, is from a large family. She finished tenth grade in a nun's school and completed the rest of her education through travel and her profession—prostitution. She lives and works in the Red Light District in Amsterdam, the Netherlands, where I interviewed her. In her testimony, her father is one of those who have the last word, who is sometimes violent. However, she does describe a "good family life" and an especially good relationship with her mother. Family union and loyalty seem to be the reality she retains in memory, as the family is the protector of female children against the evils of men and the outside world. Protection notwithstanding, she reveals her exploitation by men: sexual abuse by a relative, a priest, and involvement in prostitution, partly impelled by her husband. Rosie is, nevertheless, a woman of immense dignity, one who feels proud of her genuine accomplishments, despite remorse for the profession that enables them. Rosie brings up a concealed issue, the sexual abuse of children by adults, in this specific case, the abuse of girls by male relatives and priests. Children are embarrassed and confused by their experiences, and afraid to speak up because they might be punished. And this fear is real. Embarrassed, or horrified, by the prospect of sex crimes committed by trusted individuals, against their girls, parents refuse to confront reality.

Instead they blame children, for inventing stories. The frequency of female child abuse, recounted by Rosie, and in Part I of this chapter, reported by a doctor working in the Aguablanca district, in Cali, indicates the imperative that parents pay serious attention to children's complaints.

Interview

"Tell me about your life as a child. Please discuss your relationship with your father, mother, and siblings. Talk about your school and family life."

"First of all, I want you to know that I'm a very decent woman. . . . I went to the Sisters of Charity's day school until I was seventeen years old. I had two brothers and two sisters. We were very, very poor. . . . My father was a policeman, but later he changed professions and became a carpenter. He wanted to earn a better salary. Our family was large, and we had so many needs. . . .

"At times, my father could be violent. We children tried never to make him mad. Once he got upset with something I did and hit me in the face. Nevertheless, we did have a good family life. Because my father was from Greece, not Colombia, we returned there before his death—struggling for a decent life. Sometimes we went back to Colombia to visit our mother's family: our grandmother, uncles, and aunts. My Mom was a wonderful mother. She continuously thought about her children. I had a good relationship with my mother; we were very good friends. We always spoke Spanish, which is why I speak good Spanish. I also speak Greek and English. My mother died three years ago. I miss her very much. My parents took great care of my sisters and me because, they said, girls have to be supervised more than boys. My sisters and I weren't allowed to enter nightclubs or cafés nor participate in parties or dances. Because we had relatives in the United States, we moved there after my father died, to see if we could have a better life. I had just turned eighteen. So, my mother, my brothers, my sisters, and I all moved to America.

"I was the eldest of the five children. Thus, I had to help my mother educate and care for my brothers and sisters. My mother, who was a nurse, found an excellent job at a hospital in Rochester, Minnesota. The Mayo Clinic it was called. Meanwhile, I was sent to Miami where we had relatives; I had to work and help with the family finances, and in Florida, I was introduced by some friends to dancing clubs.

"What is a dancing club? It's a place where men go to see girls dance. Girls dance, and men give them tips. You see, it all started in an easy, simple way. I learned to make money the way I always earned it from an early age: one receives something in return for what one gives. Therefore, I went to a bar to dance; I looked at a man I liked, and he looked back at me. . . . If he was fascinated by me, I knew he was trying to start a relationship of some kind; he was trying to reach me by just looking in a special way. This is the way things work with men!

"But let us go on with what I was telling you before. With the salary of my mother's job in the hospital and my work in the dancing bars, one of my sisters was able to study archaeology, and the other one learned veterinary medicine. My brothers have been in the United States twenty-two years, and both have good jobs. My sisters are married, and they live in Greece.

"As you can see, I started my life near men. I have always believed that I belong to men. My friends in Miami convinced me that it was the only way to earn good money—by being near men and working for them. I needed to help my mother, no matter what. But, at the same time, I always felt very, very *lonely*. Really, I didn't know anything about sex. I thought sex meant kisses and superficial caresses. I did not know that in 'sex' our bodies had to be so much involved. I hated sex and the sexual act. The first time I did it, I bled terribly; it hurt me very much. I didn't like it at all. For a long time, I always did it without the lights on. As for love, well, I only loved one man: the person I married who is the father of my children. He is also Greek. He was a sailor when I met him in a dancing bar in Germany; his ship had anchored at a seaport there. I moved to Germany when I left the United States.

"My husband was terrible to me. He liked women; he was a womanizer. He also had lots of friends, and he drank. When he left the navy, he was never able to get a good, stable job again; instead, he wanted me to work for him. He always left me alone with our three children—two girls and a boy. He knew about my 'profession,' and didn't mind at all what I did. He only cared about the money I made. He was also violent and very abusive. He hurt me physically and morally; he made me lose my good judgment and led me to prostitution and drinking. We were married when I was only twenty-two years old.

"My eldest daughter is twenty-four years old and is married to a lawyer in Greece. They have a little girl, my first granddaughter. My second daughter will be married soon to a nice, young man. I have taken very good care of my two daughters and always gave them good advice about how they should behave with men. My son is seventeen and is studying to be an electrician. My three children are very intelligent! They all had a good education, and I am an excellent mother.

"Those children are my whole life, my joy, my love. I speak to them over the phone almost every day and send them all the money I can. They don't know anything about my life. They think I'm a waitress who earns good money because I work in Amsterdam. Their father has never given them anything; I'm the one who gave them everything they need. At the moment, I'm in the process of divorcing my husband; we haven't lived together for many years. He says he has a right to more than half my earnings. Can you believe it?

"Now I feel affection for someone else. He is Oriental. He's sweet and kind but extremely quiet and doesn't like to speak about his personal life. He says that he is divorced, but who knows if he does not have anyone else. He is not very generous. We go out to dinner sometimes. When I was a little girl, I dreamt that I was going to have my own, beautiful house someday with a husband and children. But life punished me: my family life is in shambles. This is what I think when I sit on that chair, waiting for the clients to come. I feel sad and nervous: nervous because sometimes I'm afraid that I can't earn enough to pay my debts and send money to my children. Each day I pay one hundred and fifty guilders to rent this room. I miss the peace of mind I had when I was a little girl. Sometimes the men who come here treat us badly; they are rough and disagreeable. They tell me, for example, that I'm old. Really, I am working to see if I can make enough money to retire and go live in Greece with my daughters, son, and granddaughter. I would like to have a small business there and live in peace."

"Why do you think men go to prostitutes?"

"Well, because prostitutes are more free with sex, with their own sexuality, which they can express better than other women; marriage ruins the relationship between a man and woman. The wife, after some time and because of innumerable reasons, gets cold and stops wanting to have sex with her husband. Or simply, the woman stops liking it, and when the husband looks for the wife, she lies there in bed without feeling anything. And husbands, well, they forget about their wives' needs. They do not make love to them. For example, they drink and want to have drunken sex; thus, wives cannot respond to the lovemaking."

"Tell me, Rosie, do you go to church?"

"Do you want me to tell the truth? Well, no, I don't go to church, but I believe in God. I love Jesus Christ, and I have faith in the Virgin Mary, who I think helps us with our needs. I also pray to Saint Cipriano for he is the saint who makes the devil go away. On the other hand, God is the great energy that helps us to go on. I pray to Him constantly. I do not have time to go to church, and I don't like confession. Once, when I was only eleven years old, I took some money from my grandmother's purse because I wanted to buy a pair of shoes. Mine were full of holes. I went to confession because I felt guilty for what I had done. The following Sunday, the priest stood up on the pulpit and, after finishing the sermon, told the parishioners what I had done. This public humiliation was my punishment. Since then, I don't trust priests. Another time when I was still a child, I went to church and asked the priest for his blessing. Suddenly, I realized he was touching me in a strange way: first he touched my head while reciting a prayer; next his hands went down to my breasts, which I developed at an early age, and from there he went to my waist, lifted my skirt, and touched my private or secret parts. I asked him what he was doing, and he answered that he was just blessing me in the name of God. Another time in Greece, the day before an operation, I went to ask the priest of the Orthodox Church to bless me, and he refused, simply because I was Catholic. Priests are liars. This has been my experience. No, I don't go to church.

"I had an uncle, my mother's eldest brother, who used to visit us. I was very young, I remember, and my uncle liked to sit me on top of his legs while we were watching television. It was always very dark. He used to touch my genitals and make me touch his penis. I was very frightened and never said anything to anyone. This situation continued for a long time. Afterwards, he used to give me gifts—shoes, dresses, toys—in order to please me and keep me quiet. One day I told the nuns who, when they heard my story, wanted me to stay and live with them. But my mother did not agree. My mother was informed by my teachers about what her brother was doing, and she forbade him to come to our house. She never told my father, who would have killed her brother.

"I was very sad, at first, when my uncle stopped visiting us, because I thought he was a wonderful, generous person. Little by little, I came to understand what he had been doing: he wanted pleasure, and he paid for it. Since I was a little girl men have tempted me. At the same time, I felt dirty and had great remorse. I was pure, but the devil does exist, and the worst of it all is that we pay for our bad actions. I have really paid for mine. Later in life, men gave me drinks, food, and money, which—as I told you before—were the returns for my work: one receives something in exchange for what one gives. It is a trade in benefits. Nothing else is expected from either of the two parties."

"Rosie, what would you say today by way of advice to an eighteen-year-old woman?"

"I would tell her to take care of her body, not let anyone touch her, and be careful of men. Usually, when a woman gives herself to a man, he stops desiring her. I would warn her to be on guard and not let men touch her without any reason. She should try not to sleep with her boyfriend before marriage and not to drink—especially hard liquor. Drinking will keep her from thinking straight and using good judgment. She should always be in control of herself. If she isn't careful, the devil, too, will possess her, and then she will be lost. I would tell her not to go to nightclubs and drink. She should always watch her behavior and keep a good head on her shoulders. Also, I would recommend that she not become promiscuous because if she does, afterwards, she won't like to be with just one man; she will start comparing the way different men make love and begin looking for men who can please her better."

"Do you consider yourself to be a free person? If so, tell me why as clearly as possible."

"Yes, I definitely consider myself a free woman. I am free to do what I wish. I work if I need to do so. I go out with whom I choose. I choose my clients. I made enough money to educate my children very well. I have my own house, and I can think of retiring quite soon after being here in Amsterdam for seventeen years. No one tells me what to do or where to go. I am an independent woman, yes." (Rosie finished her sentence with an affirmative nod of her head.)

Part I: The Virgin Mary, Mother and Woman: A Semiotic Metaphor in Aid of Colombian Women

There is no doubt that the blessed Virgin received the gift of wisdom to an exceptional degree. . . . [She] had the use of wisdom in contemplation, but she did not have the use of wisdom with regard to teaching. . . . [Teaching] is not suitable for the female sex.

Thomas Aquinas, *Summa Thelogie* III q.27 a.5 ad 3
(Ranke-Heinemann, 345–46)

Traditional Virgin Mary: The Immaculate Conception

In light of Kristeva's thoughts on the Virgin Mary and the importance of semiotic elements in language, ideas that go beyond current scholarship will be presented and developed. They concentrate on the Virgin as a model for Catholic women and on semiotic components that, by influencing and changing meaning, can "open up the possibility of explaining cultural change" (Oliver 1993: 10) while providing a revolutionary discourse to benefit women. The image of Mary is a useful model that may help Colombian women, in a society where men largely control secular and religious laws that intrinsically and surreptitiously benefit males, at the expense of females.

In Mary, Catholic women see an archetype that differs literally and symbolically from the one traditional in Christianity. As Kristeva insists, the image of the mother of the social order—whose body has only "milk and tears" and who only listens—must be replaced by a loving, conscious, "desiring" mother. This maternal image is the one the child knew before the mirror stage from the beginning of the individual's history when the world seemed to be filled with music, love, and laughter (Oliver 1993: 34–37). It is a mother who indulges in pleasure, relishes and enjoys gratification. This mother recognizes her *jouissance* and is in control of her body and mind. Through this model, the maternal semiotic element is introduced into language. Such a maternal metaphor owns an *avant-garde*, revolutionary, poetic language that will not accept a discourse based only on the Law of the Father. Revolutionary poetic language, as mentioned, speaks from the unconscious (in this case, the female unconscious), which relies on the mother's archaic law that prefigures for the child the Law of the Father (patriarchal culture). The mother's language is a heterogeneous discourse that accepts alterity, love, and the self-in-process. The self-in-process is a dissident from the Symbolic order (Kristeva 1981: 299) but stays always within the Symbolic Law. The self-in-process is a *radical*. She or he will not accept the given and is always looking for other answers. With the aid of the semiotic, one can refuses the tyranny of the Law. This approach allows women to modify the social realm while retaining current cultural rules until another ethical system is created—a more heterogeneous and loving law that accepts the other's needs, desires, pleasures, and differences, along with the knowledge that the self is never finished but always evolving.

Eve and the Virgin Mary

In a rich and detailed study of early Catholic doctrine, Joyce Salisbury presents a succinct analysis of how the theme of virginity developed in the Christian world. Her book *Church Fathers, Independent Virgins* (Salisbury 1991: 11–25) re-counts how the rules and dogmas of the Catholic Church were organized by six "theological giants": Tertullian, St. Cyprian, St. Ambrose, St. Jerome, St. Augustine, and Isidore of Seville. This process began at the end of the second century following Christ's death and lasted until Augustine's death in the fourth century. By that time, Christian doctrine was particularly well structured; it has prevailed to this day, with some modification based on more modern exegesis. Among the doctrines developed at the time of the early Christian Church were the myth of *paradise*, the *fall* caused by Eve's disobedience, the belief that *original sin* was inherited by all humanity (except the Virgin Mary), and the concept that *redemption* is provided through the birth and death of Jesus Christ (Hamington 1995). Genesis (1: 28–38) relates the myth of the world's creation, including the creation of the first man and woman and their banishment from the Garden of Eden, because of disobedience. God interprets the act of eating the forbidden apple as a sign that human beings want to be like God. The story relates how a serpent told Eve that the prohibited fruit had powerful characteristics and enticed her to eat the apple, which she shared with Adam. Christianity interpreted this tale as a "fall from grace" that was passed down to subsequent generations. The Catholic theologian Uta Ranke-Heinemann, writes in her book *Eunuchs for the Kingdom of Heaven* (1990: 90), "Punishment for the fall was first exacted on the realm of sexuality. The attitude of the Church's celibate hierarchy is that the locus par excellence of sin is sex, a view based on Augustine's pleasure-hating fantasies." The female of the species was denigrated because of the sinful actions of Eve—the first woman and hence the mother of all humanity (Hamington 1995).[1]

From then on, all blame falls on Eve. Theologians, philosophers, and historians have not mentioned the possibility that Adam could have refused the apple. Could such an interpretation have been made only by a woman? As a counter-figure to Eve, Catholicism constructed the religious image of a virgin mother in Mary. She was considered a "perpetual virgin" who never lost her innocence. Always virginal, she is believed to have been sexually pure with an intact hymen before, during, and after the birth of Jesus (Hamington 1995: 57). Although only two evangelists, Mathew and Luke, spoke about Mary's virginity, the Church fathers declared this doctrine sacred. Since humanity sinned because of a woman, the human race must be redeemed with the aid of another woman. In Church teachings, Mary replaced Eve as the "good mother." The sin committed by Adam and Eve, namely arrogant disobedience, was thought to eliminate the innocent, natural state of human beings.[2] Therefore, the new Eve had to be a virgin. St. Jerome believed that the Virgin's body was the "temple of God" (Salisbury 1991: 13) and a "fountain sealed" (Hamington 1995: 64), and emphasized that Mary's virginal nature defined the essence of female worth. To be accepted, woman had to be reconstructed differently from Eve (Hamington 1995: 63–65; Rodriguez Sehk 1986: 73–90; Salisbury 1991: 11–25).

According to Catholic dogma, Mary was placed on a pedestal high above other mortals. Religious paintings of the Virgin Mary often depict her literally sitting on such a throne that cannot be reached by followers worshipping from below. Mary's deification, based on her divine nature, left ordinary women with an impossible role model (Hamington 1995: 25). Unable to match such perfection, Christian women were left to identify with Eve, whom they were simultaneously taught to reject as evil. Mary's unattainable image alienated Catholic women, who could not consider themselves worthy within a system that denigrates femaleness. The Church disparaged the essence of womanhood as lustful, weak, and carnal by nature (Salisbury 1991: 22). Female sexuality was debased as the origin of human sinfulness, unhappiness, and, ultimately, as the source of death (Hamington 1995: 126). Uta Ranke-Heinemann complements this consideration by adding the thinking of Thomas Aquinas about women's nature:

> Thomas says that women do not correspond to "nature's first intention," which aims at perfection (men), but to "nature's second intention, (to such things as) decay, deformity, and the weakness of age". . . . Thus woman is a substitute that comes into existence when nature's first intention, the creation of a male, comes to grief. She is a developmentally retarded man.

The theory is illustrated as Esperanza describes the way her father thinks about women and speaks to men, how he portrays the debasement of what is female and what is admirable of the male. She says,

> Father treated my brothers differently. Perhaps because I was a girl and the eldest, he treated me with indifference and harshness; his behavior towards my brothers was different. He cared for them; he didn't care for me. On the contrary, he despised me. . . . My father [always] thought that I was some kind of a prostitute. My father thought that women were all prostitutes—even my three daughters. He went to prostitutes, so he projected his experiences onto all women. My father was mean to women. His attitude towards men was different. He was polite and all smiles whenever he was in front of a man—old or young.

The Church idealized men as strong, thoughtful, and spiritual. The theologians who formulated these images projected all evil onto women. Men had only one hindrance: woman's seductive nature that worked against male spirituality. Saint Jerome (Salisbury 1995: 23) says, "Woman's love in general is accused of ever being insatiable. It bursts into flame . . . give it plenty, it is again in need; it enervates a man's mind, and engrosses all thought except for the passion which it feeds." According to such thinking, the only way to control women's weak, sexual, sinful nature was through maintaining her virginity and, thus, repressing her body and mind (Salisbury 1991; Hamington 1995). Through her virginity and her maternity, Mary was meant to redress such faults of the female character.[3] But this form of motherhood was inaccessible because of its unreachable virginal idiosyncrasy. Through the normal process of reproduction, all women are rejected as devouring mothers or Medusas.[4]

Kristeva seeks to redress this argument by separating maternity from other aspects of femaleness. Kristeva proposes to deconstruct Mary as a woman and mother, returning to her the right to be human, rather than "alone of all her sex," as Marina Warner (1976) describes her. The maternal experience of pregnancy and birth helps create a mother's "her-ethics," part of which is to nurture her daughter.

Two of the women I interviewed had particularly good relationships with their mothers, whereas they learned to keep secrets from their fathers. Clara portrays this special kind of relationship between mother and daughter with a specific understanding between them, which entails a clear maternal code.

> My mother didn't bother with rules and (she) let us be responsible for ourselves. Throughout my adolescence, she told me that marriage was a terrible bondage and I should never get married. . . . After completing school, I looked for a job so I wouldn't have to stay home. . . . After work, I used to go around the small villages on my bicycle. I was trying to recapture the freedom I lost at fifteen. Father didn't know about my afternoons rides, but Mother did. When I returned home, I always brought her flowers. . . . I wanted to leave the prison in which I lived and go away. . . . [My mother] understood me, agreed with me, and ceaselessly tried to help me. In the end, my own mother . . . realized that if I wished to find new horizons in my life, I had to get married. . . . Like me, my mother was a rebel. . . . I represented the rebellion she had to stifle within her heart. She permitted my rebellion to construct and guide my life.

Susana is another good example of the special relationship a mother might have with her daughter, against the strictness of an irascible father and his law.

> From an early age, I heard my mother discuss my father's bad temper, his indirect supervision over our lives, and his iron will over our obedience to his law.

. . . My mother told me I could do anything I wished, if my father didn't know! I grew up learning how to keep secrets from my father. In a way, my mother was teaching me to be independent and exert my own will. She was also telling me not to let any man, not even my father, mistreat me. My mother's advice was that I had to be "secretive" to be free. This was the type of interaction I saw in my house: my mother always obeying my father without questioning his orders! So I grew up with the idea that women had to obey men, but behind their backs we could do whatever we liked!

The mother-child dyad is the "foundation for all social relations. It provides the basis for an ethics of love that operates outside the Law of the Father but within the symbolic" (Oliver 1993: 65).

In Kristeva's texts on the Virgin Mary, the desire of this French philosopher and theoretician is to rescue Mary as a political feminist figure and model. The archetype offered by Kristeva may serve women better than the Catholic figure of Mary constructed as the virginal mother of Jesus. Kristeva tries to replace Mary's self-effacing image with an active one, projecting power and self-assurance. Furthermore, what Kristeva constantly emphasizes is that only a different discourse can modify the master narrative of the Symbolic order. A new image of Mary could indicate how the mother's body—with its semiotic drives filled with love—can influence symbolic discourse. Kristeva allows us to imagine an image of a Mary who represents first, woman, and then, the mother of Jesus. At this time in history, Mary's virginity is not important. What is important is her femaleness and her humanity; her having been virgin and mother is secondary. Nevertheless, Mary's virginity *could* be used as a conscious metaphor to designate her as a "special woman," one who had a different discourse to disturb and change the world.

Thus, the Virgin Mary represents the metaphor for the semiotic side of signification in language. The Symbolic order or social realm organized by patriarchal law hides the semiotic chora (represented like a receptacle or a womb), which is the "place of the maternal law before the Law" (Oliver 1993: 46), in order to keep the strict Symbolic (cultural) Law functioning, unmolested by disruptive elements. Mary, according to the church, has to be thought of as a Virgin rather than as a woman, sister, or mother in her own right. She has to be silenced and kept in the shadow. Instead, following Kristeva, the Virgin Mary can be imagined as a righteous poet, a dissident who brings forth music, love, color and fairness to life, which is why she would be feared by the Symbolic order. She handles a poetic language filled with feelings, love, forgiveness, and respect for the different Other. Mary's aesthetic and loving discourse would be one that searches for different answers to change the social order. As Audre Lorde (1984:1–26) says,

> Poetry is the way we help give name to the nameless so it can be thought. . . . Poetry coins language to express and charter this revolutionary awareness and demand. In the forefront of our move toward change, there is only our poetry to hint at a possibility made real.

The time has come, in Colombia, to uncover the semiotic element of the mother's law and discourse, as Kristeva proposes. A different maternal metaphor will help empower women, as they participate actively within the social realm, with a different feminine discourse. It is important that women, as Mary did in the wedding at Canaan, speak up about their ideas and opinions on what is happening in women's rights in their country. And so they did on August 17, 2006. The twenty-five women who are in the Congress (the lowest feminine quota in the last fifteen years), no matter to which party they belonged, united and asked for a law that would protect women and children from any kind of violence. They demanded that violators be severely sanctioned. Also, they asked that political posts be shared by men and women in equal terms: 50 percent for each, not 30 percent for women, as the Colombian law has it today. To this date Colombia has to legislate a law to give equal participation to men and women in political posts. As for those who abuse women and children the law is being more firm than before, but still there is much to accomplish to make it optimal.

Rethinking Mary's different ethics might, thus, open up a political, social, and cultural debate. The influence of poetry on culture is supported by Kristeva's theories of desire, writing the body, and speaking from and with the aid of the semiotic.[5]

María del Socorro, another of the interviewees, is a good example of one who finds through her poetry that she has been able to accept and love herself and establish communication with others. She says,

> I have learned to love myself [and accept my body] more, thanks to my poetry. You see, I write poetry, and now I have published a book! Having my poetry published and applauded has helped me a lot in terms of self-esteem. I would like to fall in love with my work and stop thinking about others. And yet, I think that giving up relationships would be a way of accepting that I had bad experiences with men and women and that I am unable to communicate with either.

The semiotic and its poetic language is a way by which the social can become a "social-in-process, and human life . . . an open system" (Oliver 1993:

184).When Colombian women, with the knowledge acquired through their experiences begin speaking their own minds, fearlessly and radically, that society will start to change.

Following Jones (1985: 371), one could ask,

> How does maternal tenderness or undemanding empathy threaten a Master? The liberating stance is, rather, the determination to analyze and put an end to the patriarchal structures that have produced those qualities without reference to the needs of women.

It is an outspoken Mary who speaks with a "different voice" that empowers her discourse, who is an advocate, protector, tender heart, redeemer, and even savior (Kinsley 1989: 242) of those in need, and who could assist Colombian women in disrupting the Law of the Father and its patriarchal context, and open for women the space in history that is theirs, in their own right.[6]

Looking back over this book, what I have to say is this: it is time for women in Colombia to break their silence and start a different discourse that will encompass their lives, their ideas, their drives and desires, their entire beings, as their bodies will delineate the path on which they walk together with all the women in the world. Women in Colombia have to stop being afraid of being punished by the Law. They have to enjoy knowing that they are in the right path while they construct their own histories with joy, in a world that belongs to all: men and women, each with his or her particular differences, none suffering from discrimination. It will be an adventurous journey, the one men and women create by being able to answer the questions of life through thought and language, as they decipher the meaning of language and, with it, the meaning of life, which is what Julia Kristeva proposes. In other words, to live as conscious individuals who answer all the "whys?" they encounter throughout time (Oliver 1993: xii–xiv). Perhaps, the biblical Mary did not speak much, but whenever she did, it was a conscious, loving, and friendly discourse geared to redressing whatever was not right, or to comment about her feelings and ideas. Imagine what she might have said to her other sons and daughters, whether she had them or not.

In exploring the possibilities of a friendly discourse, by interviewing women, one observes what the women interviewed think about life in general and what their thoughts are on the ways women can empower themselves, their daughters or other younger women, and each other; and which actions will help to surmount the obstacles that obstruct a large number of women from "having [a] satisfactory personal and social life," such as Asuncion Lavrin (1987: 113) invokes. The question about what they would say to younger women to help them envision a better life was especially pertinent in stimulating thinking about such issues.

For the inteviewees, reaching for a better life entails caring for their daughters and sons, advising them to cherish their bodies, and, as Maria del Carmen affirms, to "love themselves." Manuela expresses that idea, too.

> I would say that the most important thing is for a woman to trust her desires and wishes. To a daughter I would tell her not to be afraid to explore, to take risks, to experiment with life. Doing so is part of living. It is important for a woman to follow her heart and live consciously. By experimenting, she will learn what she likes and dislikes. To be autonomous will help her not to be influenced by the wishes of others. She should strive for as much education as possible. Education will give her freedom, especially economic freedom, and she won't need to marry a "rich man" in order to survive! A woman who depends economically on a man will be under his grip. I would tell my daughter or another young woman that having a man at her side isn't very important compared to having valuable experiences to enrich her life. If she lives with someone, she shouldn't let that person mistreat her. Instead, that person should understand her and be a companion and a friend.

Being in control of themselves by living consciously and being ethical, honest, independent, and responsible, and having high ideals and goals is mentioned throughout the interviews. Some also stress the importance of teaching other women to love their families, their work, and not to be violent or aggressive with others. Women should "not allow husbands or companions to humiliate them."

Several of the interviewees also express the idea that men do not wish women well, that women, therefore, have to protect themselves from men's antagonisms. Women have to think of ways that will help them evade suffering. For many, this taking care means not permitting anyone to mistreat or harm them, in any way.

Dora: "Blind-folded in the World"

Introduction

Chapter 9, Part II, introduced by Dora, speaks of the Catholic Church and the influence it has over the faithful and specifically, in the education of girls. In her interview, Dora relates her childhood, shrouded in ignorance, thought to be innocence, over the realities of life under the protection of loving adults and kindly nuns who educated her. Both at the convent school and at her mother's house, she is taught how to live in an idyllic, unrealistic world. They never tell her that her father abandons her family for another woman. Orphaned at sixteen and unprepared, Dora marries a man who destroys all illusions with beatings, verbal and sexual violations, and unfaithfulness. With four children and conflicted by her religious and family upbringing—she has been taught to "respect and forgive" such a husband—she does not leave him.[7] She recognizes that "For me, the world of God and the real world were merged. These connections account for why I suffered so much."[8] Experiences like Dora's still take place, as practicing Catholics try to reconcile realities of their lives with traditional Church teachings. In Part I, Julia Kristeva and other theorists show how religious symbolism has been misused to abrogate the rights of women, and how that symbolism may be acquired by women to reverse the patriarchal order. The Virgin Mary, once submissive and silent, becomes a loving and relentless mother, acting in defense of her daughters. Part II of this chapter shows how, with a broader education and an open mind, men and women confront openly what they were taught as children. Many do practice artificial birth control, for example. Recently, the government has permitted legal abortion, under limited circumstances, unthinkable, not long ago when Church authority was incontestable. Even some clergy and religious women today question certain church laws and principles.

Interview

"Tell me, Dora, what do you remember about the way you were raised? Tell me as much as you wish, the good and the bad memories, too."

"I was raised in a home where there were no boys. We were two sisters. I was three years older than my sister. My father left us when I was very small. Unfortunately, my mother died when I was only seventeen years old. What I remember is that my sister and I had a lovely childhood. Our parents took care of us in an exaggerated way. To begin with, we never were allowed to go out of our homes alone; my mother thought that girls were always in great danger of being harmed. Men were bad; they wanted to harm women. For example, there were men who exposed themselves to women. Usually, our mother came along with us everywhere we went, even to our parties. Later we were sent to a nun's boarding school because my parents considered that it was the only place where they would take good care of us, especially from all the dangers one faces every day. And also, the nuns were going to give us the best ethical and moral education. I was eight years old when I went to study with the nuns. We spent all my childhood in school, which I only left when I finished high school. The atmosphere in our boarding school was ideally beautiful, but at the same time, it was not the real world. After having been there in the convent for so many years, we came out into the world blindfolded, and we did not know the real world at all. Everything was so different, and quite shocking.

"My mother's problems with my father started at the time we were sent to boarding school. At the time, he started a relationship with another woman, whom he later married. My mother wanted to spare us the disagreeable atmosphere in our family, another reason we were sent to the convent school. My mother didn't want us to know about the immoral situation, as she called it, that our family was undergoing. She cried a lot because my father was not living with her, but with the other woman. The abandonment we suffered from our father affected my mother tremendously. When she knew that my father married the other woman, my mother died of heart failure. She was forty-two years old. My mother was a wonderful woman: dynamic, a good business woman, and very hard working. My father never gave us any economic support; he had another family to take care of.

"We girls were raised differently from boys, but it never crossed my mind that life would have been easier for me if I had been a boy, simply because I was raised in a household where there were no men. Only when I grew and became an adult, I realized things in the world were different for men and women. My mother, who supervised us at all times, kept reminding us that we had to be very feminine, like she was. For example, we were not allowed to jump, because jumping was a 'masculine' way of behaving. We were not allowed to ride bicycles because something bad could happen to a girl riding a bicycle, like losing our virginity. We never used vulgar language. We had to be respectful of adults. To be loved by adults, we had to be obedient and quiet. We never socialized with adults; whenever they came to visit, we were sent away because the adult's world was not supposed to intermingle with the children's world. My mother's main concern was to teach us about all the things that would make us become desired young women. The nuns also told us how a woman should behave and be: sweet, delicate, not to jump around, be well groomed, but they also told us that our main concern were our studies. For my mother, too, studying was the only important thing we had to think about. She did not mind if we did not know how to cook, but she did want us to be academically well prepared, in case we needed it later on in life. My mother did hear our opinions, but at the end we kept quiet and did what she told us to do. On the other hand, my mother never spoke or explained to us the facts of life or menstruation. The nuns did tell us about menstruation, saying that it was a normal physiological thing that happened to women, that we should not worry, only, that during those days, we had to take good care of our bodies and be very clean. The only thing on which the nuns were very clear was about our 'having particular relationships' with other girls. The nuns did not consider it correct for girls to be too close to each other. Until today, I don't know why this was so. The same thing happened with sexual life. No one ever told us about it. When my sister married (she was sixteen), I remember that she came back from her honeymoon with her virginity intact. She came back very worried, speaking about 'all the things' she had to do with her husband and she did not understand why. Before the marriage, we spoke about her dress, the party, but nothing about what was going to happen in the honeymoon. It was the last thing we would think to talk about. The nuns did tell us about how we had to behave with boys: taking care of our virginity and our purity, something that we had to give to our husbands the day we married. No one could touch us before our wedding day. But they never went deep into the subject; nothing was clear, everything was kind of shady, and we never asked. We listened and we kept silence. My friends were the ones who told me about 'those things.' A friend spoke about menstruation as *that thing* that made her ill. To be raised in ignorance, is bad. What people think is children's innocence, at the end it is ignorance, which can be harmful. We had no curiosity about adults' lives; our children's world was very structured and happy; we didn't ask for more. But as children, we had no intimacy with ourselves. We were like an open book for those who educated us. Even if we wished to keep to ourselves, we could not do so, as those adults would constantly search into our souls.

"I married shortly after my mother died. She did not like my boyfriend because he seemed to be an abusive male type, and she was right. He was eleven years older than I. When my mother died, I stayed alone, in shock and great distress; I had no other way to survive my loss and my loneliness, aside from getting married. I was ignorant about life; I didn't know about what goes on between human beings. It was horrible. My education was so bad; it was lacking in many aspects. I didn't know what was going to happen to me. I was not prepared for married life. I did not know anything about raising babies or being a housewife. I did not know anything about men. People had told me that men were bad, but this statement had sexual connotations for me. I never liked our intimate relationships. My husband did not know how to please me. How can a man go directly to the physical act without a kiss or a caress? This process was terrible for me—liked a violation of my body, of my intimacy.

"We had four children. The terrible thing about my marriage was that my husband beat me up. He was wild, a savage. He used to attack me for the smallest incidents—because I did not know how to cook, for example. If I cried, because he used gross language against me, he hit me all over my body and face. The bruises lasted up to a month. I was just eighteen years old. Imagine: no one ever had touched me; remember that I did not have a father.

And my mother, when she touched me, was only to show me her love and affection. No one ever had mistreated me. I grew up in a secluded and loving atmosphere. My sister was going through a similar situation, so she could not help me. I had no friends; I didn't tell anyone about my suffering. My sister and I we did not know how to defend ourselves.

"My husband had other women, too. He left me alone every night. When he got tired of being away, he came back and I received him, because I had been taught that I should respect and forgive my husband, no matter what he did. Now I see how bad and unrealistic those teachings were. Finally, my husband left. My aunts did not approve of my staying alone without a husband and caring for four children. My home and my school education were linked. For me, the world of God and the real world were merged. These connections account for why I suffered so much.

Part II: The Catholic Church: Incursions on the Laws of the Prelates

> Woman is less qualified than man for moral behavior. . . . [W]oman knows nothing of fidelity. . . . [W]oman is a misbegotten man and has a faulty and defective nature. . . . [H]er feelings drive woman toward every evil, just as reason impels man toward all good.
>
> Albert the Great, *Quaestiones super animalibus* XV q.11
> (Ranke-Heinemann 178–79)

Colombia is a Catholic country (95 percent according to Cabal, Lemaitre, and Roa et al. 2004: 6). From the beginning of Colombian history the church has been a strong force for organizing society, its culture, its values and beliefs. Ecclesiastical authority and its religious philosophy have been, and still are, relevant in promoting traditional Catholic values for all of its members. Nevertheless, the understanding is that women are to follow the rules strictly, while men do whatever they wish. Masculine nature is held to be more erratic than women's, when dealing with religious regulations. Men are more immature in keeping the laws of the church, whereas women are more reliable, because they follow the example of the Virgin Mary.

Undoubtedly, ideas have changed. But, given the church's history and its own structure, patriarchy is its natural organization. Ecclesiastical authority has *silently* accepted certain values for women only: humility; obedience to God, father, brother, husband or priest and to religious precepts; a modest demeanor, and chastity. Presumably, all religious values are intended for men

Modern Virgin Mary. An Artist's view of a New Mary, by Fray Juan Jairo Rendón O.F.M. At the Church of Cristo Señor de la Vida Aguablaca, Cali, Colombia. A Model for Women: one who has Love and Poetry in her heart.

too. Nevertheless, society and the church hold women responsible to uphold those patterns of behavior, while freeing men from severe responsibility. Thinking comes from the Bible's legend of Adam and Eve: Eve failed God by promoting disobedience, by eating the forbidden fruit as she led Adam to do likewise,[9] affixing the mark of woman-as-sinner.

Women, and numerous men in Colombia, for that matter, are challenging, openly, the religious and cultural norms armed against women, especially those involving the abysmal behavior of men. As the church and the political system look away from, and keep silent over abuse of women, criticism comes not only from male and female faithful, but also, from many of the clergy and religious men and women who are not afraid of speaking up or being chastised by their superiors. Catholic individuals do recognize their rights and do work in and around the Church to make profound legal and cultural changes.

The issues are innumerable. The abuse of women at home, the office, public places or streets never stops; illegal abortions are abundant 300,000 per year (*El Tiempo*, August 29, 2006); reproductive rights and rights of women over their bodies are few. In Colombia, where many men create multiple families, bigamy is legal. The Church never openly addresses pedophilia by priests; nor does it overtly confront priests who have secret families. These activities are treated as sins (i.e., they can be pardoned by confession, discarded, and forgotten).

On the issue of abortion, the Catholic Church is immovable; abortion for any reason is a sin: it is murder. In 2006, however, Colombia's Constitutional Court accepted abortion in three instances: (1) severe deformity of the fetus, (2) when the pregnancy is caused by rape or incest, or (3) when the pregnancy threatens the mother's life.[10]

Colombia's first legal abortion was performed in August 2006, on an eleven-year-old girl who had been raped since age seven by her stepfather, with the knowledge of her mother. At first, the doctors hesitated to do the procedure on the child, because the court had not yet published its ruling. Later, when a second ruling was issued, the doctors were compelled to comply. The Church's response was one of abhorrence. Monsignor Libardo Ramirez, president of Colombia's Ecclesiastical Tribunal, referring to canonical law, stated that "excommunication was applied to anyone who participated in the 'murder of a child in the womb.'" Cardinal Alfonso Lopez Trujillo, president of the Vatican's Pontifical Council for the Family also held responsible (and subject to excommunication: exclusion by the church to receive the Sacraments) "relatives, politicians and lawmakers . . . protagonists in this abominable crime." (ibid.).

The prelates had nothing to say about the welfare of the abused eleven-year-old, whom they would have experience the physical and psychological distress of childbirth and caring for a newborn. They mentioned nothing about women who are raped, who are "stigmatized and are denied the opportunity to work and are even thrown out of their homes" (Castaño, *El Pais*, May, 14, 2006). Cardinals and priests did not speak about the girl's reputation, or about the professional medical team they excommunicated, their reputations and careers. Worse, they said nothing about the man who raped the little girl for four years or the child's mother who silently allowed him to do so. They condemned "criminals" whom they punished by throwing them out of the church. The above case of juvenile sexual abuse is neither selective nor rare. *El Pais*, Cali's leading newspaper reports,

> A doctor from the Aguablanca district assures that pregnancies of raped minors are more common than you think. The professional swears he has seen that little girls of twelve, thirteen, and fourteen years old, having been abused, must manage the drama of being made pregnant by their own fathers, brothers, uncles, and grandfathers. (Castaño, *El Pais*, May 14, 2006)

Likewise, psychologist Margarita Villa of the government family planning organization Profamilia, finds frequent evidence of incest in Cali's neighborhoods. Mothers come to Profamilia to ask for contraceptives for their minor daughters, so that they will not become pregnant, in case they are abused (ibid.). On this matter the church keeps quiet. It turns its head the other way and continues with its hypocritical and unrealistic sermons that help no one. One mother of an adolescent tells of how "everything came out all right," after her neighbor helped her daughter obtain a home abortion.

> The method . . . consisted in pricking the womb with a stick covered by the casing used to stuff a sausage. Bleeding lasted three days because it seems that, in trying to abort, the young lady (who performed the operation) tore the uterus. The official numbers reveal that the second leading cause of death for women is the botched abortion. (Castaño, *El Pais*, May 14, 2006)

Fernando Sanchez de Torres, fellow of the Colombian Academy of Medicine, a body that consults with and advises the Colombian government on matters of public health and medical education, affirms that the high incidence of maternal mortality is caused by untrained people who perform abortions in unsanitary conditions. He agrees with the law that makes abortion legal under the three criteria ("El Aborto y la Academia de Medicina," *El Tiempo*, June 1, 2003).

The church, however, persists in its conviction. The official word by Pope Benedictus XVI was reported in the *New York Times*, November 20, 2007: "Abortion is a crime," he reminded the faithful, and "no Catholic can go through it without being punished." Nevertheless, the woman who has the abortion and the medical group who performs the procedure are excommunicated; husbands, lovers, or rapists of the women are not. The church has solutions for not performing an abortion: children born out of abuse or not desired are put up for adoption. Because so many of these children are born, this solution cannot often be followed.

In March 2006, when the law that a woman could have an abortion was not yet passed, *El Tiempo* reported another serious case of a woman who needed an abortion. This time, she was a mother of three girls, who had terminal cancer. The doctors did not want to treat her with chemotherapy and radiation, for they feared that it would terminate her pregnancy of six weeks. The result of that decision was to leave the mother Martha Sulay, at age thirty-four, abandoned by her husband, living in one room with four children and an irreversible cancer. To treat her would involve the doctors in legal problems. However, the National Academy of Medicine and legal experts concurred that since abortion was not the objective of such treatment, it should have been allowed. The woman had sought treatment to save her life and not leave her daughters orphaned. But because the child might not have died but might have been born malformed, the doctors decided to wait until the baby was born (*El Tiempo*, March 26, 2006; *El Tiempo*, March 28, 2006).

Martha Sulay died, leaving her daughters orphaned. Maria de Brigard, expert in medical legislation, said speaking of Ms. Sulay's cancer and pregnancy,

> A medical committee cannot recommend . . . [such an] error. This example has to open up a discussion on therapeutic abortion. It is a stupidity to make [it] a religious debate. (Ibid.)

Florence Thomas, coordinator of *Mujer y Sociedad* (Woman and society) writes in her weekly column of *El Tiempo*, February 22, 2006 ("Regresa Monseñor Builes?") as she blames the Catholic Church for its insensitivity on the response it gives to the violence against women, particularly to their opposition to the law permitting limited abortions. Furthermore, at the time, the church asked Catholic men and women not to vote for candidates who supported the new abortion law.

> If the Church really listened to women, it would understand the dimension of a decision on the limits they can accept and how traumatic is the deci-

sion for them, but always taken in conscience from their most internal authority. To return to those limits, they need an unrestricted moral support, a therapeutic empathy from which could emanate a humanist and generous religion. . . . [A]nd I ask myself: From which religion do these men of the Church speak with their words of censure? A religion that speaks of a merciful and generous God or of a punishing deaf God who has finished by alienating so many women from this Catholicism, dogmatic and closed to history, to daily life and its dramas?

Thankfully, a great deal of support for views such as those of Florence Thomas comes from the Catholic clergy. The Franciscan friar Father Luis E. Patiño (*El Pais*, November 18, 2006) enunciates complaints unmentioned by the high echelons of the Church: "The praxis of our society and of the Church regarding women is clearly discriminatory and even violent." He speaks of the workplace, where a woman's worth is devalued; in the political sphere, where men take charge of the legislature as well as the justice system. The very state is governed, he affirms, by a "masculine mentality." Antifeminist violence is institutionalized, he says. Further, he points to the church itself:

There is violence too in the Church and in the name of God. They [women] fill the temples but they have no power of decision . . . women must only obey and always say amen. Women are victims, at times unknowing, of clerical violence sanctified in the confessional and in the moral official who invades her intimacy.

One learns at home that father rules and,

How many times and in what very hypocritical manner does one live in conjugal intimacy, when the *macho* believes himself in the right in using and abusing the feminine body for his egostistical pleasure, without keeping in mind the woman's right to dispose freely of her own body. (ibid.)

Father Patiño, who writes frequently in *El Pais*, also makes many controversial assertions on the church and sex (*El Pais*, February 17, 2006).

- "Sexuality and genitalia" he writes, "are not necessarily for procreation, but for the personal growth of the couple as an expression of love and compromise."
- To bring children into the world to suffer "hunger, ignorance and abandonment" is immoral (suggesting a need for family planning).

- Although the celibate, masculine Catholic Church denies contraception, except the natural kind, most Catholics use artificial controls. They reject the idea that such methods are sinful.
- The traditional rule that Catholic men and women must come into marriage as virgins is likewise rejected as anachronism, as is the idea that pre-marital sex is a sin. As long as the relationship is "stable" and the couple is truly in love, love and conscience are the guiding forces.
- When the feelings of the faithful are in conflict with church teachings the "voice of God" is distorted.
- As the faithful adapt to changes brought on by advances of science, psychology and anthropology, the Church must "blend the official formulations of its ecclesiastical teachings." . . . "One even speaksof the evolution of Dogmas." (Ibid.)

Father Patiño makes his comments freely and publishes them openly in a major Colombian newspaper, apparently with no censure. Likewise, sister María Luisa feels at liberty to speak critically of the Catholic Church. To my question, *"Has women's political situation in Colombia changed in any way in the last one hundred years?"* the sister in the first part of her answer, refers exclusively to women *vis a vis* the Catholic Church. She says,

The Catholic Hierarchy, not the church itself, supports with its enormous power the patriarchal diagram of man-to-woman subordination—a situation also applied to the disparity of moral concepts and behavior demanded from women and men. The so-called Patriarchs of the Church moralize and chastise women for the ways they conduct themselves and the ways they treat their bodies. It is as if sin has only been applied to women. Females still carry the burden of Eve's guilt on themselves. The Catholic community organization model comes from the Catholic patriarchs' belief that women were only suited to perform as secretaries, cooks, cleaners. It is easy to verify this by entering the Vatican jobs scheme to check what women hold which positions. As a consequence, all the decisions and concepts in this organization are issued and produced by men, with their own partial judgment and excluding the rest of humankind. Thus, we cannot assert that women's situation inside the Catholic Church has, in effect changed, even if Catholic women themselves have evolved.[11]

These words suggest that the Catholic hierarchy works as if God gave men the whole responsibility for religious matters and forgot about women.

On the subject of birth control, also considered a sin by the church, there are planning organizations, such as Profamilia and the Instituto de Bienestar

Familiar, that have been operating openly for years, even at the time when the government and church worked in concert. Nowadays, major political figures may admonish the church, publicly, to keep out of politics (*El Tiempo*, February 23, 2006).

In his newspaper article "Don't tell the Pope" (*International Herald Tribune*, November 27, 2003), Nicolas D. Kristof reports from El Salvador on the humanitarian work the Catholic Church and related organizations are doing in that country, and elsewhere, to prevent AIDS. He describes how Catholic priests work in remote, "desperately poor" villages, distributing condoms and teaching safe sex to villagers, including young students and prostitutes. They teach how to use condoms and how to run AIDS clinics. The Vatican opposes condom use even in marriage when a husband or wife has contracted HIV. But, this journalist reports, Catholic organizations provide "25 percent of AIDS care worldwide." Ignoring the church, Catholics perform humanitarian services the blindsided church would oppose, if they could. Kristof writes, "Their humanitarian work is a reminder that the Catholic Church is much greater than the Vatican."

Extrapolating from the El Salvador example, it is possible to see how thoughtful people, clergy and ordinary Catholics alike, who are tired of the pronouncements of aloof, tiresome, old-fashioned men, could work, inside the church and out, to create a humanitarian revolution that would reform the church for the better.

In this way, Colombian women might indeed co-opt the Virgin Mary as a new model for womanhood. Julia Kristeva's vision for a world where women are empowered to speak of their desires, to say "yes" and to say "no," to speak the poetry and love in their hearts, to break their millenary silence, to own their bodies, and to realize the active and potent lives they envision for themselves, may yet be realized.

What Do Colombian Women Want?

A more humane Virgin Mary replies: Women Want . . .

- To be integrated in their country's development, as active decision makers in social, economic, political, and cultural spheres
- To be free of oppression in all its forms—by gender, class, or race
- To be protected by the rule of law
- A woman's responsibilities at home to be recognized, respected, and remunerated appropriately, since the welfare of the family depends on her contribution

- Women's rights and needs to be honored in a national policy emphasizing access to resources: education based on cultural and social values; preparation for work outside the home; and gender interests directed towards female well-being
- Gender discrimination, a social evil that destroys women's health, to be eradicated from the social fabric. Likewise, the traditional division of labor, which locates women in a secondary place, to their disadvantage, should be abolished, along with machismo and marianismo, contributors to asymmetrical cultural values
- Colombian men to accept that a woman's life and body belongs to her, not to her father, brothers, husband, companion, sons, or religious men, freeing women to make decisions about their lives, their health, and how many children they wish to have or not have
- Women to organize, to break their silence, to speak their experiences, desires and sorrows, to begin a transforming cultural revolution, for the benefit of all men and women without distinction of social classes, races, religious creeds

Notes

1. In Genesis (3, Col16) the words of God/Yahweh speak of His wrath on "woman" after the fall, and her punishment: "I will multiply your pains in childbearing . . . you shall give birth to your children in pain. Your yearning shall be for your husband, yet he will lord over you."

2. Mayr Nyquist in her article "Gynesis, Genesis, and the Formation of Milton's Eve," in Marjorie Garber, editor, *Cannibals, Witches, and Divorce: Estranging the Renaissance* (Baltimore, MD: 1987) describes in great detail the two versions of the story of the creation of Adam and Eve, and the consequences suffered by Eve for having been created, either out of Adam's rib, or equal to him at first, loosing all prerogatives later on, when the male and the female took different roles in society.

3. Chapter 5 refers to Eve, Mary, the Fall, and Redemption as it came from Spain to influence the formation of the Colombian symbolic imagination.

4. See Freud's essay "Medussa's Head," in *Standard*, Vol. xviii, 273.

5. Hélène Cixous in her essay "The Laugh of the Medusa" in *New French Feminisms* (New York, Schocken Books, 1981): 250, speaks about the importance of women's writing: "Write your self. Your body must be heard. Only then will the immense resources of the unconscious spring forth. . . . It is by writing, from and toward women, and by taking up the challenge of speech. . .that women will confirm women in a place other than that which is reserved in and by the symbolic, that is, in a place other than silence. Women should break out of the snare of silence."

6. St. Paul's I Epistle to the Corinthias (14, col 34, 35), says clearly that women must keep silent and listen by law to men and their church. "Let your women keep silence in the churches: for it is not permitted unto them to speak; but *they are commanded* to be under obedience, as also saith the law. And if they will learn any thing, let them ask their husbands at home: for it is a shame for women to speak in the church".

7. In the Epistle of St. Paul to the Ephesians (5. 22, Col. 3, 18) he writes about the duties of wives towards husbands: "Submitting yourselves one to another in the fear of God. Wives, submit yourselves unto your own husbands, as unto the Lord. For the husband is the head of the wife, even as Christ is the head of the church: and he is the savior of the body. Therefore as the church is subject unto Christ, so *let* the wives *be* to their own husbands every thing . . . and wife see that she reverence *her* husband."

8. The First Epistle of St. Paul to the Corinthias (2 Col. 3, 7, 8, 9) makes emphasis of what he wrote to the Ephesius about the wife's duties to the husband. "But I would have you know, that the head of every man is Christ; and the head of the woman *is* man; and the head of Christ *is* God . . . the woman is the glory of the man. For the man is not of the woman; but the woman is the glory of the man. Neither was the man created for the woman; but the woman for the man."

9. In Genesis, (2, Col 7, 18, 21, 23) God, after he created earth and animals said, "And the Lord God formed man of the dust of the ground and breathed into his nostrils breath of life; and man became a living soul . . . [and] the Lord God said, *It is* not good that the man should be alone; I will make him an help meet for him . . . [and] the Lord God caused a deep sleep to fall upon Adam, and he slept: and he took one of his ribs [and] . . . the rib, which the Lord God had taken from the man, made he a woman, and brought her unto the man. And Adam said, This *is* now bone of my bones, and flesh of my flesh: she shall be called Woman, because she was taken out of Man."

10. See Stephanie Hepburn and Rita J. Simon, *Women's Roles and Statuses the World Over*, 2006, their chapter on Latin America and the section on Colombia (54–64), which gives a perspective about its politics, internal conflicts and wars, work force, education of its people, health care, law, rules on abortion before it was legalized in August 2006, and the like. The authors give a good overview on Colombia and its political, legal, and cultural institutions.

11. See Ranke-Heinemann, chapter IX in *Eunuchs for the Kingdom of Heaven* (1990: 125–36), where she explains why and how Roman Catholic priests and monks decided to suppress women from their lives and the world in general. Through celibacy they have searched for perfection, for the love of God, and for their salvation.

CHAPTER TEN

Conclusion: Life as a Work of Art

If I have a message . . . it is to lay out an alternative to what our grand-mothers and mothers, our teachers and priests wanted us to be, and what the men we are to marry feel most comfortable with. Marriage and motherhood, although important in whatever we decide to do, from getting married to getting pregnant, can feel as natural an imperative as going to Mass, to lunch, to the hairdresser. The Virgin Mary and Miss Colombia cannot continue being our role models. We need to intro-duce an alternative to the dichotomy between a "good woman" and *una mala mujer* (a bad woman); there is something between mother and whore. The definition of good need not entail being virginal and sub-missive. To be self-assured and independent does not mean that we are whores.

(Paternostro 1999: 37)

The strongest and most secure nets of our society are woven by women. The day of the woman is every day of the year. While we men invest our entire life in pleasure, war and alcohol, they silently prevent the coun-try from sinking in chaos and uncertainty. . . . Ideally, they would take charge of the principal entities procurement: fiscal, national defense, mayoralities, presidency of the Republic.

(Mendoza, *El Tiempo*, July 3, 2004)

Sister María Luisa: We are Ready!

"Don't the Pope's directives to women also have a practical justification? Don't they protect women from becoming a new kind of fair game for male sexuality? Don't they give the man, through the command of chastity, of consideration of women, greater possibility of a necessary spiritual compensation for his animal instincts?" (Ranke-Heinemann 1990: 284).

❧

"Has the woman's situation changed in any way during the last ninety years?"

"The question is very complex. When asking several women belonging to certain socioeconomic levels, or groups lucky enough to participate in self-esteem and personal growth seminars, and other consciousness raising groups, such women feel there has been a change in their lives compared to their mothers' and grandmothers' lives, status, and personal conditions.

"They have the feeling of being freer and of having more opportunities to choose from and make decisions about themselves and their bodies. But I believe that there is a big difference between what they feel and the actual reality. We only have to take a closer look at the number of women hired in governmental positions. In spite of the "share-agreement" of May 30, 2000, between the political parties that pretend to reach an equilibrium between opportunities for men and women (although what was negotiated was to give women only the thirty percent of governmental positions versus fifty percent to men), we can observe that, in general, the important governmental positions are occupied by men, while women are given less influential jobs.

"How do we reach a fair equilibrium and where is the instability? I believe there are two main powers in our social institutions: the Catholic hierarchy and the economic power.

"The first one, the *Catholic Hierarchy*, not the church itself, supports with their enormous power the patriarchal diagram, man-to-woman subordination, the situation also applied to the disparity of moral concepts and behavior demanded from women and men. The so-called Patriarchs of the Church moralize and chastise women for the way they conduct themselves and the way they treat their bodies. It is as if sin has only been applied to women. They still carry the burden of Eve's guilt on themselves. The community organization model comes from the Catholic Patriarch's belief that women are only suited to perform as secretaries, cooks, cleaning women. It is easy to verify this by entering the Vatican jobs scheme to check which positions women hold.

"As a consequence, all the decisions and concepts in this organization are issued and produced by men, with their own partial judgment and excluding the rest of humankind. Thus, we cannot assert that women's situation inside the Catholic Church has, in effect, changed, even if Catholic women themselves have evolved.

"And the economic power is the other enormous obstacle for women's liberation in the twenty-first century. Even if women have grown in their self-esteem, even if they are aware of their rights and belong to feminist groups, if *they still depend economically on men*, there is no way for them to reach an equilibrium in their relationship—woman-husband-companion at home, or woman-boss in the working place. If she is the wife of an important man, she is expected to follow him, make him feel superior, act as the jewel to enhance his made-up personality and to act as his 'pet.' Many women, if alone, have to endure a relationship with their boss or the boss's wife, often against their will, a situation that can be violent, if not desired. They do it for one reason: economic support. They fear losing their job or being left with a home to support and children to raise and educate. Many decide to live under the heel of *machismo* and even endure irregularities in their personal lives.

"If we Colombian women were capable of holding the position we are entitled to within the Catholic Church, we would be able to be part of the decision-making process, to be heard, and to help other women of our society rise from the ashes, work towards a very much needed change and become valuable citizens. We have been preparing ourselves to reach this goal for many years. We are now, also, ready to participate actively in the Catholic Church!"

The Path Ahead

This study has observed what women want, what they deserve, and what they are capable of attaining. Women themselves can, and do find the ways by which to reach their desires to benefit their lives and the lives of their loved ones. Women usually try to work toward their objectives at home, in the workplace, at church and in other community organizations.

Education, key to advancement, creates possibilities, not only for economic success and political power but also for opening minds and learning to ask and answer questions. And education begins at home. Men are usually raised by women. Even the most disadvantaged mother can talk and teach her sons about treating women with respect. No mother should allow herself to be facilitator of a philosophy that hurts all, men and women.

Many women have attained professional education. They are or can be leaders. Even with everyone occupied in her own affairs, advancing and managing family and career responsibilities, some will find time to help in tracing new roads for women and their well-being. Women work on behalf of women, whether locally in family planning organizations or other institutions for the advancement of females, impelling the government to recognize and enforce existing laws in favor of women. Every step adds to a major contribution.

One dedicated woman can make a large difference. Attorney Patricia Guerrero, educated at Columbia University in New York City, returned to Colombia to found the League of Displaced Women and to organize *La Cidudad de las Mujeres* (The city of the women). Apparently taking as a model former U.S President Jimmy Carter's Habitat for Humanity, she collected donations to build homes for women displaced by violence. These women had watched as family members were senselessly gunned down before their doors, as their own lives disintegrated, plundered by armed groups. In the new city, they work together to build homes, to reconstruct a safe community for themselves and their families (Semana, 2006: 20–27).

In another instance, former prostitutes from the city of Popayan, under the auspices of Mayor Libardo Ramirez, have renounced that profession, having been contracted to keep the streets clean. Some resorted to prostitution when their husbands abandoned them and their children, leaving them without a means of support. Now, in addition to sweeping the streets, they have formed a cooperative, to sell in city-run retail stores, sometimes selling the crafts they make themselves. And, the mayor's wife has initiated a scholarship fund for them to pursue technical studies (*El Pais*, March 21, 2006).

That men and women cooperate to promote the interest of women is not new in Colombia. The nation's original suffragettes created alliances with a few male supporters to win their rights (*El Tiempo*, *UNperiodico* 2004). Countering those who defile themselves by war, drink, and bigamy are practical and fair-minded men like Mayor Libardo Ramirez, models for other decent men to follow.

Breaking the Chains of Culture

> The radical being of women is very much an Otherworld journey. It is both discovery and creation of a world other than patriarchy. Patriarchy appears to be "everywhere."
>
> Mary Daly, *Gyn/Ecology* (1990: 1)

The process of achieving liberation within society does not occur without struggle. Plato beautifully demonstrated this truth in his myth of the cave, describing a man who had been bound to a wall—along with other men—for many years. One day, the unfortunate individual freed himself, because he wanted to emerge and behold another source of "light" other than the one reflected on the cave wall, as well as the world illuminated by that light. After leaving the cave, the man's life changed. The shadows he had seen previously were cast by a bonfire behind him, yet now this light no longer served to define the boundaries of his existence. Concrete realities shaped his life. After so much time in the dark, could his eyes adjust to sunlight? Confusion and chaos enveloped the man, for whom control and organization formerly prevailed.

Like the cave in Plato's allegory, cultural forces limit thought for people who spend their lives within social enclosures. Cultural forces hinder thinking and obstruct change. Mental restriction leads to a static life that inhibits the flow of ideas. By contrast, intellectual freedom is the road to self-knowledge and new possibilities. Analysis can alter a person's perspective on the meaning of life, whose "essence"—according to Cassirer (1944: 3, 5)—"does not depend on external circumstances" since men and women "may be described and defined only in terms of their consciousness." When an individual decides to change, as a result of introspection, and accepts the inevitable risk of being in conflict with society, all security for the self is brought into question. However, an active life becomes rich with options that can replace the protected, established existence where innovation has no place. Questioning and criticizing culture to uncover political violence, which for Foucault is the only worthy political act, is the way to "alter power relations" (Foucault 1984: 6). Human beings add value to their lives because, through "this fundamental faculty of giving a response to himself and to others, man becomes a 'responsible' being, a moral subject" (Cassirer 1944: 6).[1] To become a thinking creative individual requires a daily, conscious struggle with the present; a re-evaluation of the past; and a search for renewal of the self in the future, as means of existence (Zuleta 1980: 46). Thus, says Davies (1990: 508),

> Woman can be a subject who realizes, speaks, writes her subjectified condition and searches out how the patterns holding that subjectification in place can be subverted, turned to her own ends, toward reclaiming herself as a whole, entire, capable of loving not from lack or need, but from a desire located in the whole of her embodied being. She moves thus to a celebration of desiring—as opposed to being a desirable object—playing with new words, new patterns, new meanings, breaking up old patterns . . . finding the texts of words, of body, of interaction, that make the idea and the ideal of a whole, embodied woman as *active subject a lived reality* (my emphasis).

Further, as Lavrin (1987: 121) envisions, it is then the beginning of a revolution that will break with the past seeking for a better future that inquires into the needs of men and women. But only the individual who risks everything, even life, will be able to participate actively in a cultural revolution that searches for a different status quo.

Artistically Speaking

As Foucault said at the end of his life, "What strikes me is the fact that in our society, art has become something which is related only to objects and not to individuals. . . . But couldn't everyone's life become a work of art?" (Didier 1991: 355). Sartre, too, envisioned turning life into a work of art.[2] If women had more possibilities, were better educated, and could participate in every aspect of social, political, and economic life, we would expect them to enjoy such a goal. But it is one that can only be achieved in a society that allows women to be autonomous, safe from violence, and the owners of their bodies and discourse. In a more just society, women will have the opportunity to profit from every possibility offered to men.[3] Women would be able to create wonderful lives if the social contract were revised. Both women and men envision a better world. Utopia is a dream that gets people to face in the right direction and "stop devising social utopias for the needs of one sex alone" (Lavrin 1987: 121). The work of a utopia is to open possibilities in fields where acceptance of the given seems unmovable (Cassirer 1944: 62). Furthermore, human freedom and commitment are not insignificant, abstract themes. They deal with "culture creation, culture revision, and human potentialities" (Thompson 1965: 167). What feminists want, like all social scientists searching for a better world, is a more suitable social reality, with a greater measure of justice in which power relations have been modified, regardless of gender, race, religion, class, and sexual preference.

Lastly, the lesson I have learned through these interviews and the conversations that surround them is that envisioning should start with ideas generated in women's imaginations. It is our responsibility to develop women's insights into life perspectives that offer a better future to all members of the social community—a future that can become tangible through a daily review of social mores and of reality, that is conscious and responsible and that benefits each member of the society, with no exception. The human sciences and feminism share one goal: the liberation of the individual from the harm of social constraints and the grip of a lethal technology and a prosaic and senseless life, based today on a globalized and violence based economy (see Henry

1963). Max Weber (1976: 182) anticipates this concern, writing of "the mighty cosmos of the modern economic order . . . the iron cage [in which] specialists without spirit, sensualists without heart, [are] caught in the delusion that [they] have achieved a level of development never before attained by mankind" while they have forgotten about what is inherent to human beings, their humanness. Furthermore, women have the responsibility to "create a safer world for women" (Bell and Klein 1996–1997: xxvii). This responsibility entitles women to "an exploration of the ideology of male supremacy and female subordination" (Lavrin 1987: 110, 112), and to correct this odious state of affairs.

Radical feminism gives women the courage to be daring and to question the world around them; to work for social change in order to transform their destinies and to dismantle the oppression that structures female lives (see Rowland and Klein 1997; Morgan 1997). As Bell and Klein say, it "is a commitment to transforming society so that women may enjoy their full personhood." Thus, women using their own empowering tools—their experiences, their special way of knowing, their consciousness, and their discourse that names as it creates their woman's world and contexts (Rowland and Klein 1997: 32)—constantly re-create themselves, their lives, their material realities. Following Chris Weedon, let us not forget that

> [s]ocial meanings are produced within social institutions and practices in which individuals, who are shaped by these institutions, are agents of change, rather than its authors, change which may either serve hegemonic interests or challenge existing power relations. . . . [H]ow we live our lives as conscious thinking subjects, and how we give meaning to the material social relations under which we live and which structure our everyday lives, depends on the range and social power of existing discourses, our access to them and the political strength of the interests which they represent. (1987: 25–26)

Women through language, through thought, and through desire acquire the vital energy needed to construct their everyday existence; they make and unmake themselves and speak as assertive, independent individuals in their own right. Radical feminist practice and theory are intertwined (Rowland and Klein 1997: 25) because their theory results from women's experiences. Accordingly, "[r]adical feminism creates an original political and social theory of women's oppression, and strategies for ending that oppression which come from women's lived experiences" (Rowland and Klein 1997: 9). The main concern and process of such theory is the reconstruction of women's lives, which it seeks to achieve by utilizing females' specificities, differences, similarities, and consciousness as an Ariadne's thread[4] in the transformation of the social world, to fit women's interests and needs. Most important,

> [w]omen's power to refuse to accept a downgrading of our opinions, our rights, our demands, is the beginning of a fundamental change in the way we are seen and the way the world operates. We need the courage to continue to speak out loudly again and again against violence and aggression in whatever form it takes. (Scutt 1997:110)

Radical feminists' social and political roles, choices, and revolutionary activities are, thus, based on the transformation of the world. Radical feminists do have the courage to go on speaking and fighting. They are conscious of how change comes about through their archeological endeavors in the study of "particular historical phenomena for analysis," as Foucault proposed, in order to understand the origin of ideas, of human, social, and cultural history and of institutions.

Notes

1. Human collectivity creates moral characteristics, which constitute what Mauss in *The Gift*, 23, termed *la personne moral* (the moral person) or social person.

2. Mercedes Hanabergh's *Mardoqueo* (Espana: Publidisia, 2007) is an exemplary recent work by a Colombian woman who, through questioning herself and a homeless man deeply and fearlessly about life, thought, and desires, creates, with the aid of language, a work of art. Her book is a poem that may open her way to other searching inquiries.

3. Lavrin, "Women, the Family, and Social Change," 121, says on this subject, "Above all, the integration of women at all levels of social policy and civic participation is an idea ripe for implementation, and an objective worth working for. This necessitates a reassessment of social and ethical values aimed at a just recognition of women's participatory activities in society."

4. See Mary Daly *Gyn/Ecology* (Boston: Beacon Press, 1990), 389. She says about spinning, "Sapping requires spinning. . . . Understood in a cosmic sense it describes the whirling movement of creation. According to Merrian-Webster, *spin* is connected in its original Latin term *sponte*, meaning 'of one's own free will, voluntarily.' Thus Spinning implies spontaneous movement, the free creativity that springs from integrity of being." Most interesting is Daly's chapter "Spinning: Cosmic Tapestries," 385–424.

Appendix I: Statistical Indicators

Below are statistics currently available, relative to discussions of Economics, Politics, and Reproductive Health, in chapter 6.

In 2007, Colombia's population was 51.2% female and 48.8% male.
Source: The World Bank Reproductive Health 2007: 100.

Economics
Life Expectancy, 2000–2005
Women: 76.9 years; Men 64.0 years

Women and Men Over 15 Years Old Engaged in Economic Activity (estimated)
2000: Women   38%;   Men: 66%
2001–2005:   Women: 49%;   Men   73.9%

Unemployment, 2005
Women: 31.7%; Men 16.9%

Distribution of Women and Men in the Labor Force by Sector, 1994
Women: Agriculture, 3%;   Industry, 20%;   Services, 77%
Men: Agriculture, 37%;   Industry, 25%;   Services 38%
Source: National Administrative Department of Statistics (DANE)

Politics
Women in Public Life

Ministerial seats women occupy (percentages):*
Mono-cameral or lower chamber, 1987:   0%
Upper chamber, 2004–2007 (DANE)   12%
Mono-cameral or lower chamber, 2004–2007 (DANE)   14%
Mayors (Source Cabal, Lemaitre, and Roa 2001)   .6%
*In 2007, 23% of cabinet ministers are female

Women in decision-making positions in Government Ministries

Ministerial level, 2002/2006	women:	46.15%	men:	53.85%
Mayors 2002/2006	women:	7.50%	men:	92.50%
State Governors 2002/2006	women:	6.25%	men:	93.75%
Senate	women:	11.76%	men:	88.24%

Source: DANE

Reproductive Health
Contraceptive use by women of reproductive age, 2005:
Any method: 76%
Modern methods: 69.2%

Maternal mortality ratio (per 100,000 live births), 2000:   71

Infant mortality per 1,000, 2002–2007:   24.10
Source: *Instituto Colombiano de Bienestar Familiar* (ICBF)

Births per woman:
1990:   3.1
2005:   2.4

Births per 1,000 adolescent women, ages 15–19, 2005:   75

Unmet need for contraception, Married Women, ages 15–49, 2000–2005:   6%

Contraceptive prevalence rate, Married Women, ages 15–49, 2005–2005:   78%

Pregnant women receiving prenatal care, 2000–2005:   94%

Births attended by skilled health staff:
1990–1992:   82%
2000–2005:   96%
Source: *World Development Indicators* (The World Bank Reproductive Health 2007:100.)

Bibliography

Acosta-Belen, Edna, and Christine E. Bose. *Researching Women in Latin America and the Caribbean*. Boulder, CO: Westview Press, 1993.

Amnesty International. *Colombia: Cuerpos marcados, crimenes silenciados: Violencia sexual contra las mujeres en el marco del conflicto armado* (Colombia: Wounded bodies, silenced crimes: Sexual violence against women in the view of the armed conflict). October, 2004.

Andrade, Arturo, ed. *Cartas de Amor entre Manuelita y Bolívar* (Love letters between Manuelita and Bolivar). Bogotá: Círculo de Lectores, 2000.

Arango, Luz Gabriela, Magdalena Leon, and Mara Viveros, eds. *Genero e Identidad: Ensayos Sobre lo Femenino y lo Masculino* (Gender and identity: Essays on the feminine and the masculine). Bogotá: Tercer Mundo, 1995.

Arenal, Electa, and Amanda Powell. *Sor Juana Inés de la Crúz: The Answer/La Respuesta*. New York: The Feminist Press, 1994.

Atwood, Margaret. *The Handmaid's Tale*. New York: Anchor Books, 1998.

Barreto Gama, Juanita. "Estereotipos sobre la Femineidad: Mantenimiento y Cambio" (Stereotypes on feminine sexuality: Maintenance and change). In *Consejeria Presidencial para la Política Social: Las Mujeres en la Historia de Colombia Tomo I* (Women in Colombian history, Volume I). Magdala Velásquez Toro, ed. Bogotá: Editorial Norma, 1995: 362–78.

Baruck, Elaine Hoffman. "Feminism and Psychoanalysis." In *Julia Kristeva: Intreviews*. Ross Mitchell Guberman, ed. New York: Columbia University Press, 1996: 113–33.

Beckman, Peter, and Francine D'Amico, eds. *Women, Gender and World Politics: Perspectives, Policies and Prospects*. Westport, CT: Bergin and Garvey, 1994.

Behar, Ruth, and Ruth A. Gordon, eds. *Women Writing Culture*. Berkeley, CA: University of California Press, 1995.

Belenkey, Mary Field, Blyth McVicker Clinchey, Nancy Rule Goldberger, and Jill Tarule. *Women's Way of Knowing*. New York: Basic Books, 1986.

Bell, Diane, and Renate Klein, eds. *Radically Speaking: Feminism Reclaimed*. Melbourne: Spinifex Press, 1996–1997.

———. "Forward—Beware: Radical Feminists Speak, Read, Write, Organise, Enjoy Life, and Never Forget." In *Radically Speaking: Feminism Reclaimed*. Diane Bell and Renate Klein, eds. Melbourne: Spinifex Press, 1996: i–xx.

Benedict, Ruth. *Patterns of Culture*. Boston: Houghton Mifflin, 1934.

Beneria, Lourdes, ed. *Women and Development: The Sexual Division of Labor in Rural Societies*. New York: Praeger Special Studies, 1985.

Beneria, Lourdes, and Gita Sen. "Gender Inequalities and Women's Roles in Economics Development—Theoretical and Practical Implications," *Feminist Studies* 8, No.1 (Spring 1982): 157–76.

Benjamin, Jessica. *The Bonds of Love: Psychoanalysis, Feminism and the Problem of Domination*. New York: Pantheon Books, 1988.

Berger, Marguerite, and Mayra Buvinic, eds. *La Mujer en el Sector Informal* (Women in the informal sector). Caracas: Editorial Nueva Sociedad, 1985.

Bermudez, Suzy. *Hijas, Esposas y Amantes* (Daughters, wives, and lovers). Bogotá: Ediciones Uniandes, 1992.

———. *El Bello Sexo: La Mujer y la Familia Durante el Olimpo Radical* (The beautiful sex and the family during the radical olympus). Bogotá: Eco Ediciones, 1993.

Billson, Janet Mancini. "The Progressive Verification Method: Toward a Feminist Methodology for Studying Women Cross-Culturally," *Women's Studies International Forum*. Vol. 14, No. 3 (1991): 201–15.

———. *Keepers of the Culture: The Power of Tradition in Women's Lives*. New York: Lexington Books, 1995.

Billson, Janet Mancini, and Carolyn Fluehr-Lobban. *Female Well-Being: Toward a Global Theory of Social Change*. London: Zed Books, 2005.

Blum, Claudia. Personal communication. 2001.

Bonilla, Elsy, ed. *Mujer y Familia en Colombia* (Woman and the family in Colombia). Bogotá: Plaza y Janes, 1985.

———. *Texto y Contexto: Simbología Femenina y Orden Social*. Bogotá: Universidad de los Andes, No.7, January–April 1986.

Bordo, Susan. "The Body and the Reproduction of Femininity: A Feminist Appropriation of Foucault." In *Gender/Body/Knowledge*. Alison Jaggar and Susan Bordo, eds. New Brunswick, NJ: Rutgers University Press, 1989: 13–33.

Borja, Jaime Humberto. "Sexualidad y cultura femenina en la Colonia" (Sexuality and feminine culture in Colonial times). In *Las Mujeres en la historia de Colombia* (*Women in Colombian History*). Vol. 3. Santa Fé de Bogota, Colombia: Consejería presidencial para la política social, 1995: 47–71.

Bose, C. E., and Edna Acosta-Belen, eds. *Women in the Latin American Development Process.* Philadelphia, PA: Temple University Press, 1995.

Boserup, Ester. *Woman's Role in Economic Development.* New York: St. Martin's Press, 1970.

Boucquey, Eliane. "*Unes femmes,*" The Woman Effect. In *Julia Kristeva: Interviews.* Ross Mitchell Guberman, ed. New York: Columbia University Press, 1996: 103–12.

Bourque, Susan C., and Kay Barbara Warren. *Women of the Andes.* Ann Arbor, MI: University of Michigan Press, 1981.

Bowles, Gloria, and Renate Duelly Klein. *Theories of Women's Studies.* New York: Routledge and Kegan Paul, 1983.

Bracher, Mark. *Lacan, Discourse, and Social Change: A Psychoanalytic Cultural Criticism.* Ithaca, NY: Cornell University Press, 1993.

Brandes, Stanley. "Like Wounded Stags: Male Sexual Ideology in an Andalusian Town." In *Sexual Meanings.* Sherry Ortner and Harriet Whitehead, eds. New York: Cambridge University Press, 1981: 216–39.

Brocke-Utne, Birgit. "Women and third world countries—What do we have in common?" *Women's Studies International Forum.* Vol. 12, No. 5, 1989.

Bunch, Charlotte. "Transforming Human Rights from a Feminist Perspective." In *Women's Rights Are Human Rights.* Julia Peters and Andrea Wolper, eds. New York: Routledge, 1995.

Bushnell, David. *The Making of Modern Colombia: A Nation in Spite of Itself.* Berkeley, CA: University of California Press, 1993.

Butler, Judith. *Gender Trouble: Feminism and the Subversion of Identity.* London: Routledge, Chapman and Hall, 1990.

Buvinic, Mayra. "Women in Poverty: A New Global Underclass." *Foreign Policy,* Fall, 1997: 38–25.

Cabal, Luisa, Julieta Lemaitre, and Mónica Roa, eds. *Cuerpo y Derecho: Legislación y Jurisprudencia en América Latina.* Bogotá: Editorial Temis, 2001.

Cardenas, Consuelo, Morales Maria Fernanda, and Pilar Fernandez. "Entre el Poder y los Tacones" (Between power and high heels). *El Espectador.* March 11–17, 2007.

Cassirer, Ernst. *An Essay on Man: An Introduction to a Philosophy of Human Culture.* New Haven, CT: Yale University Press, 1944.

———. *Language and Myth.* New York: Dover Publications, 1946.

———. *Symbol, Myth, and Culture: Essays and Lecutures of Ernest Cassirer, 1935–1945.* Donald Phillip Verene, ed. New Haven, CT: Yale University Press, 1979.

Castaño, José Alejandro. "El anborto no puede volverse un método de planificación." *El Pais.* Bogotá: August 27, 2007.

Castellanos, Gabriela. "Eva y Maria—La mujer en la tradcion judeo-cristiana" (Eve and Mary—Woman in the Judeo-Christian tradition). *La Cabala.* No. 8: 4–6. Cali, Colombia: September 1985.

Castellanos, Gabriela, and Simone Accorsi. *Sujetos Feminos y Masculinos* (Feminine and masculine subjects). Bogotá: Editorial Manzana de la Discordia, 2001.

Castro, Carvajal Beatríz. "Policarpo Salavarrieta." In *Las Mujeres en la Historia de Colombia* (*Women in Colombian History*). Vol. 1. Santa Fé de Bogotá, Colombia: Consejría Preseidencial para la Política Social, 1995: 117–31.

Caws, Peter. *Structuralism: The Art of the Intelligible*. Atlantic Highlands, NJ: Humanities Press, 1991.

Centre for Reproductive Law and Policy (CRLP). *Women of the World: Laws and Policies Affecting Their Reproductive Lives, Latin America and the Caribbean*, 1997, 2000.

CEPAL. See www.eclac.cl/publicaciones (accessed 2001).

Chaney, Elsa. *Supermadre: Women in Politics in Latin America*. Austin, TX: University of Texas Press, 1979.

Charlton, Sue Ellen M. *Women in Third World Development*. Boston: Westview Press, 1984.

Cherpak, Evelyn. "The Participation of Women in the Independence Movement in Gran Colombia 1780–1830." In *Latin American Perspectivas*. Asuncion Lavrin, ed. Westport, CT: Greenwood Press, 1978: 220–50.

———. "Las mujeres en la independencia: Sus acciones y sus contribuciones" (Women in the independence: Their actions and contributions). In *Consejeria Presidencial: Mujeres en la Historia de Colombia* (Women in Colombian history). Magdala Velásquez Toro, ed. Bogotá: Editorial Norma, 1995: 83–116.

Chodorow, Nancy. *The Reproduction of Mothering*. Berkeley, CA: University of California Press, 1978.

Cixous, Hélène. "The Laugh of the Medusa." *Signs: Journal of Women in Culture and Society* 1, No.1 (1976): 874–93.

———. "Castration and Decapitation." *Signs: Journal of Women in Culture and Society* 7, No.1 (1981): 36–55.

Clark, Suzanne, and Kathleen Hulley. "Cultural Strangeness and the Subject in Crisis." In *Julia Kristeva: Interviews*. Ross Mitchell Guberman, ed. New York: Columbia University Press, 1996: 35–38.

Cole, Michael, and Silvia Scribner. *Culture and Thought: A Psychological Introduction*. New York: John Wiley and Sons, 1974.

Collins, Patricia Hill. *Black Feminist Thought*. Boston: Unwin Human, 1990.

Consejeria Presidencial para la Equidad de la Mujer. See www.presidencia.gov.co /equidad/observatorio_genero.htm

Cordoba, Piedad. *Mujeres en el Congreso de Colombia* (Women in the Colombian Congreso). See www.fescol.org.C/DocPdf/mujeresenelcongreso.pdf (accessed 2004).

Corpoeducacion. *Situación de la educación en basica, media y superior en Colombia* (What is going on in Colombia in basic, median, and superior education). Bogotá: Litocamargo, 2002.

Cottingham, Jane, ed. *United Nations Report on Health*. New York: United Nations, 1983.

Craske, Nikki. *Women and Politics in Latin America*. New Brunswick, NJ: Rutgers University Press, 1999.

Daly, Mary. *Gyn/Ecology: The Metaethics of Radical Feminism.* Boston: Beacon, 1990.

Dallerie, Arlene B. "The Politics of Writing (The) Body: *Ecriture Feminine.*" In *Gender/Body/Knowledge.* Allison Jagar and Susan Bordo, eds. New Brunswick, NJ: Rutgers University Press, 1990: 52–67.

DANE (Departamento Administrativo Nacional de Estadisticas). *Proyecciones anuales de poblacion por sexo y por edad 1985–2015.* Bogotá: DANE, 2007.

DANE Estadisticas DE Genero. See www.dane.gov.co/censo/htm.

Davies, Bronwyn. "The Problem of Desire." *Social Problems* 37, No. 4, 1990: 501–16.

Davies, Miranda. *Third World/Second Sex.* London: Zed Books, 1987.

De Beauvoir, Simone. *The Second Sex.* New York: Vintage Books, 1952.

Deere, Carmen Diana, and Leon de Magdalena Leal. "Peasant Production, Proletarization, and the Sexual Division of Labor in the Andes." *Signs: Journal of Women in Culture and Society* 7, No. 2, 1981: 338–59.

"De Faldas Tomar" (To Hold the Skirts). *Poder* (Power Journal). October 21, 2006.

De Los Ríos, Gloria. "Condición Jurídica de las Mujeres" (The juridical condition of women). In *Consejeria Presidencial para Polítical Social: Las Mujeres en la Historia de Colombia.* Magdala Velásquez Toro, ed. Bogotá: Editorial Norma, 1995: 421–30.

De Vault, Marjorie. "Talking and Listening from Women's Standpoint: Feminist Strategies for Interviewing and Analysis." *Social Problems* 37, No. 1. February 1990: 96–116.

Devereux, George. *From Anxiety to Methods in the Behavioral Sciences.* The Hague: Mouton, 1967.

Diagnostico Nacional De Salud Sexual y Reproductiva. See www.col.ops-oms.org / familia/Maternidad/3cifras.htm.

Didier, Eribon. *Michel Foucault.* Betsy Wing, trans. Cambridge, MA: Harvard University Press, 1991.

Dilthey, Wilhelm. *Introduction to the Human Sciences.* Ramon J. Betanzos, trans. Detroit, MI: Wayne State University Press, 1988.

Dinnerstein, Dorothy. *The Mermaid and the Minotaur: Sexual Arrangements and Human Malaise.* New York: Harper Colophon Books, 1975.

Dirección Nacional de Equidad Para Las Mujeres: Los Derechos de la Mujer en Colombia. Bogotá: Imprenta Nacional de Colombia, 1997.

DNP (Departamento Nacional de Planeacion). Bogotá. See www.eltiempo.com/ salud/noticias/articulo-web-nota_interior.html (accessed 2002).

Dobash, Emerson, and Russell Dobash. *Violence Against Wives.* New York: Free Press, 1979.

Douglas, Carol Anne. "I'll Take the Low road: A Look at Contemporary Feminist Theory." In *Radically Speaking: Feminism Reclaimed.* Diane Bell and Renate Klein, eds. Melbourne: Spinifex Press, 1996–1997: 417–20.

Douglas, Mary. *Purity and Danger.* Boston: Routledge and Kegan Paul, 1966.

Du Bois, Barbara. "Passionate Scholarship: Notes on Values, Knowing and Method in Feminist Social Science." In *Theories of Women's Studies.* Gloria Bowles and Renate Duelli Klein, eds. New York: Routledge and Kegan Paul, 1983: 105–16.

Dueñas Vargas, Guiomar. "La Ruta del Sugragio Femenino" (The route to the feminine vote). *UN Periodico* (Newspaper from the National University). Bogotá: August 22, 2004.

Durkheim, Emile. *Rules for the Explanation of Social Facts*. In *High Points in Anthropology*. Paul Bohannan and Mark Glazer, eds. New York: Alfred A. Knopf, 1938: 233–52.

Dowrkin, Andrea. *Woman Hating*. New York: Dutton, 1974.

"Editorial: Mujeres quieren tener cuota 50%/50%" ("Women wish to have a 50%/50% of political cuotas"). *El Tiempo*. Bogotá: August 17, 2006.

Ehrenreich, Barbara, and Deirdre English. *For Her Own Good: Two Centuries of the Expert's Advice to Women*. New York: Anchor Book, 2005.

Eisenstein, Hester, and Alice Jardin, eds. *The Future of Difference*. New Brunswick, NJ: Rutgers University Press, 1980.

Eisenstein, Zillah R. *Capitalist Patriarchy and the Case of Socialist Feminism*. New York: Monthly Review Press, 1979.

El Tiempo. See www.eltiempo.com//opinion/columnistas/florencethomas/ARTICULO-WEB-NOTAINTERIOR.html.

Engels, Frederick. *The Origin of the Family, Private Property and the State*. New York: International Publishers, [1972] 1985.

"Ex prostitutas de Popayan 'barrieron' cons su pasado" (Ex-prostitutes from Popayan got rid of their past). *El Pais*. Cali, Colombia: March 21, 2006.

Fansworth-Alvear, A. *Dulcinea in the Factory: Myths, Morals, Men and Women in Colombia's Industrial Experiment, 1905–1960*. Durham, NC: Duke University Press, 2000.

Féral, Josette. "The Powers of Difference." In *The Future of Difference*. Hester Eisenstein and Alice Jardin, eds. New Brunswick, NJ: Rutgers University Press, 1985: 88–94

Flax, Jane. "Mother-Daughter Relationships." In *The Future of Difference*. Hester Eisenstein and Alice Jardin, eds. New Brunswick, NJ: Rutgers University Press, 1985: 20–40.

Flores, Angel, and Kate Flores. *The Defiant Muse: Hispanic Feminist Poems from the Middle Ages to the Present: A Bilingual Anthology*. New York: The Feminist Press, 1986.

Foucault, Michel. *The Order of Things: An Archaeology of the Human Sciences*. New York: Vintage Books, [1970] 1973.

———. *The History of Sexuality: An Introduction*, Volume I. New York: Vintage Books, 1974.

———. *Discipline and Punish*. New York: Vintage Books, 1979.

———. *The Foucault Reader*. Paul Rabinow, ed. New York: Pantheon Books, 1984.

Fox Keller, Evelyn. *Reflections on Gender and Science*. New Haven, CT: Yale University Press, 1985.

Franco, Jean. *Plotting Women: Gender and Representation in Mexico*. New York: Columbia University Press, 1988.

Fraser, Avron S. *The U.N. Decade for Women Documents and Dialogue*. Boulder, CO: Westview Press, 1987.

Frechette, Barbara. *El Poder Compartido* (Sharing power). Bogotá: Editorial Norma, 1999.

French, Peter, Theodore E. Uehling, Jr., and Howard K. Wettstein. *Midwest Studies in Philosophy, Volume XV: The Philosophy of the Human Sciences*. South Bend, IN: University of Notre Dame Press, 1990.

Freud, Sigmund. *The Standard Edition of the Complete Psychological Works of Sigmund Freud*. Edited and translated by James Strachey. London: The Hogarth Press, 1986.

Frielich, Morris. "Manufacturing Culture: Man the Scientist." In *The Meaning of Culture*. Morris Frielich, ed. Lexington, MA: Xerox College Publishing, 1972: 267–325.

Fuller, Norma. "En Torno a la Polaridad Marianismo-Machismo" (Around the polarity *marianismo-machismo*). In *Genero e Identidad: Ensayos sobre lo Feminino y lo Masculino* (Gender and identity: Essays on the feminine and the masculine). Lúz Gabriela Arango, ed. Bogotá: Ediciones Uniandes, 1995: 26–30.

Gadant, Monique, ed. *Women of the Mediterranean*. New Jersey: Zed Books, 1986.

Gallop, Jane, and Carolyn Burke. "Psychoanalysis and Feminism in France." In *The Future of Difference*. Hester Eisenstein and Alice Jardin, eds. New Brunswick, NJ: Rutgers University Press, 1980: 106–14.

Gebara, I. *El rostro oculto del mal* (The Hidden Face of Evil). Madrid: Editorial Trotta, 2002.

Gelb, Joyce. *Feminism and Politics*. Berkeley, CA: University of California Press, 1989.

Geertz, Clifford. *The Interpretation of Culture*. New York: Routledge, 1975.

Gil, Rosa María, and Carmen Inoa Vasquez. *The María Paradox: How Latinas Can Merge Old World Traditions with New World Self-Esteem*. New York: Perigee Press, 1996.

Gilligan, Carol. *In a Different Voice*. Cambridge, MA: Harvard University Press, 1982.

Goldsmith-Clermont, Luisella. *Economic Evaluations of Unpaid Household Work: Africa, Asia, Latin America and Oceania*. Geneva: UNFPA, 1987.

Greer, Germaine. *The Whole Woman*. New York: Alfred A. Knopf, 1999.

Grosz, Elizabeth. *Jacques Lacan: A Feminist Introduction*. New York: Routledge, 1990.

———. *Volatile Bodies: Toward a Corporeal Feminism*. Bloomington, IN: Indiana University Press, 1994.

———. *Space, Time and Perversion*. London and New York: Routledge, 1995.

Guberman, Ross Mitchell, ed. *Julia Kristeva: Interviews*. New York: Columbia University Press, 1996.

Guhl, Mercedes. "Las Madres de la Patria: Antonia Santos y Policarpa Salavarrieta (Mothers of our nation: Antonia Santos and Policarpa Salavarrieta). In *Las Desobedientes* (The desobedients). María Mercedes Jaramillo and Betty Osorio de Negret, eds. Bogotá: Panamericana Editorial, 1997: 118–30.

Gutiérrez de Pineda, Virginia. *Familia y Cultura en Colombia* (Family and culture in Colombia). Bogotá: Instituto Colombiano de Cultura, 1975.

Gutiérrez de Pineda, Virginia. *La Familia en Colombia: Transfondo Historico*. Medellin, Colombia: Ministerio de Cultura, Editorial Universidad de Antioquia, [1963] 1997.

Gutting, Gary. "Foucault's Geneaological Method." In *Midwest Studies in Philosophy Volume XV: The Philosophy of the Human Sciences*. Peter Finch, Theodore E. Uehling, Jr., Howard K. Wettstein, eds. South Bend, IN: University of Notre Dame Press, 1990: 327–43.

Hall, Edward. *Beyond Culture*. Garden City, NY: Anchor Press, 1976.

Hamington, Maurice. *Hail Mary? The Struggle for Ultimate Womanhood in Catholicism*. New York: Routledge, 1995.

Hammond, Innes. *The Conquistadors*. New York: Alfred. A. Knopf, 1969.

Hanabergh, Mercedes. *Mardoqueo*. España: Publidisa, 2007.

Harding, Sandra. *The Science Question in Feminism*. Ithaca, NY: Cornell University Press, 1986.

———, ed. *Feminism and Methodology*. Bloomington, IN: Indiana University Press, 1987.

———. *Whose Science? Whose Knowledge? Thinking from Women's Lives*. Ithaca, NY: Cornell University Press, 1991.

———. *The Racial Economy of Science*. Sandra Harding, ed. Bloomington, IN: Indiana University Press, 1993.

Harstock, Nancy. *Discovering Reality*. London: D. Reidel Publishing Co., 1983.

Heisi, Lori. "The Global War Against Women." *Washington Post—Outlook*, B4, 9 April 1989.

Heisi, Lori, Jacqueline Pitanguy, and Adrienne Germain. "Violence Against Women: The Hidden Health Burden." *World Bank Discussion Papers*, No. 255, 1994.

Henry, Jules. *Culture Against Man*. New York: Random House, 1963.

Hepburn, Stephanie, and Rita Simon. *Women's Roles and Statuses the World Over*. Lanham, MD: Lexington Books, 2007.

Herman, Judith Lewis. *Father-Daughter Incest*. Cambridge, MA: Harvard University Press, 1981.

Heyzer, Noeleen, Sushma Kapoor, and Joanne Sandler, eds. *A Commitment to the World's Women: Perspectives on Development for Beijing and Beyond*. New York: UNIFEM, 1995.

Hoff, Joan. "The Pernicioius Effect of Post-Structuralism on Women's History." In *Radically Speaking. Feminism Reclaimed*. Diane Bell and Renate Klein, eds. Melbourne: Spinifex Press, 1996–1997.

Holy Bible. King James Version. London: Oxford University Press, n.d.

Hooks, Bell. *Feminist Theory: From Margin to Center*. Boston: South End Press, 1984, 2000.

Hoschild, Arlie. *The Second Shift*. NewYork: Avon Books, 1989.

Humm, Maggie. *The Dictionary of Feminist Theory*. Columbus, OH: Ohio State University, 1989–1995.

Howell, Irving A. *Culture and the History of Man.* In *The Meaning of Culture.* Morris Frielich, ed. Lexington, MA: Xerox College Publishing, 1965: 199–213.

Hoff, Joan. "The Pernicious Effect of Post-structuralism on Women's History." In *Radically Speaking: Feminism Reclaimed.* Diane Bell and Renate Klein, eds. Melbourne: Spinifex Press, 1996–1997: 393–412.

IDB (Inter-American Development Bank). *Too Close to Home: Domestic Violence in the Americas.* A. R. Morrison and M. L. Biehl, eds. Washington, D.C.: 1985.

———. *Working Women in the Americas.* Washington D.C.: Inter American Bank Publishers, 1990.

———. *Women in the Americas: Bridging the Gender Gap.* Washington, D.C.: The John's Hopkins University Press, 1995.

———. *Too Close To Home: Domestic Violence in the Americas.* Andrew R. Morrison and María Loreto Biehl, eds. Washington D.C.: Inter-American Bank Publishers, 1999.

Inter-American Commission of Women. *Violence in the Americas—a Regional Analysis Including a Review of the Implementation of the Inter-American Convention on the Prevention, Punishment and Eradication of Violence Against Women.* Belem do Para, Brazil (Executive Summary 7/23/04 1–22).

Irigaray, Luce. *This Sex Which Is Not One.* Catherine Porter and Caroline Burke, trans. Ithaca, NY: Cornell University Press, 1985.

Isaacs, Jorge. *María.* Medellín: Editorial Bedout S. A., 1984.

Jaggar, Alison, and Susan Bordo. *Gender/Body/Knowledge.* New Brunswick, NJ: Rutgers University Press, 1990.

Jaquette, Jane, ed. *The Women's Movement in Latin America.* Boston: Unwin Hyman, 1989.

———. "Women in Power: From Tokenism to Critical Mass." *Foreign Policy.* Fall 2007.

Jaramillo Castillo, Carlos Eduardo. "Muejeres en Guerra" ("Women at War"). In *Las Muejeres en la Historia de Colombia* (*Women in Colombian History*). Vol. 2. Santa Fé de Bogotá, Colombia: Consejería Presidencial para la Política Social, 1995: 359–86.

Jaramillo, María Mercedes, and Betty Osorio de Negret, eds. *Las Desobedientes* (The disobedients). Bogotá: Panamericana Editorial, 1997.

Jardin, Alice. *The Future of Difference.* New Brunswick, NJ: Rutgers University Press, 1980.

———. Introduction to Julia Kristeva's "Women's Time." *Sign,* Vol. 7, No. 11, 1981, 10–12.

Jary, David, and Julia Jary. *Sociology: Harper Collins Dictionary.* New York: Harper Perennial, 1991.

Jolly, Clifford J., and Fred Plog. *Physical Anthropology and Archaeology.* New York: Alfred A. Knopf, 1982.

Jones, Ann Jocelyn. "Writing the Body: Toward an Understanding of *l'Ecriture Fémi-nine*." In *Feminist Criticism: Essays on Women, Literature and Theory*. Elaine Showalter, ed. New York: Pantheon Books, 1985: 361–77.

Joyce, James. *A Portrait of the Artist as a Young Man*. New York: Bantam Books, 1992.

Kelly-Gadol, Joan. "The Social Relation of the Sexes: Methodological Implications of Women's History." In *Feminism and Methodology*. Sandra Harding, ed. Bloomington, IN: Indiana University Press, 1987: 29–36.

Kinsley, David. *The Goddesses' Mirror: Visions of the Divine from East and West*. New York: State University of New York Press, 1989.

Kitzinger, Celia. "Therapy and How It Undermines the Practice of Radical Feminism." In *Specially Speaking: Feminism Reclaimed*. Diane Bell and Renate Klein, eds. Melbourne: Spinifex Press, 1996–1997: 92–101.

Kramarae, Chris, and Paula A. Treichler, eds. *A Feminist Dictionary*. Boston: Pandora Press, 1985.

Kristeva, Julia. "Women's Time." *Signs: Journal for Woman in Culture and Society*. Translated and with an introduction by Alice Jardin. Vol. 7, No. 1 (Autumn 1981): 4–35.

———. *Desire in Language*. Leon Roudiez, ed. Thomas Gora, Alice Jardin, and Leon Roudiez, trans. New York: Columbia University Press, 1982.

———. *Tales of Love*. Leon Roudiez, trans. New York: Columbia University Press, 1983.

———. *Revolution in Poetic Language*. New York, Columbia University, 1984.

Kristof, Nicholas D. "Don't tell the pope." *International Herald Tribune*. November 27, 2003.

Kvale, Steiner. *InterViews: An Introduction to Qualitative Research Interviewing*. London: Sage, 1996.

Lacan, Jacques. *ECRITS: A Selection*. Alan Sheridan, trans. New York: W. W. Norton and Company, 1977.

Lara, Patricia. *Mujeres en la Guerra* (Women in the war). Bogotá: Editorial Planeta, 2000.

Laub Coser, Rose. "Reflections on Feminist Theory." In *Feminism and Sociological Theory*. Ruth Wallace, ed. London: Sage, 1989: 200–07.

Lavrin, Asuncion. *Latin American Women: Historical Perspectives*. Westport, CT: Greenwood Press, 1978.

———. "Women, the Family, and Social Change in Latin America." *World Affairs* 150, No. 2 (Fall 1987): 109–28.

Leal, Magdalena. *Poder Y Empoderamiento De Las Mujeres* (Power and women's empowerment). Bogotá: Tercer Mundo Editores, 1988.

———. *Mujeres y Participacion Politica: Avances y desafíos en America Latina*. (Women and political participation: advances and defiance in Latin America). Bogotá: Tercer Mundo Editores, 1994.

Lengerman, Patricia, and Jill Niebrugge-Brantley. "Feminist Sociological Theory." In *Frontiers of Sociological Theory: The New Synthesis*. George Ritzer, ed. New York: Columbia University Press, 1990: 316–44.

Lerner, Gerda. *The Creation of Patriarchy*. New York: Oxford University Press, 1986.

Lévi-Strauss, Clauss. *Elementary Structures of Kinship*. Boston: Beacon Press, 1969.

———. *Tristes Tropiques*. John and Doreen Wightman, trans. New York: Pocket Books, 1973.

Linton, Ralph. *The Study of Man*. New York: D. Appleton Century Company, 1936.

Lipkowitz, Ina, and Andrea Loselle. "A Conversation with Julia Kristeva." In *Julia Kristeva: Interviews*. Ross Mitchell Guberman, ed. New York: Columbia University Press, 1996: 18–34.

Lorde, Audre. "Poetry is not a Luxury." In *The Future of Difference*. Hester Eisenstein and Alice Jardin, eds. New Jersey: Rutgers University Press, 1984a: 125–27.

———. *Sister Outsider*. New York: The Crossing Press, 1984b.

Luna, Lola. *Los Movimientos de Mujeres en America Latina y la Renovacion de la Historia Politica* (Women's movements in Latin America and the renovation of political history). In *Centro de estudios de genero mujer y sociedad*. Cali, Colombia: Universidad del Valle, Editorial la Manzana de la Discordia, 2001.

———. "Cincuenta *Anos del Voto Femenino en Colombia: Compañera y no Sierva*" (Fifty years of the feminine vote in Colombia: partner, not serf). *El Tiempo, UNPeriodico*. Bogotá: August, 22, 2004.

MacKinnon, Catharine. "Feminism, Marxism, Method and the State: An Agenda for Theory. Toward Feminist Jurisprudence." In *Feminism and Methodology*. Sandra Harding, ed. Bloomington, IN: Indiana University Press, 1987: 135–53.

———. "From Practice to Theory, or What is a White Woman Anyway?" In *Radically Speaking: Feminism Reclaimed*. Diane Bell and Renate Klein, eds. Melbourne: Spinifex Press, 1996–1997: 45–54.

Mair, Lucille Mathurin. "Women: A Decade is Time Enough." *Third World Quarterly*, 8, No. 2, April (1986): 583–93.

Marcuse, Herbert. *Eros and Civilization*. Boston: Beacon Press, 1955.

Marks, Elaine. "Women and Literature in France." *Signs* 4 (1978): 841.

Marks, Elaine, and Isabelle de Courtivron. *New French Feminisms*. New York: Schoken Books, 1981.

Márquez, Gabriel García. *Crónica de una Muerte Anunciada* (Chronicle of a death foretold). Bogotá: Editorial Norma, 1981.

Martin, Luther, Huck Gutman, and Patrick Hutton eds. *Technologies of the Self*. Amherst, MA: University of Massachusetts Press, 1988a.

———. "Truth, Power, and Self: An Interview with Michel Foucault." Amherst: University of Massachusetts Press, 1988b: 8–12.

Marx, Karl, and Frederick Engels. *The German Ideology: Part One*. Edited by C. J. Arthur. New York: International Publishers, 1970.

Mauss, Marcele. *The Gift*. New York: W.W. Norton and Company, 1967.

"Medicos que practicaon aborta a niña de 11 anos fueron excomulgados por la Iglesia Catolica" (Doctors who performed an abortion on an 11 years old girl were ex- communicated by the Catholic Church). *El Tiempo*. Bogotá: August 29, 2006.

Medrano, Diana, and Cristina Escobar. "Pasado resente de las organizacions feministas en Colombia" (Past and present of the feminist organizations of Colombia). In *Mujer y familia en Colombia* (Woman and Family in Colombia). Bogotá: Plaza and Janes, 1985.

Mendoza, Mario. "Ellas: El pais esta sostenido sobre los hombres de las mujeres" (They: our country is being sustained in the women's shoulders). *El Tiempo*. Bogotá: July 3, 2004.

Mies, María. "Toward a Methodology for Feminist Research." In *Theories of Women's Studies*. Gloria Bowles and Renate Duelli Klein, eds. New York: Routledge and Kegan Paul, 1983: 117–39.

———. *Patriarchy and Accumulation on a World Scale*. London: Zed Books, 1986.

Mies, María, Veronika Benholdt-Thomsen, and Claudia von Werlhof, eds. *Women: The Last Colony*. London: Zed Books Ltd., 1988.

Miles, Marilyn. *The Woman's History of the World*. London: Michael Joseph, 1988.

Mill, John Stuart. *The Subjection of Women*. Greenwich, CT: Fawcett Publications, 1971.

Miller, Nancy K., ed. *The Poetics of Gender*. New York: Columbia University Press, 1986.

Millet, Kate. *Sexual Politics*. New York: Avon Books, 1969.

Mitchell, Juliet. *Woman's Estate*. New York: Vintage Books, 1973.

———. *Psychoanalysis and Feminism*. New York: Perseus Publishing, 2000.

Mitchell, Juliet, and Jacqueline Rose. *Feminine Sexuality*. New York: Pantheon Books, 1982.

Moi, Toril. *Sexual/Textual Politics*. London: Methuen, 1985.

———. *French Feminist Thought: A Reader*. New York, Basil Blackwell, 1987.

———, ed. *The Kristeva Reader*. New York: Columbia University Press, 1988.

Molyneux, Maxine. "The Chimera of Success: Gender *Ennui* and the Changed International Policy Environment." In *Feminisms Contradictions, Contestations and Challenges in Development*. Andrea Cornwall, Eliszabeth Harrison, and Ann Whitehead, eds. London: Zed Books, 2007.

Momsen, Janet Henshall. *Women and Development in Third World*. New York: Routledge, 1991.

Morgan, Robin, ed. *Sisterhood Is Global: The International Women's Movement Anthology*. New York: Anchor Books, 1984.

———. "Light Bulbs, Radishes, and the Politics of the 21st Century." In *Radically Speaking: Feminism Reclaimed*. Diane Bell and Renate Klein, eds. Melbourne: Spinifex, 1997: 325–38.

Moser, Caroline O. "Gender planning in the Third World: meeting practical and strategic gender needs." In *World Development*, 17 (11): 1,799–1,825 (1989).

Murphy, Yolanda, and Robert F. Murphy. *Women of the Forest*. New York: Columbia University Press, 1985.

National Geographic. "Colombia." *National Geographic Atlas of the World*, 7th edition. Washington, D.C: National Geographic Society (1999).

NCADV (National Coalition Against Domestic Violence). *Fact Sheets*, Washington, D.C.: NCADV, 1985.

Nicholson, Linda. *The Second Wave. A Reader in Feminist Theory*. New York: Routledge, 1997.

Nyquist, Mary. "Gynesis, Genesis, and the Formation of Milton's Eve." In *Cannibals, Witches, and Divorce: Estranging the Renaissance*. Marjorie Garber, ed. Baltimore: Johns Hopkins University Press, 1987.

Nye, Andrea. "The Voice of the Serpent: French Feminism and the Philosophy of Language." In *Women, Knowledge and Reality: Explorations in Feminist Philosophy*. Ann Garry and Marilyn Pearsall, eds. Boston: Unwin Hyman 1989: 233–49.

OAS/CIDH. "Comision Interamericana de Derechos Humanos" (Inter-American Commission on Human Rights), 'Informe de la Comision Interamericana de Derechos Humanos de la Mujer en las Americas (Inter-American Report on Women's Human Rights in the Americas). Washington, D.C.: 1997–1998.

Obeyesekere, Gananath. *The Work of Culture: Symbolic Transformation in Psychoanalysis and Anthropology*. Chicago: University of Chicago Press, 1990.

OIM/ANEC (Organizacion Interncional para las Migraciones, y Asociacion Nacional de Enfermeras de Colombia, Secional de Antioquia). *Colombian Country Report*. Bogotá: Union de Empleados Bancarios, 2002.

Oliver, Kelly. *Reading Kristeva*. Bloomington, IN: Indiana University Press, 1993.

———, ed. *The Portable Kristeva*. New York: Columbia University Press, 1997.

Ortiz, Lucía. "Genio, figura, y ocaso de Manuela Saenz" (Personality and Disappearance of Manula Saenz). In *Las Desobedientes* (The disobedients). María Mercedes Jaramillo and Betty Osorio de Negret, eds. Bogotá: Panamericana Editorial, 1997: 83–117.

Ortner, Sherry. "Is Female to Male as Nature Is to Culture?" In *Women, Culture and Society*. Michelle Zimbalist Rosaldo and Louise Lamphere, eds. Stanford, CA: Stanford University Press, 1974: 67–87.

Ortner, Sherry, and Harriet Whitehead. *Sexual Meanings*. New York: Cambridge University Press, 1981.

Paget, M. A. "Unlearning to Not Speak." *Human Studies* 13, 1990: 147–61.

PAHO. *Health in the Americas*. See www.paho.org (accessed 1998).

Palma, Milagros. *La Mujer es Puro Cuento: Feminidad Aborigen y Mestiza* (To be a woman is mere fantasy: Aborigine and "mestiza" femininity). Bogotá: Tercer Mundo Editores, 1992.

Paternostro, Silvana. *In the Land of Man and God: A Latin Woman's Journey*. New York: Penguin, 1999.

Peristiany, Jean. *Honor and Shame: The Values of Mediterranean Society*. Chicago: Chicago University Press, 1966.

Perkins Gilman, Charlotte. *The Home: Its Work and Influence*. New York: McClure, Phillips, and Company, 1903.

Pescatello, Ann. *Female and Male in Latin America*. Pittsburgh, PA: University of Pittsburgh Press, 1973.

Peters, Julie, and Andrea Wolper, eds. *Women's Rights, Human Rights: International Feminist Perspectives*. New York: Routledge, 1995.

Pitt-Rivers, Julian, ed. *Mediterranean Countrymen: Essays in the Social Anthropology of the Mediterranean*. Paris: Mouton, 1966.

Plummer, Ken. *Telling Sexual Stories: Power, Change, and Social Worlds*. New York: New York: Routledge, 1995.

Prescott, William H. *History of the Reign of Ferdinand and Isabella: The Catholic Kings of Spain*. London: George Routledge and Sons, 1837.

Psycho and Group. "Woman Is Never What We Say." In *Julia Kristeva: Interviews*. Ross Mitchell Guberman, ed. New York: Columbia University Press, 1996: 95–102.

Ramirez, Marta Lucia. "Senadora le pide al Presidente ampliar la cuota femenina" (Senador asks the president to enlarge the female quota). *El Tiempo*. Bogotá: December 22, 2007.

Ranke-Heinemann, Uta. *Eunuchs for the Kingdom of Heaven: Women, Sexuality and the Catholic Church*. New York: Double Day, 1990.

Rayna, Reiter R., ed. *Toward an Anthropology of Women*. New York: Monthly Review Press, 1976.

Reinharz, Shulamit. "Experiential Analysis: A Contribution to Feminist Research." In *Theories of Women's Studies*. Gloria Bowles and Renate Duelli Klein, eds. New York: Routledge and Kegan Paul, 1983: 162–91.

Reinharz, Shulamit, and Lynn Davidman. *Feminist Methods in Social Research*. New York: Oxford University Press, 1992.

Restrepo, Roberto. "Las mujeres en las sociedades prehispánicas" (Women in pre-hispanic societies). In *Conserjeria Presidencial para la Política Social Las Mujeres en la Historia de Colombia*. Magdala Velásquez Toro, ed. Bogotá: Editorial Norma, 1995: 1–42.

Rico De Alonso, Ana. *Madres Solteras Adolescentes* (Unwedded adolescent mothers). Bogotá: Plaza and Janes, 1986.

Ricoeur, Paul. *Hermeneutics and the Human Sciences*. Edited and translated by John B. Thompson. New York: Cambridge University Press, 1981.

Rich, Adrienne. *Of Woman Born: Motherhood as Experience and Institution*. New York: Norton Books, 1977.

Rilke, Rainer Maria. *Letters to a Young Poet*. New York: Vintage Books, 1986.

Ritzer, George, ed. *Frontiers of Sociological Theory: The New Synthesis*. New York: Columbia University Press, 1990.

Rodriguez, Pablo. "Las mujeres y el matrimonio en la Nueva Granada." In *Las Mujeres en la Historia de Colombia* (Women in Colombian History). Santa Fé de Bogotá, Colombia: Consejería Presidencial para la Política Social, 1995: 241–91.

Rodriguez Sehk, Penelope. "La Virgen-Madre Simbolo de la Feminidad Latinoamericana" (The virgin-mother symbol of Latin American feminity). *Texto y Contexto: Simbología Femenina y Orden Social*. Elsy Bonilla, ed. No.7. (April 1986): 73–90.

Rodriguez-Vergara, Isabel. "María de los Angeles Cano Márquez: Del sindicalismo al socialismo subvertiendo las leyes del padre" (María de los Angeles Cano: From sindicalism to socialism subverting the father's law). In *Las Desobedientes* (The disobedients). María Mercedes Jaramillo and Betty Osorio de Negret, eds. Bogotá: Panamericana Editorial, 1997: 230–53.

Rogers, Barbara. *The Domestication of Women: Discrimination in Developing Societies*. New York: Tavistock Publications, 1980.

Roheim, Geza. *Psychoanalysis and Anthropology: Culture, Personality, and the Unconscious*. New York: International Universities Press, 1950.

Rosaldo, Michelle Zimbalist. "Woman, Culture, and Society: A Theoretical Overview." In *Woman, Culture and Society*. Michelle Zimbalist Rosaldo and Louise Lamphere, eds. Stanford, CA: Stanford University Press, 1974: 17–42.

Rosaldo, Michelle Zimbalist, and Louise Lamphere. *Woman/Culture and Society*. Stanford, CA: Stanford University Press, 1974.

Rousseau, Jean Jacques. *An Essay on the Origins of Languages*. Victor Gourevitch, trans. New York: Harper and Row, 1987.

Rowland, Robyn, and Renate Klein. "Radical Feminism: History, Politics, Action." In *Radically Speaking: Feminism Reclaimed*. Diane Bell and Renate Klein, eds. Melbourne: Spinifex, 1997: 9–36.

Rubin, Gayle. "The Traffic in Women: Notes on the 'Political Economy' of Sex." In *Toward an Anthropology of Women*. Rayna R. Reiter, ed. New York: Monthly Review Press, 1975: 157–210.

Rubinstein, Roberta. *Boundaries of the Self, Gender, Culture, and Fiction*. Urbana, IL: University of Illinois, 1987.

Sacks, Karen. "Engels Revisited: Women, the Organization of Production, and Private Property." In *Toward an Anthropology of Women*. Rayna R. Reiter, ed. New York: Monthly Review, 1975: 207–22.

Safa, Helen. "Women's social movements in Latin America." In *Women in the Latin American Development Process*. C. E. Bose and E. Acosta-Belen, eds. Philadelphia, PA: Temple University Press, 1995.

Safford, Frank, and Marco Palacios. *Colombia: Fragmented Land, Divided Society*. New York: Oxford University Press, 2002.

Saint Augustine. *Confessions*. Translated with an introduction by R. S. Pine-Coffin. New York: Penguin Books, 2002.

Salamanca, Juana. "Mujeres Castigadas" (History of punishing women). *El Tiempo*. Bogotá: March 25, 2006.

Salisbury, Joyce E. *Church Fathers, Independent Virgins*. New York: Verso, 1991.

Saltzman Chafetz, Janet. "Gender Equality: Toward a Theory of Change." In *Feminism and Social Change*. Ruth Wallace, ed. London: Sage, 1986: 135–60.

Sanchez de Torres, Fernando. "El aborto y la academia de medicina" (Abortion and the academy of medicine). *El Tiempo.* Bogotá: June 1, 2003.

Santacoloma, Luis E. Patiño. "Mujer y Varón los Creó" (He created them woman and man). *El Pais.* Cali, Colombia: November 18, 2006.

———. "Los Derechos de la Mujer" (Women's Rights). *El Pais.* Cali, Colombia: March 17, 2007.

Sawicki, Jana. "Foucault, Feminism and Questions of Identity." In *Michel Foucault's Archaeology of Scientific Reason.* Gary Gutting, ed. Cambridge: Cambridge University Press, 1989: 132–50.

Schechter, Suzanne. *Women and Male Violence: The Vision and the Struggles of the Battered Women's Movement.* Boston: South End Press, 1982.

Schneider, Jane. "Of Vigilance and Virgins: Honor, Shame, and Access to Resources in Mediterranean Societies." *Ethnology*, Vol. 10, 3. July 1–24, 1971.

Schopp-Schilling, Hanna Beate, and Cees Flinterman, eds. *The Circle of Empowerment: Twenty-Five Years of the UN Committee on the Elimination of Discrimination against Women.* New York: The Feminist Press, 2007.

Scutt, Jocelynne A. "The Personal is Political." In *Radically Speaking: Feminism Reclaimed.* Diane Bell and Renate Klein, eds. Melbourne: Spinifex Press, 1996–1997: 102–10.

Segura, Cristina Graiño. "Las mujeres castellanas de los siglos XV y XVI y su presencia en América (Castillian women in the fifteenth and sixteenth centuries and their presence in America). In *Consejeria Presidencial para la política social: Las Mujeres en la historia de Colombia,* Tomo I (Women in Colombian history, Volume I). Magdala Velásquez Toro, ed. Bogotá: Editorial Norma, 1995: 43–59.

SEMANA. "La Ciudad de las Mujeres" (Women's City). Bogotá: March 20–27, 2006.

Sen, Gita, and Caren Grown. *Development, Crisis, and Alternative Visions: Third World Women's Perspectives.* New York: Monthly Review Press, 1987.

Sen, Amartya. *Development as Freedom.* New York: Anchor Books, 1999.

Showalter, Elaine. *Feminist Criticism: Essays on Women, Literature and Theory.* New York: Pantheon Books, 1985.

Slocum, Sally. "Woman the Gatherer: Male Bias in Anthropology." In *Toward an Anthropology of Women.* Rayna R. Reiter, ed. New York: Monthly Review Press, 1975: 36–50.

Smith, Dorothy E. *Everyday World As Problematic: A Feminist Sociology.* Boston: Northeast University Press, 1987.

———. "Sociological Theory: Methods of Writing Patriarchy." In *Feminism and Sociological Theory.* Ruth Wallace, ed. London: Sage Publications 1989: 8–22.

Sommer, Doris. *Foundational Fictions: The National Romances of Latin America.* Berkeley, CA: University of California Press, 1993.

Spender, Dale. "Theorizing about Theorizing." In *Theories of Women's Studies.* Gloria Bowles and Renate Klein, eds. New York: Routledge and Kegan Paul, 1982: 27–31.

Stamatopoulou, Elissavet. "Women's Rights and the United Nations." In *Women's Rights, Human Rights: International Feminist Perspectives.* Julie Peters and Andrea Wolper, eds. New York: Routledge, 1995: 36–48.

Stanley, Liz, and Sue Wise. "'Back into the Personal' or: Our Attempt to Construct 'Feminist Research.'" In *Theories of Women's Studies.* Gloria Bowles and Renate Duelli Klein, eds. New York: Routledge and Kegan Paul, 1983: 162–91.

Stanton, Domna. "Language and Revolution. The Franco-American Dis-Connection." In *The Future of Difference.* Hester Eisenstein and Alice Jardin, eds. New Brunswick, NJ: Rutgers University Press, 1985: 73–87.

———. "Difference on Trial: A Critique of the Maternal Metaphor in Cixous, Irigaray, and Kristeva." In *The Poetics of Gender.* Nancy K. Miller, ed. New York: Columbia University Press, 1986: 157–82.

Steiner, George. *On Difficulty and Other Essays.* New York: Oxford University Press, 1978.

Stephan, Nancy Lee. "Race and Gender: The Role of Analogy in Science." In *The Racial Economy of Science.* Sandra Harding, ed. Bloomington, IN: Indiana University Press, 1993: 359–76.

Stevens, Evelyn. "*Marianismo:* The Other Face of *Machismo* in Latin America." In *Female and Male in Latin America.* Ann Pescatello, ed. Pittsburgh, PA: University of Pittsburgh Press, 1973: 9–16.

Sulay, Martha. "No pudo abortar aunque tenía cáncer y ahora ya no tiene cura" (She was not allowed to abort and now she will not be healed). *El Tiempo.* March 26, 2006.

———. 'Martha Sulay abre debate sobre el aborto" (Martha Sulay opens a debate on abortion). *El Tiempo.* Bogotá: March 28, 2006.

Sulemain, Susan Rubin, ed. *The Female Body in Western Culture.* Cambridge, MA: Harvard University Press, 1985.

Suphi, Mehmet. "The Expulsion of Safarad Jews: Regression in the Development of Modern Society." *Mind and Human Interaction* 4, No.1, December 1992: 40–51.

Thomas, Florence. "A Propósito de: La Virgen-Madre como Simbólo de la Femenidad Latinoamericana" (On Regard of the: virgin-mother as symbol of Latin American feminity). *Texto y Contexto: Simbiologia Femenina y Orden Social.* Elsy Bonilla, ed. No.7, Bogotá (Enero-Abril 1986): 199–201.

———. *Los Estragos del Amor: El Discurso Amoroso en los Medios de Comunicación* (Loves' ravages: The love discourse in the media). Bogotá: Editorial Universidad de los Andes, 1999.

———. "La Bigamia en Colombia" (Bigamy in Colombia). *El Tiempo.* Bogotá, 2001.

———. *La Mujer Tiene la Palabra* (Woman has the word). Bogotá: Aguilar, 2001.

———. *Palabras en el Tiempo* (Words within Time). Bogotá: Aguilar, 2003.

———. "Ciudadana" (Female Citizen). *El Tiempo.* Bogotá: August 25, 2004.

———. "Regresa Monseñor Builes" (Monsignor Buils is back). *El Tiempo.* February 22, 2006.

Thompson, Laura. *Toward a Science of Mankind*. New York: McGraw-Hill, 1961.

——. *Culture and Freedom*. In *The Meaning of Culture*. Morris Frielich, ed. Boston: Xerox College Publishing, 1965: 155–67.

Tirado Mejia, Alvaro, director científico y académico. *Nueva Historia de Colombia* (A new history of Colombia). Bogotá: Editorial Planeta, 1989.

Tokatlián, Juan Gabriel. "Feminismo y Geopolítica" (Feminism and geopolitics). *El Tiempo*, section 6A. Bogotá: August 16, 1998.

Turbay, Catalina, and Ana Rico. *Construyendo Identidades: Niñas, Jovenes, y Mujeres en Colombia; Reflexiones sobre Socializacion de Roles de Genero* (Constructing identities: Girls, young women, and women in Colombia; reflections on the socialization of gender roles). Bogotá: Unicef, Consejeria Presidencial para la juventud, la Mujer y la Familia, 1994.

Turner, Victor. *The Forest of Symbols: Aspects of Ndembu Ritual*. Ithaca, NY: Cornell University Press, 1970.

UNESCO Institute for Statistics. See www.uis.unesco.org (accessed 2002).

UNICEF. *The Official Summary of the State of the World's Children 2003*. See www.unicef.org/infobycountry/Colombia.html/

UNIFEM. *The Human Cost of Women's Poverty: Perspectives from Latin America and the Caribbean*. Mexico City: UNIFEM, 1995.

——. "Promoting gender equality and empowering women, Colombia." In *The Millenium Development Goals in Latin America and The Caribbean*. United Nations: New York, 2003.

United Nations. *Violence against Women in the Family*. New York: United Nations, 1989.

——. *The Worlds Women 2000: Trends and Statistics*. New York: United Nations, 1989.

——. *Strategies for Confronting Domestic Violence: A Resource Manual*. New York: United Nations, 1993.

——. "Report on women's human rights." *El Espectador*. August 21, 2004.

Vance, Carole S., ed. *Pleasure and Danger: Exploring Female Sexuality*. Boston: Routledge, 1984.

Velásquez Toro, Magdala. "Condición Jurídica y Social de la Mujer" (Women's legal and social conditions). In *Nueva Historia de Colombia*, Tomo I (New history of Colombia, Volume I). Alvaro Tirado-Mejia, ed. Bogotá: Editorial Planeta, 1989: 77–100.

——. "La Republica liberal y la lucha por los derechos civiles y políticos de la mujer" (The liberal republic and the struggle for the civil and political rights of woman). In *Consejeria Presidencial. Las Mujeres en la Historia de Colombia*, Tomo I (Women in Colombian history, Volume I). Magdala Velásquez Toro, ed. Bogotá: Editorial Norma, 1995: 183–228.

Velásquez Toro, Magdala, and Catalina Cardenas Reyes. "Proceso Historico y Derechos de las Mujeres Años, 50 y 60" (Historical process and women's rights in the 50s and 60s). In *Consejeria presidencial: Las Mujeres en la Historia de Colombia*,

Tomo I (Women in Colombian history, Volume I). Magdala Velásquez Toro, ed. Bogotá: Editorial Norma, 1995: 229–57.

Villareal Mendez, Norma. "El Camino de la Utopia Feminista en Colombia 1975–1991" (The road to a utopian feminism in Colombia 1975–1991). In *Mujeres y Participación Política: Avances y Desafíos en América Latina* (Women and political participation: Advances and defiances in Latin America). Magdalena León, ed. Bogotá: T. M. Editores, 1994: 234.

———. "Mujeres y Espacios Políticos: Participación Política y Análisis Electoral" (Women and political spaces: Political participation and analysis on elections). In *Consejería Mujeres en la Historia de Colombia*, Tomo I (Women in Colombian history, Volume I). Magdala Velásquez Toro, ed. Bogotá: Editorial Norma, 1995: 319–47.

Wallace, Ruth A., ed. *Feminism and Sociological Theory*. London: Sage, 1989.

Warner, Marina. *Alone of All Her Sex: The Myth and the Cult of the Virgin Mary*. New York: Alfred A. Knopf, 1976.

Weber, Max. *The Protestant Ethic and the Spirit of Capitalism*. Talcott Parsons, trans. London: Allen and Unwin, 1976.

Weedon, Chris. *Feminist Practice and Poststructuralist Theory*. Oxford: Basil Blackwell, 1987.

Williams, Daniel, and Alan Cooperman. "Vatican Letter Denounces 'Lethal Effects' of Feminism." *The Washington Post*. Washington D.C.: August, 1, 2004.

Wills Obregón, Maria Emma. *Inclusion Sin Representacion. La irrupcion politica de las mujeres en Colombia 1970–2000* (Inclusion without representation: Colombian women's irruption into politics 1970–2000). Bogotá: Grupo Editorial Norma, 2007.

Wittig, Monique. "The Mark of Gender." In *The Poetics of Gender*. Carolyn G. Heilbourn and Nancy K. Miller, eds. New York: Columbia University Press, 1986: 63–73.

———. "One is Not Born a Woman." In *The Second Wave: A Reader in Feminist Theory*. Linda Nicholson, ed. New York: Routledge, 1997: 265–71.

Wollstonecraft, Mary. *A Vindication of the Rights of Women*. New York: Dover, 1996.

Woolf, Virginia. *Three Guineas*. New York: A Harvest Book, 1974.

World Bank. *Violence in Colombia: Building Sustainable Peace and Social Capital*, World Bank Country Study. Washington, D.C: World Bank, 1999.

———. *World Development Indicators 2007*.

Zuleta, Estanislao. *Sobre la Idealización en la Vida Personal y Colectiva, y Otros Ensayos*. Bogotá: Nueva Biblioteca de Cultura, 1985.

Zúñiga, Luis. *Manuela: Una Novela Sobre la Vida de Manuelita Saénz* (Manuela: A Novel on Manuelita Saénz's Life). Bogotá: Círculo de Lectores, 2000.

Index

About the Author

Elena Garcés is a feminist, activist, researcher, and consultant in Colombia and the United States. She earned her PhD in human sciences from George Washington University, Washington, D.C., with a dissertation titled *The Construction of Radical Feminist Knowledge: Women in Colombia as an Example*. She is a co-founder of Mujeres Pazificas, a feminist group in Colombia that works for peace. She is also co-founder and editor of a feminist magazine, *Cabala*, published in Cali, Colombia.